The Scale of Perfection

AND THE ENGLISH
MYSTICAL TRADITION

The Scale of Perfection

AND THE ENGLISH MYSTICAL TRADITION

JOSEPH E. MILOSH

THE UNIVERSITY OF WISCONSIN PRESS

MADISON, MILWAUKEE, LONDON, 1966

Published by
The University of Wisconsin Press
Madison, Milwaukee, and London
U.S.A.: Box 1379, Madison, Wisconsin 53701
U.K.: 26–28 Hallam Street, London, W. 1

Printed in the
United States of America
by Kingsport Press, Inc., Kingsport,
Tennessee
Library of Congress
Catalog Card Number 66–22857

TO SYLVIA

N̲ot by visions alone

PREFATORY NOTE

Walter Hilton's *Scale of Perfection* is one of the most important mediaeval contemplative works; it is also a valuable measure for judging other literature in the mystical tradition, since it espouses a contemplative *via media*. The purpose of this analysis is to provide a basis of appreciation for *The Scale* itself and for the work as a measure. To this end, I compare Hilton's views with those of critics and other contemplatives, especially his contemporaries, while I explicate his teachings.

The analysis is not directed solely to the specialist, but to the general student of mystical literature, mediaeval English literature, or the history of ideas as well. Technical terminology is defined as it appears, and background materials sufficient for an immediate understanding of Hilton's teachings are included when necessary. A portion of Chapter I, moreover, treats three of the most vexing general problems of criticizing mystical literature and the relevance of these problems to *The Scale*, in part as an aid to the reader lacking a background in such studies.

Translations of Middle English, Latin, and French works are given in the text. The notes, however, are arranged for the convenience of those who might wish to look further at primary sources. References to *The Cloud of Unknowing* and *The Book of Margery Kempe* are by chapter as well as page, so that any edition, including the EETS original, may be consulted; other notes, for important, frequently cited works, include page references to the original as well as to the translated text.

What I have gained from previous scholarship, both on mysticism generally and on special topics, is evident in my notes. For particular aid, I am heavily indebted to the late Professor Roland M. Smith, of the University of Illinois. Because of his extensive early criticisms, many difficulties were surmounted and my own goals were more clearly set. Finally, I wish to thank Professor Helen C. White for the suggestions and encouragement which she so kindly gave during the process of revision. Her help substantially affected the progress of my work.

JOSEPH E. MILOSH

Madison, Wisconsin
January, 1966

CONTENTS

The Scale of Perfection

AND THE ENGLISH
MYSTICAL TRADITION

I

A BACKGROUND

Of the fourteenth-century English books on contemplation, the spiritual process leading to a special knowledge of and union with God, Walter Hilton's *Scale of Perfection* is one of the most influential. The number of extant manuscripts (over forty for Book I and at least twenty-four for Book II) suggests that *The Scale* was one of the most widely read of mediaeval mystical works. The first printed edition, brought out by Wynkyn de Worde in 1494 at the command of the mother of Henry VII,[1] and the four subsequent editions by 1533 reflect a further expansion of the popularity of *The Scale*, an expansion permitted by the development of printing in England. Moreover, Father Augustine Baker's high praise and recommendation of *The Scale* in the seventeenth century and the many modern editions of it from the nineteenth century on, including a translation into French and a recent paper-covered modernization, indicate that *The Scale* has had a continuing popularity.

This popularity is due primarily to Hilton's teachings. A portion of *The Scale* is concerned with the ascetic life as a basis for contemplation, and for that portion Hilton makes great use of the religious-handbook tradition, a tradition explaining the means that lead to the simple and devout Christian life attainable by almost any person with a reasonably strong desire for it.[2] While Hilton's use of the religious-handbook tradition attracts those who are just beginning a life centered about spiritual goals,

3

his doctrines on the contemplative life seem to admit one at once to at least the fringes of a relationship with God while encouraging him to advance, with God's grace, to a higher stage as quickly as he can. Finally, both the elements which Hilton uses from the religious-handbook tradition and his teachings on the contemplative life proper are so permeated with moderation that the means and goals Hilton sets do not seem to be highly unnatural. Contemplation never becomes the prerogative of extraordinary personalities, achievable only by those whom God is inclined to knock from their horses and convert with lightning and thunder. In fact, by derogating physical manifestations and in general what the layman might think of as "matters of the occult," like extraordinary weeping or séance-like visions, and by emphasizing meekness and charity as the best indications of one's progress towards perfection, Hilton gives a hope of contemplation and perhaps of eventual mystical union with God to any sincere person willing to reject the world and devote his life to their pursuit.

But besides his teachings, Hilton's method of presentation attracts and encourages readers. Unlike the author of *The Cloud of Unknowing*, who does not deal with the early stages of one's progress towards God and who in his prologue is almost harsh enough to frighten an aspiring contemplative from reading his book because of its high matter,[3] Hilton not only begins his *Scale* at a level which any good Christian can achieve, but helps the reader to ascend the gradual steps towards perfection. He divides his teachings into units which can be assimilated one at a time, and he tells the reader not to try to force his way to God's side. Understanding, and consequently progress, must come naturally, bit by bit: "And if it [*The Scale*] comforteth thee not or else thou takest it not readily, study not too long thereabout; but lay it beside thee till another time, and give thee to thy prayer or to other occupation. Take it as it will come, and not all at once" (I, xciii, p. 222).[4] A final important technique of presentation in *The Scale* is Hilton's interweaving of ascetic and contemplative material. Hilton emphasizes constantly that the contemplative must not forget about the essentials of Christian life. He knows that to teach, one must repeat, and he repeats his most important and basic exhortations and caveats systematically, keeping the contemplative's life balanced, providing comfort and reassurance when they are necessary, and caring for the progressing soul encountering difficulties so that it will not slip backwards. Hilton guides his pupils carefully, and part of his popularity is certainly the result of his pupils' realization that the methods of presentation in *The Scale* encourage them while keeping them secure in their advancement.

Finally, Hilton's personality, as revealed by his attitudes and directions, is responsible for part of the continuing appeal of *The Scale*. His own humility corresponds with his emphasis on the virtue in his writings, suggesting author-reader co-operation in spiritual progress. After a chapter which Hilton thinks is perhaps discouragingly difficult, he stops to clarify, but his clarification is not filled with anything like alienating condescension: "And therefore if thou think that I have herebefore spoken too high to thee, for thou mightest not take it nor fulfill it as I have said or shall say, I will now fall down to thee as low as thou wilt, for my profit as well as for thine" (I, xliv, p. 103). The concluding words are addressed to the reader as a peer capable of accomplishing goals with Hilton, not as an unquestioning disciple of a great master who can be troubled to set down only a few harsh orders which, if the disciple can interpret them correctly, will lead to progress. Hilton, in fact, tells the reader to surpass *The Scale's* teaching: ". . . but do as I have said, and better if thou might" (I, xxxix, p. 91). If Hilton does succeed in encouraging and leading the aspiring contemplative towards perfection, if his guide is effective, and if the reader seems ready to thank him, Hilton quietly backs away, disclaiming credit and humbly refusing to accept thanks even as the creator of a helpful instrument: "And therefore if any word be therein that stirreth or comforteth thee more to the love of God, thank God, for it is His gift and not of the word" (I, xciii, p. 222). Hilton's humility is not mere embellishment. Rather, it is so true that it produces an atmosphere encouraging to the reader, a tone pervading the book and inviting participation, a feeling for the reader which makes difficult goals seem attainable.

Despite Hilton's careful teachings, his use of effective techniques of presentation, and the appeal which stems from his own attitudes, and despite the obvious popularity of *The Scale* as shown by the number of extant manuscripts and printed editions, scholars have not given much critical attention to *The Scale*. While it is true that William Inge as early as 1907 devoted a chapter to Hilton in his *Studies of English Mystics* and, to the discontent of Hope Emily Allen,[5] not one to Rolle, and while recent works on the English mystics by Knowles,[6] Pepler,[7] and Colledge [8] include a chapter on Hilton and often accord him much merit, no extended study of this major work has been made. In fact, Helen Gardner's short essay published in 1937 [9] has remained one of the best critical commentaries on Hilton's guide.

There are explanations for the relative lack of interest in Hilton. In the first place, there is no curiosity-provoking or sensational quality in Hilton's work. Rolle startles us with his sensible fire and amuses us by running off with the two kirtles he took from his sister, who thought he was mad. The author of *The Cloud of Unknowing* startles us with his imagery and appears to be offering an intellectual challenge with his often harsh and daring tone. Julian of Norwich's sickness and subsequent visions with their graphic details and her feelings of disbelief in her own experiences present a concrete foundation for her reflections as well as a puzzle whose explanation is perhaps partly psychological and partly psychosomatic. And the *Book of Margery Kempe*, with its travels to foreign lands, homely problems, phallic temptations, passionate tears, and general audacity could be easily edited into a best seller. If Hilton has an outstanding quality, it is moderation, and by no twisting of words can moderation be called sensational. In the second place, the excellence of *The Scale* is seen only after dissection. Its apparent simplicity as a guide is the result of Hilton's excellence as a teacher, of his being able to present bits of teaching large enough to produce growth but small enough not to satiate, of his foreseeing problems and interweaving solutions. Contemplatives inspired by *The Scale,* as many have been, perhaps realize its value without understanding why the guide succeeds, but the critic can realize *The Scale*'s excellence only after he has analyzed its constitution.

The purpose of this study is to analyze the constitution of *The Scale* and thus to provide an appreciation of Hilton's teachings and methods. In addition, it is my hope that an explanation of the meaning and importance of *The Scale* will cause scholars generally to recognize Hilton's position as the principal contemplative of the fourteenth-century English school, a position long accorded him by many spiritual readers.

Various initial difficulties confront the critic of *The Scale,* some particularly associated with Hilton and others pertaining to the general study of contemplation. First, almost nothing personal about Hilton which can aid in a further understanding of his works is known. He died in 1395/6, probably on March 23, though some manuscripts indicate the vigil of the Annunciation, March 24.[10] Perhaps from Yorkshire or Nottingham,[11] he was an Augustinian canon in Thurgarton priory, near Southwell. Several manuscripts call him master, and one suggests expressly that he was a Doctor of the University of Paris,[12] calling him *"Parisius."* [13] While the Paris degree seems improbable, it is likely that Hilton had a degree in Canon Law, as Joy Russell-Smith has pointed out.[14] Other references to him in manuscripts, calling him *"Sanctus vir in opere et sermone"* and commenting on miracles produced at his tomb, and in works like the *Speculum Spiritualium,* citing *"Venerabilis Hilto"* with Bernard, Augustine, and other doctors of the Church,[15] are brief and serve only to indicate the extent of his reputation.

Moreover, Hilton's works themselves tell the critic little about him that can be helpful in analyzing *The Scale*. It is hardly true, as Inge suggests, that "Walter Hylton keeps his own individuality in the background" [16] or that he is writing a cold, analytical treatise, for Hilton's humility, moderation, warm concern for his pupil, and willingness to teach on any level obviously reveal much of his personality. But it is true that Hilton nowhere sets down autobiographical passages or even interjected comments on his background or education. As for a single autobiographical, interpretive tool for *The Scale* derived from the text itself (for example, that Hilton was a trained theologian), the dangers inherent in extracting a few similar passages from the complexity of *The Scale*, forming a conjecture on the basis of these passages, and turning the conjecture into a theory with which the entirety of *The Scale* is explained are great. A *parti pris* is too easily gotten. Evelyn Underhill, perhaps on the basis of Hilton's use of the religious-handbook tradition, which she seems not to differentiate as a tradition separate from the contemplative one, concludes that despite parallels with learned works in *The Scale*, Hilton was not highly educated: "It would be a mistake, in spite of these many parallels with their evidence of reading, to consider him a learned man. The 'Scale' requires, on the literary side, no more than the ordinary stock-in-trade of the religious writer and preacher of his day." [17] On the other hand, Father Conrad Pepler, perhaps on the basis of the initial divisions in Book I and the final chapters of Book II of *The Scale*, writes in a recent study that Hilton "is at once the most learned and the most analytical of all these writers [Rolle, the author of *The Cloud*, and Mother Julian]." [18] Such disparate evaluations might be avoidable, of course, if scholars had definite biographical information about Walter Hilton.

But the critic of *The Scale* lacks not only biographical data to aid him; he lacks an exact text also. Textual studies of *The Scale* were begun some years ago by Evelyn Underhill for an edition of the work published in 1923, but Miss Underhill examined only ten manuscripts. On the basis of her examination she chose for her copy text Harley 6579, a manuscript containing two features which might not have appeared in Hilton's original text. The first of these, which she calls "brief Christo-centric additions and expansions," [19] consists of short phrases, often repetitive or superfluous, which refer to the name of Jesus or to the humanity of Christ. Miss Underhill argues that the Christo-centric additions are Hilton's, but that they are a part of his alteration of an early Book I:

At a later period, perhaps because his own spiritual experience had deepened and taken a more warmly Christo-centric colour, perhaps because too great an encouragement of abstract contemplation of the Godhead was regarded as dangerous, Book I was revised and though its general plan was undisturbed, numerous brief Christo-centric additions and expansions were made to it.[20]

In an essay published in 1936, however, Helen Gardner, on the basis of a textual study and literary analysis, argues carefully and convincingly that the short expansions in many manuscripts are due not to Hilton, but to later owners of the manuscripts, perhaps Carthusians at Syon or Sheen, who glossed Hilton's text:

Their effect [the effect of the expansions] upon the subject matter is not so far-reaching as Miss Underhill suggests. They are rarely more than a phrase and never more than a short sentence; often they are mere repetitions to enforce a point, sometimes slight expansions of a point already made, sometimes they refer back to a slightly earlier point in the argument and sometimes they appear to have no function at all except to overload the sentence.[21]

Critics may never be certain whether the Christo-centric additions are Hilton's or not, even though Miss Gardner's study is convincing, very precise, and based on the examination of thirty manuscripts of *The Scale*.

But for a study of Hilton's teachings, certainty about the authenticity of the Christo-centric additions is not very important, for as Miss Gardner points out, the additions do not alter the meaning of the passages in which they appear. While the additions are more than pious ejaculations, they usually contain purely devotional material, material which presents the reader with a concrete and inspiring thought on which to base his action or his prayer. When Hilton is advocating that one who is being tempted should not strive too violently to put down his evil thoughts by his own power, he suggests that the good man might regard temptation as a punishment for his sins. The words in brackets represent the expansion:

And yet if they will aye hang upon them, then it is good to them that they be not angry nor heavy for to feel them, but that they with a good trust in God will bear them, as it were a bodily pain, and a scourge of our Lord, for cleansing of their sins, as long as He will [for His love, as He was scourged and bare the Cross for their love]. (I, xxxviii, p. 87)

The addition here, a typical one, recalls from the life of Christ a particular reason for the action recommended above, but it in no way influences the action recommended. Moreover, the Christo-centric additions are basically composed of material that Hilton recommends in other chapters (I, xxxiv–xxxvi) as being the foundation of profitable meditation. Consequently, they do not present the critic with material which is not found elsewhere in *The Scale*. Also, that the basis of most of the expansions is found in chapters specifically devoted to meditation, especially on the passion, possibly gives force to Helen Gardner's argument that the expansions are by a pious monk. An annotator trying to make *The Scale* more inspiring or concrete in spots might humbly hesitate to add his own comments, comments not justifiable by reference to the text of the master. By re-using parts of *The Scale* to emphasize other parts, the interpolator might defend his inspiring expansions as already accepted, *totidem verbis*, by Hilton. But again, the expansions need not be definitely ascribed or not ascribed to Hilton. Since they do not alter the meaning of the passages in which they appear and since the material they are composed of is basically what Hilton discusses elsewhere, the expansions do not affect an analysis of Hilton's teachings.

However, a second feature of Harley 6579 and its group, an extension of chapter xliv of Book I, does affect Hilton's teaching. Fortunately, critics and textual scholars have agreed on its authenticity. The extension, about four printed pages long, is commonly called the "passage on the Holy Name." Sometimes praised for exactly the opposite of what it teaches, the passage is both important and, although it contains material not found elsewhere in *The Scale,* consistent with Hilton's teachings. Helen Gardner, agreeing with Evelyn Underhill, argues that the passage on the Holy Name can be shown to be authentic from internal and external evidence:

> There can be no doubt that the passage on the Holy Name is genuine. Both style and matter are typical of Hilton at his best. He is adopting his favourite method of giving every man his due and of rationalizing the more extravagant expressions of mysticism.
>
> . . . .
>
> Internal evidence suggests that the passage was in the original text and was afterwards omitted. Chapter xlv begins with a strong warning against presuming on the mercy of God. This follows quite naturally after the passage on the Holy Name with its promise of salvation to all who desire ghostly health. But it does not follow on well to the end of chapter xliv if the long passage is omitted.
>
> . . . .
>
> The external evidence for the authenticity of the passage and for its presence in the original text is that it is part of the text in the Vernon and Simeon manuscripts, which date from the end of the fourteenth century, that is possibly from Hilton's own lifetime. On the other hand two manuscripts which are dated as late fourteenth-century also, Harley 1022 and Dd. v. 55, omit it.
>
> Stronger evidence is that this passage is included in the text of the Latin translation.
>
> . . . .
>
> It is also worth noting that the Thornton manuscript in the Cathedral Library at Lincoln, which contains chapter xliv as an independent and unascribed tract, does not give the disputed passage alone, but gives the whole of chapter xliv with the last

sentence of chapter xliii. There is thus no evidence that the disputed passage ever existed independently of the main text.[22]

Of these two particular textual problems of *The Scale*, then, the first, concerning the Christo-centric additions, need not be solved, while the second, concerning the passage on the Holy Name, has been solved. But the lack of a critical text of *The Scale* continues to pose a difficulty. There are modernizations of *The Scale*, but perhaps because of the number of manuscripts that would have to be collated for this longest of the fourteenth-century contemplative works, no one has yet produced a definitive edition.[23]

For a number of reasons this study is based on Evelyn Underhill's text, first published in 1923 and put through a second impression in 1948. In the first place, the Underhill text follows very closely Harley 6579, the manuscript which contains both the Christo-centric passages and the passage on the Holy Name and which S. S. Hussey has chosen as the copy text for his edition of Book II.[24] Miss Underhill's modernization, also, consists mainly of spelling modernizations; it is not a rewriting of Hilton in current English, and, in fact, it follows the sentence structure of Harley 6579 rather exactly. The Underhill edition, moreover, is a standard text of *The Scale*. It is probably the one most commonly used by the critics of the contemplatives, and it supplies the quotations in perhaps the best known work on the English contemplatives, Knowles' *The English Mystical Tradition*. Finally, the second impression of it is presently available.

A preliminary explanation must be made here of the seeming difficulty caused by the division of *The Scale* into separate books. Wells assumed that *The Scale* contains three books,[25] evidently because some manuscripts subdivide Book II after chapter xxx.[26] This view is not accepted, but scholars do recognize within the work two books, each possessing distinguishing characteristics. Miss Underhill suggests that Book II shows "signs of an increase in spiritual maturity and surety of touch" and that perhaps it was written some years after Book I.[27] Miss Gardner maintains that "the two books are very different in treatment, though both handle the same theme."[28] And other critics seem to agree at least with Dom Noetinger's comments that the two books were not produced at the same time and that variations in tone and style differentiate them.[29] But whether Books I and II were composed separately, whether they show differences in the author's maturity, or whether they were intended for different audiences, they agree on all points of doctrine.[30] In fact, the essential qualities of each book differ so little that a critic, admitting variations resulting from the specific demands of particular materials treated, can tacitly ignore the possibility that the two books were composed at various times and treat *The Scale* as a unit. Father Pepler does this in his section on Hilton in *The English Religious Heritage.* I treat *The Scale* as a unified work and shall show in the final criticism that there are clear and definite major relations between the two books and that the two together teach a constant progress.

Besides the difficulties which stem from the lack of biographical knowledge of Hilton and from textual uncertainties, three other problems pertinent to the criticism of any contemplative work must be recognized here, even if they cannot be solved.

The first of these problems derives not from the mystics, but from their critics. In the works of some of the well-known commentators on the mystics exists a fault which causes various lacks of balance, a fault which consists of subordinating what the mystics say to an external, arbitrary thesis. William R. Inge, for example, whose Bampton Lectures of 1899 were responsible for much of the impetus given to the study of the mystics in the twentieth century, has been called the author of "excellent," "scientifically thorough" work.[31] Indeed, he is often very perceptive. Yet the Bampton Lectures, his *Studies of English Mystics,* and especially his later *Mysticism in Religion* at times seem distorted because of anti-Catholicism. In a lecture on Hilton given in 1905 he comments that "it is not a sign of Protestant prejudice to assert that the mystical literature of the pre-

Reformation period is more valuable and edifying than anything that the Roman Church has produced since."[32] This view, gratuitous in context, suggests the kind of underlying personal persuasion which easily produces inaccuracies. In his last book, published in 1948, Inge casts off all semblance of tolerance and rather patently reveals an important conviction affecting his study: that Anglicism by its nature sympathizes with mysticism while Catholicism does not.[33] When such a theory underlies the basis of one's choice of materials, his explanations of what the mystics say, and his critical comments, the resulting critique certainly must be suspect.

Opposite to the anti-Catholic critics, like Inge and Fairweather, are the pro-Catholic ones, like Colledge, who prefers to analyze the writings of the mystics in the light of modern Catholic doctrine, to praise and emphasize constantly exactly what Inge attacks, the authority of the Church, and to preach a sort of mediaeval-modern obscurantism. At the beginning of his long introduction to selections from mediaeval English contemplatives, Colledge, having stated that "inspired seekers" may reach the point at which "private illumination" can reveal certain truths about God's mysteries, immediately warns that we must beware of all speculation because of the danger of heresy:

But before those who arrive at this point proceed from it to assert that in the resemblances between the teachings of the world's great Christian and pagan mystics we have some highest common denominator which renders negligible their differences, they would do well to read on in St. Paul, to note that he is led directly from this to his statement that hitherto such speculation upon the divine mysteries has too often resulted in doctrinal error and moral perversion of the worst kind.

He is here speaking of pre-Christian religious history, but we know well that his words have been confirmed again and again during the Christian era. . . .[34]

What Colledge says is essentially true, and indeed his caveat has foundation in *The Scale* itself. Yet, to deal with only the purely orthodox mystics or to present only what a modern theologian regards as the orthodox passages from the writings of a mystic is to distort or ignore what in fact existed, a major problem between orthodoxy and the validity of private illumination. Assuming that the mystical writings which are not congruous with the orthodoxy of the Catholic Church are of no value or even dangerous because they are heretical can lead the critic, again, to an inaccurate basis of choice of materials for historical explication.

Of course, such a lack of balance is not characteristic of all the critics of the mystics. Phyllis Hodgson's work on *The Cloud* and its attendant treatises and Hope Emily Allen's work on the *Book of Margery Kempe* merit the highest praise because of their care and competence. Among the religious who write about the mystics are equally careful, generally unprejudiced critics. Father Pepler and Dom Cuthbert Butler are both willing to admit that they cannot understand certain problems and unwilling to simplify unjustly to attain a personal end dictated by religious belief. Dom David Knowles, the author of the most popular survey of the English mystics, seems never to allow his Catholicism to dictate or color explanations. And it is generally, but not always, true that the recent critics of mysticism are more disinterested and accurate than their predecessors.[35] But the colored criticism, which on certain points outweighs the disinterested criticism, presents a major problem: sorting.

Such a problem is easier avoided than solved. Relying heavily on primary sources to substantiate arguments and referring to the critics only for generally agreed upon materials or to acknowledge indebtedness will produce an analytical method which is workable and safe. Such a method, moreover, is consistent with advice given by two very competent writers on the mystics. Evelyn Underhill pointed out some years ago that the works of the mystics are "for the most part left unread by those who now talk much about mysticism" and that the mystics "can only be studied in their works." [36] And Dom Cuthbert Butler has written that there is a superfluity of books about mysticism and that "what is needed is a more objective presentation of what the mystics themselves thought about their mysticism, to be determined by a systematic study and formulation of the ideas of the principal mystics. . . ." [37]

The second difficulty pertaining to the criticism of mysticism in general proceeds from one of the major qualities of mysticism itself, ineffability. William James remarks that ineffability is an easy identifier of the mystical state, going on to explain that the quality makes the mystical experience in a certain way like feeling rather than knowing. A noncontemplative observer cannot understand the experience fully any more than, for example, one who has never loved can understand the feeling of one who loves.[38]

Ineffability is a quality of mysticism in general, not only of mediaeval mysticism. The Moslem mystics and Plotinus both noted the quality in their experiences,[39] and St. Augustine, amplifying on Moses' desire to see God in his essence, agrees that in ecstasy or a mystical experience one hears "unspeakable words that man may not utter" (2 Cor. 12:4).[40] The mediaeval contemplatives, even while they are teaching the means to achieve the mystical experience, explicitly remark that the experience proper cannot be communicated. The author of *The Cloud of Unknowing* says that he might be able to help a man who feels himself drawn by grace to achieve the experience, but that he dares not attempt to explain it with his "blabbering fleshly tongue." [41] And in *The Book of Privy Counselling* he writes,

But now, for to make satisfaction to thy proud wit, in commending of this work, truly I tell thee that if a soul that is thus occupied had tongue and language to say as it feeleth, then all the clerks in christendom should wonder at that wisdom. Yea! and in comparison of it all their great learning should seem open folly. And therefore no wonder that I cannot tell thee the worthiness of this work with my boisterous, beastly tongue. And God forbid that it should be so defouled in itself, for to be strained under the stirrings of a fleshly tongue. Nay, it may not be! And truly it will not be, and God forbid that I should covet it! [42]

Margery Kempe also found that what she learned from the Lord's visitation or from "holy contemplation" was unutterable:

They were so holy and so high that she was abashed to tell them to any creature, and also they were so high above her bodily wits that she might never express them with her bodily tongue, as she felt them.
    She understood them better in her soul than she could utter them. [43]

Walter Hilton, explaining the knowledge one gets from the mystical experience, says that it is had "with a wonderful reverence and a privy burning love and with ghostly savour and heavenly delight, more clearly and more fully than it may be written or said" (II, xxxii, p. 371).

The ineffability of the mystical experience is chiefly caused by what James and others call the noetic quality of the same experience. In a mystical experience one becomes aware of a truth beyond that to which dialectics can lead, a truth not the result of one's own efforts or of the epistemological process. This "direct encounter with absolute truth," as Evelyn Underhill calls it, [44] is totally different from any other knowledge one has. This total difference first puts the mystic in a position in which he has no words to convey the experience, since his words have meanings and associations only in the world of knowledge common to him and to the rest of humanity and not in the world of the new truth. Secondly it puts the reader or hearer of the experience in the state of the man who has never been in love but who is trying to understand the mind of a lover, as James suggests. The experience is ineffable, then, both from the point of view of the mystic who has it and of the nonmystic trying to understand it.

Moreover, if the new truth is about God, as it is in Christian mysticism, the finite mind of man is perceiving, even though perhaps only in a minute way, the infinity of the Supreme Being. As Hilton points out, such perception of the Infinite by the finite can be had only as the gift of the Infinite; consequently, even if the new knowledge could be conveyed by means of a common language, it could be conveyed only to a finite mind to which God has given the ability to perceive the Infinite. This disparity between the finite mind understanding and the Infinite to be understood also causes the quality of ineffability.

Despite the quality of ineffability, mystics have attempted to convey the nature of the experience and nonmystics have attempted to appreciate it. Inevitably misunderstanding has resulted. The mystics in general have tried to prevent misunderstanding by warning those who are not sufficiently prepared or not sincere to avoid mystical matters. The author of *The Cloud* is particularly emphatic:

> But as for worldly praters, open praisers and blamers of themselves or of any other, gossips, whisperers, tale-bearers and all manner of carpers: cared I never that they saw this book. For mine intent was never to write such thing unto them. And therefore I would that they meddled not therewith; neither they nor any of these curious learned or unlearned men. Yea, though they be full good men in active living, yet this matter accordeth nothing to them.[45]

And Hilton warns not only that *The Scale* is not for actives, but also that even contemplatives who do not readily understand it should set it aside until another time (I, xciii).

The mystics realize that it is easy to misunderstand what they say, especially since the quality of ineffability often forces them to write metaphorically. When Hilton talks of the song of angels as comforting a soul, he states that the song "may not be described by no bodily likeness, for it is ghostly, and above all manner of imagination and reason."[46] Yet he continues to refer to the comfort as song. In *The Scale*, perhaps referring to difficulties arising because of Rolle's terminology (although Rolle insists that the fire he experienced in his soul was a sensible one[47]),

Hilton warns against taking literally what is said metaphorically:

All men that speaketh of the fire of love knoweth not well what it is; for what it is can I not tell thee, save this may I tell thee, that it is neither bodily, nor it is not bodily felt. A soul may feel it in prayer, or in devotion, which soul is in the body, but he feeleth it not by no bodily wit. For though it be so, that if it work in a soul the body may turn into an heat and as it were chafen for likened travail of the spirit; nevertheless the fire of love is not bodily, for it is only in the ghostly desire of the soul. This is no doubt to no man or woman that feeleth devotion; but some are simple, and ween because that it is called fire that it should be hot as bodily fire is. And for this I say that I have said. (I, xxvi, p. 59)

Such repeated warnings must affect the modern critic. The real danger lies, of course, not in the critic's being baffled completely by the meaning of a certain passage, but in his believing that he understands when he does not.

Fortunately, the problem caused by the ineffability of the mystical experience is not so great in *The Scale* as in the works of many other contemplatives. In the first place, an important portion of Hilton's material is from the religious-handbook tradition, which is clear on such matters as preparation for the religious life and asceticism. Secondly, Hilton spends much more time with the lower levels of contemplation and with the means for the progress of the soul than with the highest level, the mystical experience proper, probably because while the lower levels of contemplative life and the means for progress can be explained, the highest level must be experienced to be understood. Finally, Hilton is generally exceedingly clear, and when he begins to leave precise, literal statement, he usually accompanies his metaphorically intended material with a warning to the reader to interpret spiritually rather than to swallow literally. The warning may be like the one in the passage from the "Song of Angels" quoted above, or it may take the form of a grammatical emphasis on the metaphor involved, as in the heading for I, xxx (p. 67): "That this manner of prayer pleaseth much God, and maketh a man to have him *as he were* drunken . . ." (italics mine). Whenever ineffability does cause difficulties, I label my explanation as conjectural or follow the example of Dom Cuthbert Butler, whose caution obliges him to say at times, ". . . the meaning of which, however, I confess is not clear to me." [48]

The last general problem pertaining to the study of the mystics —a problem which must be solved, even if arbitrarily, if any precision is desired—is the basic one of definition of terms. Scholars have realized that the great variety of definitions of "mysticism" and "contemplation" has succeeded in confusing the study of mysticism. Yet, instead of firmly adopting a set of specific terms to work with, they have usually been satisfied with including in their own studies lists of various definitions of mysticism or, as Inge does in *Christian Mysticism,* an appendix of mystical terms defined by as many people in as many ways as possible. To these definitions they normally add their own, an all-encompassing definition which seems to be an attempt not to exclude any sort of extraordinary experience rather than an effort to delineate a specific state or study.

Before 1900 Robert Vaughan, the universally disparaged author of *Hours with the Mystics,* realized the confusion over terms: "Is it not almost inevitable, when the significance of the word mysticism is so broad and ill-defined, that those who speak of it should misunderstand or be misunderstood? What two persons can you meet with who will define the term in precisely the same way? The word is in itself a not less general and extensive one than *revolution,* for instance." [49] But later critics who disparaged Vaughan did not learn from him. Arthur Edward Waite in his *Studies in Mysticism* [50] writes about everything from the mystical experience proper, as I define it, to hypnotism and table-moving séances as being part of the study of mysticism. James, talking about bringing on a mystical experience, says that "the sway of alcohol over mankind is unquestionably due to its power to stimulate the mystical faculties of human nature, usually crushed to earth by the cold facts and dry criticisms of the sober hour," and that "nitrous oxide and ether, especially nitrous oxide, when sufficiently diluted with air, stimulate the mystical consciousness in an extraordinary degree. Depth beyond depth of truth seems revealed to the inhaler." [51] The mediaeval contemplatives, who believe that the truth of the mystical experience is directly the gift of God, would hardly accord the adjective "mystical" to the "revelations" of intoxication. Even among the critics who accept the mystical experience as a religious one there is confusion. Fairweather says that mysticism is the result of "a natural impulse that leads human nature to cry out for the living God" and consequently that "in some degree, surely, every true Christian is a mystic." [52] While such a conclusion may result in the inspiration of the pious, it obviously confuses the true mystical state with the simple devotion of men of good will. Even Hope Emily Allen, when she explains her opinion of Margery Kempe, says that she has treated Margery as a mystic, that is, as having "the spiritual graces (or psychological phenomena) which are called mysticism." [53] But making "psychological phenomena" equivalent to "spiritual graces" constructs a definition of mysticism which might include Lear's ranting on the heath as well as Hilton's peace. Here Miss Allen, by not according her definition a major quality, is hardly being more precise than if she were to say that Margery was either inspired by God or demented.[54]

Besides the lack of precision in defining "mysticism," or perhaps because of it, a pejorative connotation has become associated with the word. Fairweather remarks that the word has been "too much associated with dreamy visionaries," [55] and the *Oxford English Dictionary* recognizes that the word can be used as a "term of reproach": "From the hostile point of view, mysticism implies self-delusion or dreamy confusion of thought; hence the term is often applied loosely to any religious belief to which these evil qualities are imputed." Adding to the difficulty is the popular connotation: in Robert Penn Warren's *All the King's Men* Jack Burden says that he "would study Lois with a clinical detachment and a sense of mystic regeneration" and that "almost at will" he "could produce an optical illusion"; [56] and Rachel Carson in *The Sea Around Us* describes the evolution of man as the transformation of mammals "into beings with the body and brain and the mystical spirit of man." [57] Warren uses "mystic regeneration" to mean, apparently, "heady reflection," and Miss Carson uses "mystical" to mean "inscrutable" or "supernatural," with an overtone of "mysterious."

In this analysis, "mysticism" and "contemplation" are used synonymously with the following meanings. *Contemplation* and *mysticism* will refer to a spiritual process only, not to the physical acts of fasting or the like which may occur in conjunction with it and which are properly part of asceticism. Contemplation will refer to a process purely religious in intent, a process which should culminate in a special union with God in which the soul submits completely to the Divine wish. Contemplation will refer to the entire religious process, to all stages in the process, even though various stages or divisions may have particular names. Negatively, *contemplation* and *mysticism* will never be used to refer to merely occult studies, to the work of magicians or hypnotists, or to otherwise strange or even inexplicable physical or psychological happenings. In short, contemplation will mean the total spiritual, religious process which leads to and involves, as Hilton says, "that feeling of love and ghostly knowing of God by opening of the ghostly eye" (I, xlv, p. 109).

Of the various stages in the process of contemplation, two must be given specific names at once. Meditation is a lower level of contemplation which entails considering inspiring scenes or good thoughts, especially those which are scriptural.[58] Meditation depends heavily upon images, most often caused by a voluntary effort, which lead one to a greater active love of God. Meditation, for example, is the compassionate consideration of

Lord Jhesu in a bodily likeness, as He was in earth, and how He was taken of the Jews and bound as a thief, beaten and despised, scourged and deemed to the death, how lowly He bare the cross upon His back, and how cruelly He was nailed thereupon; also of the crown of thorns upon His head, and of the sharp spear that stang Him to the heart. . . . (I, xxxv, p. 79)

At the top of the total process of contemplation is, properly, the mystical experience. The mystical experience is what Hilton calls the highest level of contemplation or perfect contemplation,[59] and it consists basically of "an experimental perception of God's Being and Presence."[60] Delacroix best contrasts the nature of meditation with that of the mystical experience:

The mystics distinguish two manners of thinking, one by means of discourse—in essence a progression of ideas—supported by images, the other by means of intuition. In religious matters, this discourse is meditation; the understanding, aided by the imagination, develops a theme, cuts out, or rather makes up, a unified whole. Discourse is logical, reflected thought which is divided into operations and is effected in discrete acts. It is applicable to all explicit Christianity, which because of the multiplicity of its dogmas and the complexity of its ethic, because of the richness of its history and its worship, is a marvelous subject for it, always diverse and always one. Intuition, on the other hand, apprehends suddenly, without ideas and without analysis, in an unresolved and undetermined way, a reality which, outside of any relation to an object or a subject, is given as absolute.[61]

In the light of the preceding background material, caveats, and terms, an examination of *The Scale* can begin.

THE THREE CHRISTIAN LIVES
AND THE LEVELS
OF CONTEMPLATION

Contemplation has been defined as the total spiritual, religious process which leads to and involves a new perception of and union with God. Contemplation, being the spiritual process and the states in it, is distinct, then, from the external or physical life of the person enjoying the process. Yet the type of external life one leads, whether that of a recluse or of a man of affairs, has been associated, since Martha served while Mary listened, with the degree of development of one's spiritual state. Mystics of all sorts, including the Desert Fathers and the members of the various sects prevalent by the fourth century after Christ, sought to achieve perfection partially by rejecting the goods and consequently the cares of the world, and eventually popular notions led to the quick association of the secluded life with a high spiritual state and the worldly life with a low one. Such associations are maintained today, though with qualifications, by the Catholic Church, which places the layman below the parish priest and the priest below the monk in its spiritual hierarchy. The mediaeval contemplatives also distinguish between those leading secluded lives and those leading active ones, and although they do not make contemplation the exclusive property of the recluse, they allow only to him the full use of the highest parts of it. The author of *The Cloud* says that even actives who are "full good men" are not to be given his book,[1] and Hilton distinguishes the active from the contemplative in the same way when he says that *The Scale* belongs "not all to a man which hath active life" (I, xciii, p. 223).

For Hilton an active is a good Christian who is generally occupied with external affairs. Citing Gregory, he distinguishes the active life as one of the two lives which may lead a man to salvation (I, ii), separating the active life from the life of a sinner, who will be damned. In regarding the active life as the life of a good Christian, Hilton is also in the fourteenth-century contemplative tradition, which, springing from the general distinction made by the Church Fathers,[2] sets up the three categories of the damned, the actives, and the contemplatives.[3] The active, as the author of *The Cloud* points out, must be occupied with "man's learning and his natural knowledge"; consequently, God is with him only in "suffering and consent," while he is with the contemplative as a motivating force, "stirring and working."[4] But again, the active unquestionably has a place in heaven. As Hilton insistently harks back, "*In domo patris mei multae mansiones sunt*"; moreover, although the active is not one of God's "darlings," he is one of God's "friends" (I, xliv, pp. 107–8). To earn his place in heaven, the active must obey the two great commandments, to love God and to love his neighbor. But as Hilton says, agreeing with Rolle's teaching in "The Form of Living,"[5] in the active's life the love must be shown "outward by good bodily works; in fulfilling of God's commandments and of the seven works of mercy, bodily and ghostly, to a man's evenchristian" (I, ii, p. 3; see also I, xli; I, lxvi). Besides, the active must practice some forms of asceticism, mortifying himself moderately to build strength to ward off temptation and to make his body subject to his spirit. The clearest comprehensive definition of the active life permitted by these characteristics is a negative one: the active life embraces all good Christian life, including clerical and religious life, that is not primarily contemplative.

The active may not be able to become a contemplative for a number of reasons. In the first place, the contemplative life is one to which a soul is invited by God; of the saved souls, some will be asked to dine with the Lord, but others will be asked to drink with him (I, xliv). That it is the invitation of God which determines one's state is emphasized by Hilton in the first sentence of *The Scale*, in which he advises the reader, a recluse, to "stand steadfastly" "in the calling [in] which our Lord hath called thee to His service." Moreover, a man's worldly obligations may restrain him from leaving the active life, as Hilton constantly suggests in his "Mixed Life"; that is, he may have "state, office, or cure over other men, and have goods for to spend" (I, ii, p. 3). Finally, one, even a contemplative, might be forced to the active life by God, perhaps to serve the Church in a particular way. Gregory, for example, although he lamented losing the time and atmosphere for contemplation, accepted the bidding of the Church to become pope.[6]

The active life, even apart from its espousal by popes and bishops called to it specially by God, is not without its rewards and importance. It leads to salvation: works of mercy or good deeds, such as building chapels or hospitals, gain merit in heaven for the charitable active (I, lxvi). In fact, since the degree of charity a Christian possesses, not his external state, determines his "sovereign and principal" reward, it is possible for an active to merit a high place in heaven:

The one [reward] is sovereign and principal, as is love and knowing of Him after the measure of charity given of God to a soul living in deadly flesh. This meed is best and sovereign, for it is God Himself; and it is common to all the souls that shall be saved in what state or degree that they be living in Holy Kirk, more or less after the quantity and the mickle head of their charity. For he that most loveth God in charity here in this life, what degree he be in, be he lewd or learned, secular or religious, he shall have most meed in the bliss of heaven, for he shall most love God and know Him, and that is the sovereign meed. And as for this meed, it shall fall that some worldly man or woman, as a lord or a lady, knight or squire, merchant or plowman, or what degree he be in, man or woman, shall have more meed than some priest, or friar, monk or canon or anker enclosed. (I, lxi, p. 147)

Also, the active life is important as a means to contemplation, for the charitable works of active life, including moderate ascetic practices, predispose one to receive the gift of contemplation by subordinating things of the body to things of the spirit (I, ii). While Hilton's teaching that the active life is a means to contemplation is traditional, Hilton does not emphasize the necessity of the active life as the Church Fathers do. Both Augustine and Gregory maintain that the active life must precede the contemplative life and that the active life is necessary while the contemplative life is "optional," perhaps a luxury.[7] Hilton, however, although he accords merit to the active life and even insists that one leading an active life may receive a higher reward than one leading a contemplative life, does not argue that the meritorious works of the active life are an absolute prerequisite for the contemplative life. For Hilton, the active life is a necessity only when worldly cares or God's appointment makes it so. Otherwise it is inferior to the contemplative life. The active life is important, finally, in that it can enable one to achieve at least the lower levels of contemplation. Usually the active can hope to attain only "the lower degree of the second part of contemplation," a fervent prayer and a "little tasting of the sweetness of the love of God" (I, vi, p. 11), but by a "special grace" an active can receive even the third or highest part of contemplation, although he cannot enjoy this gift fully (I, ix, p. 18). In maintaining that the active life allows the enjoyment of only the lower parts of contemplation, Hilton is opposed to most modern critics, like Miss Underhill, who sees in the contemplatives an ability to make contemplation and external activity coincide:

The mind, concentrated upon a higher object of interest, is undistracted by its own likes and dislikes; and performs efficiently the work that is given it to do. Where it does not do so, then the normal make-up of the subject, rather than its mystical proclivities, must be blamed. St. Catherine of Genoa found in this divine companionship the power which made her hospital a success. St. Teresa was an admirable housewife, and declared that she found her God very easily amongst the pots and pans. Appearances notwithstanding, Mary would probably have been a better cook than Martha, had circumstances forced on her this form of activity.[8]

Hilton's teachings on the active life, especially in contrast to those of his contemporaries, are both reasonable and sympathetic. Rolle believes that an active is like a stork, which has wings but cannot fly: he might have the potential to ascend towards God in contemplation, but he cannot ascend because he is weighed down with worldly affections and vanities.[9] Rolle also, starting with the principle that charity determines sovereign meed, the principle that Hilton explains in the quotation above, sets up a comparison entirely different from Hilton's. While Hilton interprets the principle as meaning that a plowman may have a higher place in heaven than an anchorite, Rolle explains it as meaning that the contemplative must have a higher place than the active or preacher, for the contemplative must have more love.[10] The difference in interpretation illustrates the difference in attitudes: whereas Rolle wants to read all as extolling the contemplative life, Hilton wants to be sure that the active life is treated justly. The author of *The Cloud*, who theoretically—or perhaps sophistically—sees a relation between the active and contemplative lives,[11] has little practical use for actives. While he says that their attacks on contemplatives should be excused because of their ignorance,[12] he also calls down the voice of the Lord to tell them not to meddle with contemplatives [13] and tells the "half-meeked souls," as he calls them, to be content with their lot, for they will be saved in some way.[14]

Hilton never attacks actives. While he reserves the higher parts of contemplation for contemplatives and while he gives the charitable contemplative more reward than the charitable active, he never feels the need to derogate the active life to emphasize the excellence of the contemplative one. Also, he is realistically sympathetic with the flaws of the actives, at one point pardoning them when he would not pardon a contemplative: actives may be "somewhat excusable" for being lukewarm in their spiritual exercises, but those who have few worldly cares, like religious, "are more for to blame for that they stand still as they were idle" (II, xviii, p. 291). Hilton's attitude toward actives is between that of Gregory and Augustine and that of Rolle and the author of *The Cloud*. He accepts the active life as necessary, but only for those bound by worldly duties; he regards the active life as inferior to the contemplative one, but he willingly accords it its proper merits.

Opposite to the active life is the contemplative life, which must not be confused with contemplation. While contemplation, again, is a spiritual process, the contemplative life is the external life led by one who wishes to devote all of his efforts to achieving the highest levels of contemplation. This external life may be cenobitic or anchoritic. For example, it may be that of a religious in a convent, like the "ghostly sister" to whom *The Scale* is addressed, or of a contemplative like Rolle, who, though not a religious, forsook the world. The characteristics of the contemplative life, then, are both internal and external. Internally, one seeks God, and externally, he rejects the world:

Contemplative life lieth in perfect love and charity felt inwardly by ghostly virtues, and by soothfast knowing and sight of God and ghostly things. This life belongeth specially to them which forsake for the love of God all worldly riches, worships and outward businesses and wholly give them body and soul up, their mights and their cunning, to service of God by ghostly occupation. Now then, since it is so that thy state asketh for to be contemplative, for that is the end and the intent of thine enclosing, that thou mightest more freely and entirely give thee to ghostly occupation: then behoveth thee for to be right busy night and day. . . . (I, iii, p. 5)

It would seem that the solitude of the contemplative life, the external characteristic, would not be nearly so important as the internal characteristic, the desire for contemplation; however, for Hilton and his contemporaries the solitude is almost of tantamount importance. Rolle says in *The Mending of Life* that "ilk man contemplative loves solitariness," [15] and Margaret Deanesly has pointed to the obvious fact that Rolle's "estimate of the worthiness of the solitary life is more mediaeval than modern."[16] Rolle specifically criticizes those who do not value the solitary life and explains who is truly alone: "Others err worse that cease not to reprove and slander solitary life, saying: *Vae soli;* that is to say: 'Woe be to a man alone'; not expounding 'alone' as 'without God,' but 'without a fellow.' He truly is alone with whom God is not. . . ."[17] The author of *The Cloud* also defends the rejection of the world, even against the critics who suggest, economically, that men should not lead contemplative lives "except they be secure beforehand of their bodily necessaries"; God will provide, he responds, either by giving the necessaries or the "strength in body and patience in spirit to bear need."[18] And Margery Kempe is in one passage advised that, if she wants to devote her life to God, she should retire from the world: "So an old monk . . . took her by the hand, saying unto her:—'What canst thou say of God?' 'Sir,' she said, 'I will both speak of Him, and hear of Him,' repeating to the monk a story of Scripture. The monk said:—'I would thou wert enclosed in a house of stone, so that, there, no man should speak with thee.'"[19] Hilton, throughout *The Scale,* stresses the rejection of the world and the solitude of the contemplative life. To "cast out full cleanly all loves and likings, sorrows and dreads of all earthly things" (I, xlvii, p. 115), the contemplative must cast off "earthly business," which dulls the lantern lighting the way to perfection (I, xlviii, p. 117). One must be like the "ghostly sister" of *The Scale,* that is, enclosed, if he wishes to appreciate fully the gift of contemplation (I, ix).

Hilton's emphasis on the necessity of solitude for high contemplation seems very clear, despite the contrary view of recent critics.[20] Joy Russell-Smith, after citing a number of passages in which Hilton assigns contemplation to those in the contemplative state, goes on to argue that the mature Hilton is interested in contemplation for Christians in all lives. Her argument is based primarily on the observation that Hilton's insistence on the necessity of solitude occurs in Book I, while in Book II, a later and more sophisticated treatise, it is lacking.[21] But such an observation does not necessarily lead to the conclusion that Hilton changed his mind in Book II. The lack of insistence on basic notions in the second book corresponds with the more advanced state of the reader addressed there, a reader who has already absorbed in Book I the division between active and contemplative together with the prerogatives of each. And that the division is a basic notion is made clear by Mrs. Russell-Smith's own ample quotation from Book I. Moreover, if Hilton had changed his mind in Book II, we might expect some revision of Book I, or at least a specific statement in II that actives need not be put off by the earlier distinctions. Since we find neither, it is likely that Hilton continued to maintain the tie between high contemplation and solitude.

It is possible to lead a contemplative life and never achieve the heights of contemplation, especially by thwarting the purpose of the contemplative life and assuming only its external qualities. In the first chapter of *The Scale* Hilton counsels the reader that the soul as well as the body must reject the world, for "a bodily turning to God without the heart following, is but a figure and a likeness of virtues and no soothfastness" (p. 1). And those who enter a cloistered order "for a worldly cause, as for their bodily sustenance or some other such cause" are scarcely leading contemplative lives (I, lx, p. 144). Accurately defined, of course, such lives would merit only the adjective "solitary," and not "contemplative."

The rewards of the contemplative life are great. Not only does the contemplative have the sole right to the "full use" of the highest part of contemplation, but he also gets a sovereign reward according to his charity, as the active does. In addition, he receives a special reward of grace which comes from rejecting "all wilful businesses of earthly things unto the bare need," a reward for those in any state—"priest, clerk, or lewd man, widow, wife or maiden"—who give "wholly their will and their body to God's service" (I, lx, pp. 144–45). Finally, he gets an "accidental meed," aureole, generally understood as especially for celibates,[22] but according to Hilton for martyrdom, preaching, celibacy, and "other special good deeds," like "enclosings of ankers" (I, lxi, p. 148). Indeed, *"Maria optimam partem elegit . . ."* (I, xlv, pp. 109–10).

Besides the active life and the contemplative life, there is a third kind of life which a good Christian may lead, the mixed life. Definitions and evaluations of the mixed life vary greatly throughout the Middle Ages and among the mystics generally, and the exact meaning of the term is often elusive. The mixed life is not dealt with by name in *The Scale,* but Hilton does discuss its nature there, and he explains it in detail in another of his works, "The Book That Is Called Mixed Life, Which Is Drawn Out Between Active Life and Life Contemplative." [23] Hilton's concern with a mixed life was not something new or peculiar to his time. According to Pepler, "St. Thomas is not happy about the term 'mixed life', though St. Augustine does refer in this context to a *compositum.*" [24] Thomas maintains that no matter what one's external life may be, his interior life will be either active or contemplative, that is, either finding its pleasure in the business of the world or in contemplation. Although a man might perhaps alternate between these two pleasures, one of them must be the controlling force, so that a mixed life is impossible. Father Pepler, who seems unhappy about the implications of St. Thomas' pronouncement, tries to explain away the problem theoretically, mainly with the aid of a very broad definition of contemplation: "When we are reminded that all the active business and concern, if it be Christian, should of itself be leading to contemplation, it clearly establishes the fact that the Christian life in its essence is simple and never mixed, that it should always be tending to identify itself with the contemplative ideal of Mary." [25] Yet the problem of effectively combining the two lives exists, and it is excellently shown by St. John of the Cross:

Does it make any difference whether a bird be held by a slender thread or by a rope, while the bird is bound and cannot fly until the cord that holds it is broken? It is true that a slender thread is more easily broken; still notwithstanding, if it is not broken the bird cannot fly. This is the state of a soul with particular attachments: it never can attain to the liberty of the divine union, whatever virtues it may possess. Desires and attachments affect the soul as the remora is said to affect a ship; that is but a little fish, yet when it clings to the vessel it effectually hinders its progress.[26]

And Richard Rolle, who perhaps relies on personal experience for his argument, agrees with St. Thomas, though practically more than theoretically, and with St. John of the Cross:

Truly if any man might get both lives, that is to say contemplative and active, and keep and fulfil them, he were full great; that he might fulfil bodily service, and nevertheless feel the heavenly sound in himself, and be melted in singing into the joy of heavenly love. I wot not if ever any mortal man had this. To me it seems impossible that both should be together.

Christ truly in this respect is not to be numbered among men, nor His blest Mother among women. For Christ had no wandering thoughts, and He was not contemplative in a common manner, as saints in this life are contemplative; truly He needed not to labour as we need, because, from the beginning of His Conceiving, He saw God.[27]

In contrast to those who maintain that a mixed life cannot exist are those who advocate it. Gregory, amplifying on Augustine, teaches not only that the mixed life is fitting for many, but that the claims of the two lives can be reconciled, as, for example, in the life of a preacher or of a superior.[28] St. Teresa advocated the mixed life, maintaining that the spiritual marriage is to produce "work, work." [29] While she herself led an externally active life, she apparently enjoyed the mystical experience proper, the highest level of contemplation; thus she lived according to "the psychology of Christ," with "its dual character of action and fruition." [30] Regarding such mystics, William James observes that one of the results of contemplation can be a new energy in a mixed life: St. Ignatius became "assuredly one of the most powerfully practical human engines that ever lived." [31] Margery Kempe led a mixed life, for she combined her visions and talks with God with pilgrimages, debates, and sermons. Hilton himself at some time perhaps led a mixed life: while we have evidence that he was once a hermit, we know certainly that he was a spiritual director or adviser to a number of people in various states of life. Such examples suggest one of the most common interpretations of the mixed life, that it is a specially energetic and active life inspired and directed by contemplative experiences. In this case the communication of that which is contemplated, usually by preaching and instruction, often assumes an importance tantamount to the contemplation itself.

For Hilton, the definition of mixed life is simple, but very important. The mixed life is not something quibbled about with what Mark Twain might call "gold-leaf distinctions," and it is not an extraordinary new active life resulting from miraculous inspiration, like St. Paul's. Rather, it is simply the life of a man who wishes to enjoy contemplation but who cannot devote all his efforts to it because of necessary practical affairs.[32] One leading a mixed life cannot be properly called a contemplative because, as Thomas points out and as Hilton agrees, contemplatives devote all their lives to contemplation.[33] Yet, a person leading a mixed life is to be differentiated from an active because an active is generally understood as one who is so immersed in practical affairs that he may not enjoy contemplation. The mixed life is not a half-and-half combination of the active life and the contemplative life, but a joining of the active life and the lower levels of contemplation, those which can be achieved by actives. It is, then, the best active life possible, and in *The Scale* Hilton treats the mixed life under the heading of active. In "Mixed Life," it is true, he emphasizes the difference between the active life and the mixed life; but he does so there because he is trying, by giving him a medial position, to temper the zeal of a man seeking the contemplative life in spite of his worldly obligations.

The reasons for leading a mixed life are the same as those for leading an active life. A man may have "state, office, or cure over other men" (I, ii, p. 3), or he may have to leave contemplation to relieve and comfort "other men, either of their bodies or of their souls." [34] Just as Gregory teaches that a contemplative should accept an office of superiority, putting his own prayer in privacy beneath the good work he can do for others,[35] Hilton teaches that it is "villainy" to crown a man's head with gems and leave his body naked:

Right so ghostly, it is no worship to God to crown his head and leave his body bare.

Thou shalt understand that our Lord Jesu Christ as Man is head of all the ghostly body which is Holy Church. The members of this body are all Christian men: some are arms and some are feet, and some are other members after sundry workings that they use in their living. Then, if that thou be busy with all thy working in thy might for to array his head—that is, for to worship himself by mind of his Passion and of his other works in his manhood by devotion and meditation of him—and forgettest his feet that are thy children and thy servants, thy tenants and all thine even-Christians, and lettest them spill for default of keeping, unarrayed, unkept and not tended to as they ought for to be, thou pleasest him not, thou doest no worship to him. Thou makest thee for to kiss his mouth by devotion and ghostly prayer; but thou treadest upon his feet and defilest them, inasmuch as thou wilt not tend to them (for negligence of thyself) which thou hast taken the cure of.[36]

The worth and rewards of the mixed life vary in mystical literature. Gregory, following Augustine, maintains that the mixed life, as of preachers, is superior to the contemplative life, for preachers are not only holy themselves, but they lead others to be holy and instruct them in the faith.[37] St. Teresa maintains that "to give to our Lord a perfect hospitality, Mary and Martha must combine," that is, that the most perfect life one can lead is the mixed life.[38] Rolle, in *The Mending of Life,* after he has said that the "highest perfection" is achieved by solitaries raised by contemplation, has an afterthought that the mixed life—if it can exist—is the highest:

Unless it happen there be some in such state that they have come even with the height of the contemplative life, and yet they cease not to fulfil the office of the preacher. *They* pass these other solitaries —highest in contemplation and only given to godly things, not to the needs of their neighbours—their degrees being like, and for their preaching they are worthy a crown that is cleped aureola.[39]

Rolle, however, really thinks it "impossible" that both lives can exist together,[40] and he himself forsook "the business of the world" which "gnaws us as a worm" in order to devote his life to contemplation, although he evidently was a good preacher.[41] Hilton, since he maintains that the active cannot enjoy the highest levels of contemplation and since he treats the mixed life as the active life plus a devotion to the lower levels of contemplation, sets the mixed life below the contemplative life. One leading a mixed life may gain aureole for his preaching, and he will get his primary reward according to his degree of charity (I, lxi). Yet he cannot enjoy the mystical experience, the highest level of contemplation (I, ix). Even in "Mixed Life" Hilton maintains that "life contemplative alone (if they might come thereto soothfastly) were best, most speedful, most meedful, most fair, most worthy of them for to use and for to hold," although he is at the same time emphasizing that duties often demand that one not embrace the contemplative life.[42] The worth which Hilton gives to the mixed life—although it is below that given to the mixed life by the Church Fathers, by the contemplatives in general, and by modern spiritual writers and critics of the contemplative and contemplation—is consistent with his view that only the solitary can enjoy contemplation fully and with his teachings on contemplation itself.

Separate from but related to the three Christian lives is the process of contemplation, which itself is divided into levels. Like the levels of Christian life, the levels of contemplation are not of Hilton's invention. Plotinus lists three steps by which the soul can ascend towards the absolute,[43] and in the teachings of St. Paul "the life, death, and resurrection of Christ are a drama to be re-enacted in little in the life of the Christian." [44] Stages of contemplation, perhaps first roughly set up by Dionysius the Areopagite or pseudo-Denis, are accepted by Augustine, Gregory, and Thomas [45] and appear in the various "ladder" works, like *The Scale,* in Rolle's *"calor," "dulcor,"* and *"canor,"* [46] and in *The Cloud of Unknowing.* Most contemplatives and most critics of the contemplatives accept three stages in contemplation, purgation, illumination, and union; however, there are exceptions, like the Spanish mystic Molinos, who did not accept the normal three stages,[47] and the stages can be altered by subdivision, as Richard of St. Victor alters them in *Benjamin Minor.*[48] Purgation, as the word implies, involves a correction of faults and a disciplining of the soul; illumination, a new realization of God's glory accompanied by a new fervor for him; union, a close relation with God which leads to a new experience of the Infinite as a gift from God to the passive soul.

The levels or, as Hilton calls them, the "parts" of contemplation are differentiated, first, because they exist. The contemplatives, in attempting to communicate their spiritual development, have observed major levels in their progress, and they have felt that a knowledge of the levels is integral to a knowledge of contemplation. That the stages were developed as an analogy to the spiritual or physical hierarchy of the Church, that they represent "a mere juggling with the magic number, the sacred triad," [49] seems doubtful, for the levels also appear in pagan mystical literature. But that the levels were emphasized to instruct seems very likely. An entire process can often be best understood after an understanding of its components, and a spiritual director can often guide best by presenting small portions of material which can be appreciated and which consequently can provide incentive for more learning. Whatever the causes for the emphasis on the differing levels of contemplation may be, the emphasis has resulted in a difficulty.

Most critics have fortunately recognized the danger of overschematization. While Father Pepler constructs a neat, nicely subdivided chart to explain the levels of contemplation in *The Scale*, he realizes that such charts are explanatory aids rather than indicators of fine distinctions. About the author of *The Cloud* he says, "He knows nothing of the later analytical precisions of mystical writers who would divide and subdivide to the *n*th degree." [50] Dom David Knowles says that "mystical theologians" must realize that many of their categories are not "clear-cut," [51] and James comments more harshly on the chart-makers of the spiritual life: "I cannot pretend to detail to you the sundry stages of the Christian mystical life. Our time would not suffice, for one thing; and moreover, I confess that the subdivisions and names which we find in the Catholic books seem to me to represent nothing objectively distinct. So many men, so many minds. . . ." [52]

Although overschematization will lead to oversimplification and misunderstanding, the opposite vice, which refuses to see stages and regards only the total process, can be equally deluding. When Bullett says that the stages of contemplation are "separable only in analysis" and are part of a "continuing indivisible process," [53] he is ignoring the actuality of the stages most contemplatives emphasize, although perhaps he is coming close to what the relation between the stages is.

In Hilton the stages, contrary to Miss Underhill's view, are not "simple and poetic," the work of a "dreamer rather than the mapmaker." [54] Rather, they are individual but interdependent steps which, although continuity and nuances exist, represent a system of progress. [55] The *Scala Perfectionis* presents a staircase or ladder or even a scaling ladder to attain perfection with, and like a ladder it has levels or rungs which enable one to ascend and at the same time which hold the total process, or the sidepieces, together. The entire point of the ladder image is that divisions do exist, but that they all lead, one by one, to the top:

But from the lowest to the highest may not a soul suddenly start, no more than a man that will climb upon an high ladder and setteth his foot upon the lowest stave, may at the next fly up to the highest; but him behoveth go by process one after another, till he may come to the overest. Right so it is ghostly. . . . (II, xvii, pp. 288–89)

The Scale treats of three major parts of contemplation, parts which will be analyzed separately but which, it must be remembered, are linked in purpose and in construction.

For Hilton the first part of contemplation consists of what might be regarded as the common or reasoned knowledge of God possessed by men. It is gained by studying the Scriptures, by discussion, instruction, or logic. It might be the knowledge of God as displayed in the order of the universe or as conjectured on the basis of his being infinite, but it is a part of contemplation "in as mickle as it is a sight of soothfastness, and a knowing of ghostly things" (I, iv, p. 6). Coleman seems to think that this knowledge is somehow special,[56] but in fact, as Geraldine Hodgson points out, "there seems no difference between this condition and ordinary theological learning." [57] This kind of purely theological and reasoned knowledge seems so different from what is usually recognized as contemplation that Dom Butler criticizes the Dominicans for apparently seeing "some intimate connexion between the study of speculative theology and contemplation." [58] Yet, that Hilton is writing about precisely this sort of speculative theology is emphasized by his allotting the first part of contemplation especially to "lettered men, and great clerks which by long study and travail in Holy Writ come into this knowing, more or less, after the subtlety of kindly wit and continuance of study upon the general gift that God gives each man that hath use of reason" (I, iv, p. 6).

The first part of contemplation is in itself neither good nor bad, for knowledge may be possessed by heretics or hypocrites or by others who lack charity. Mere knowledge, in fact, can lead to pride and sin rather than to love and contemplation, as Hilton points out, quoting from St. Paul the same passage that Rolle and the author of *The Cloud* had previously used: "*Scientia inflat, caritas autem edificat*" (I, iv, p. 7).[59] Yet, that Hilton does accord reasoned knowledge a place in contemplation, though it may be a "shadow" of "very contemplation," contrasts him with the author of *The Cloud*, who says that a "curious knowledge of learning and of nature" usually serves only to blind clerks to contemplation,[60] and with Rolle, who thought his scholastic training of no value in trying to achieve contemplation.[61]

Hilton's acceptance of knowledge as comprising the first part of contemplation also tells us something about his view of the contemplative-scholastic relation, a relation that is now somewhat more understood than formerly. It is common to find the assertion that contemplation and scholasticism are incompatible and that, in fact, contemplation flourished in the fourteenth century as a reaction against the emphasis on dialectics in scholasticism. While modern critics like Miss Hodgson, Dom Noetinger, and Dom Knowles see that the author of *The Cloud* is not completely anti-intellectual,[62] that Hilton takes many of his definitions from St. Thomas,[63] and that scholasticism is not necessarily incompatible with contemplation,[64] there is yet a tendency to divorce all scholasticism from all contemplation. But Hilton's giving reasoned knowledge a place in contemplation and his teaching that such knowledge can be useful in the ascent of the ladder indicate an outstanding eclecticism. Perhaps as a practical spiritual director he believed that the rejection of any non-evil means to achieve his end would be wasteful. Whatever his reason, his use of scholastic materials contrasts him to the popular stereotype of the mystic as a "man of the heart" who scorns knowledge acquired by natural intelligence.

The second part of contemplation, which is almost directly opposite to the first part, consists "principally in affection, without light of understanding of ghostly things; and this is commonly of simple and unlettered men which give them[selves] wholly to devotion" (I, v, p. 9). The affection is a feeling of the "fervour of love and ghostly sweetness," a "little tasting of the sweetness of the love of God." It is comparable to

Rolle's "*dulcor*" and "*calor*" put together, for the sweetness is accompanied by a "burning love in devotion" (I, ix, p. 16). The negative characteristic of the second part of contemplation, the lack of a "light of understanding of ghostly things," is not necessarily a lack of the reasoned knowledge of the first part of contemplation, though Hilton suggests the second part is common to "unlettered men." It is the lack of the special cognition of the mystical experience, a lack of "sight in understanding of ghostly things" and "of privities of Holy Writ in special" (I, v, p. 9). One might enjoy, then, both the first and second parts of contemplation alternately. The "great trust in the goodness and the mercy of God" might proceed from "the mind of His Passion or of any of His works in His manhood" (I, v, p. 9) as gleaned from one's studies, and the fervor of love might drive a man, if he is lettered, to further study. An active may enjoy, by God's gift, a lower degree of the second part of contemplation (I, vi), which might be given "through faith and imagination of Jhesu in His manhood" in order to strengthen him in his devotion and keep him from error (II, xxx, p. 359). But the higher degree of the second part of contemplation, in which psalms, prayers, and devout sayings "are turned as it were into a ghostly mirth and sweet song," is reserved for those "which are in great rest of body and of soul" (I, vii, p. 12). It is interesting that Hilton's second part of contemplation can be just as much a starting point as his first part: perhaps because the first part of contemplation, knowledge, can be abused, Hilton does not make it a necessary primary step, though he specifically calls it "the first part of contemplation." It seems more likely, however, that he had to give both the lettered and the unlettered starting points, so that one who did not know Latin and consequently could not read the Scriptures and theological works, like the ghostly sister to whom *The Scale* is addressed (I, xv), would not be hindered in his spiritual progress.

The fervor in devotion and the affection of the second part of contemplation are achieved by meditation, prayer, and God's gift of grace (I, v). Meditation, as defined in the previous chapter, is the voluntary and compassionate consideration of teachings from the Scriptures, events in the life of Christ, the goodness of God, and like topics. Meditation is one's own effort, his "own ghostly craft," [65] as the author of *The Cloud* says, to advance by preparing himself for a fuller reception of grace. It is the door to contemplation, especially when it is a "beholding of the passion of Christ," [66] and "a man shall not come to ghostly delight in contemplation of Christ's Godhead, but he come first in imagination by bitterness and by compassion and by steadfast thinking of His manhood" (I, xxxv, pp. 80–81). Along with meditation as a means to achieve contemplation is prayer, especially ejaculations said with intensity and desire, like "Ah, Lord, heal my soul, for I have sinned against thee" (I, xxix, p. 65). These prayers, like the "SIN, SIN, SIN! OUT, OUT, OUT!" of the author of *The Cloud*,[67] must be said with "a stying [ascending] desire of the heart into God by withdrawing of the heart from all earthly thoughts" (I, xxv, p. 58), a characteristic which Julian of Norwich comments on.[68] If the prayers are vocal prayers, such as religious are often required to say, they must not be said "speedily and recklessly, as thou wert evil paid that thou art bound with them" (I, xxvii, pp. 60–61), for as Rolle points out, "What good canst thou hope may come thereof if thou lettest thy tongue blabber on the book, and thy heart run about the world in divers places where it will? Therefore, set thy thought on Christ, and He shall bind it to Him and hold it from the venom of this world's business." [69] The active means to affection, then, are prayer and meditation, and Hilton, agreeing with the Fathers,[70] says that these means, not reasoned knowledge, are the first necessary steps a contemplative must take. Grace, the final means of achieving affection, is directly the gift of God, and consequently it is responsible for the fact that actives as well as contemplatives can enjoy some of the levels of contemplation. Grace is responsible both for the purifying of meditation and prayer and for the affection which is the result of the meditation and prayer, so that the most essential element for the second part of contemplation is dependent on God's will. (Hilton's teachings on grace are analyzed in a later chapter.)

The value of affection or the second part of contemplation is greater than that of the first part. Since affection is contingent upon God's giving grace and since the burning love is a kind of charity (I, v), affection is necessarily good, unlike reasoned knowledge. Moreover, as pointed out above, affection is the first necessary part of contemplation, the highest rung at which men can begin, unless, as Rolle writes, they are fools who plan to begin at the highest level and come down to the lowest.[71] This insistence on affection as a prerequisite for the highest level of contemplation is common in Hilton and his contemporaries, occurring in Rolle's work and in *The Cloud*.[72] But while affection is a necessary state in the process of contemplation, it is not the highest, since it rests heavily on meditation, which is based on the imagination:

Thus taught our Lord Mary Magdalen, that should be contemplative, when He said thus: *Noli me tangere, nondum enim ascendi ad Patrem meum.* Touch Me not, I am not yet styed up to My Father. That is for to say, Mary Magdalen loved burningly our Lord Jhesu before time of His passion, but her love was mickle bodily, little ghostly. She trowed well that He was God, but she loved Him little as God, for she could not then; and therefore she suffered all her affection and all her thought fall in Him as He was in form of man. And our Lord blamed her not then, but praised it mickle. But after when He was risen from death and appeared to her, she would have worshipped Him with such manner love as she did before; and then our Lord forbade her and said thus, "Touch me not." That is: set not the rest nor the love of thine heart in that form of man that thou seest with thy fleshly eyes only, for to rest therein; for in that form I am not styed up to My Father. That is, I am not even to the Father; for in the form of man I am less than He. Touch Me not so, but set thy thought and thy love into that form in which I am even to the Father, that is the form of the Godhead, and love Me, know Me, and worship Me as God and man godly, not as a man manly. (II, xxx, pp. 362–63)

The love and fervor stirred by meditation, though good, are entirely different from the understanding of the third part of contemplation, and they are to be recognized as inferior. Though in affection there is a sort of knowing of God in the imagination, it is like milk for children who are not yet old enough to take whole food (I, ix; II, xxxi).[73] The second part of contemplation is not to be enjoyed in itself, and its sweetness is not to be cultivated for the pleasure of the contemplative. Rather, it is a stage the contemplative must regard as medial, and he must "look that he be aye desiring for to come to more knowing and feeling of God, in the third part of contemplation" (I, vii, p. 13).[74]

The third part of contemplation, which is the highest, consists both of knowing and loving, or "cognition" and "affection" (I, viii, p. 14). It is the state which is "verily contemplative," in which one has a "feeling of love and ghostly knowing of God by opening of the ghostly eye" (I, xlv, p. 109), and which comprises the mystical experience proper. In attributing the two characteristics of knowing and loving to the mystical experience, Hilton treats the experience as does the author of *The Cloud*, who advises the reader that in the final stages of contemplation he should let "thy blind beholding of thy naked being be gladly borne up in listiness [eager longing] of love, to be knitted and oned in grace and in spirit to the precious being of God in himself only as he is, without more." [75] While the combination of loving and knowing is also traditional, occurring in Augustine, who presents the mystical experience as "the most penetrating intellectual vision into things divine" with a "consuming passion" for God,[76] the emphasis on each of the separate elements varies. In Augustine the quest is an intellectual one, attained essentially by voluntary effort,[77] but in Hilton the attaining of the mystical experience is not primarily the result of one's own effort, and it certainly is not an intellectual process. Moreover, whereas many of the mediaeval German contemplatives tend to emphasize the idea of union in the mystical experience, coming from affection, and whereas the mystics and contemplatives most influenced by Plotinus will exaggerate the understanding or cognition in the experience, Hilton tends to balance the importance of cognition and affection in the third part of contemplation. The difficulty of establishing the exact proportional relation between cognition and affection is, of course, great, because of the ineffability of the mystical experience. Many contemplatives, as one would expect, prefer something like Ruysbroek's "wandering in the sea of divinity" [78] to an attempt at literal explanation.

The cognition of the third part of contemplation is not the reasoned knowledge of the first part, nor is it an "exalted Platonism," as Butler points out.[79] It is an entirely new understanding or enlightenment of that which cannot be understood by reason alone. It is the beginning of a perception of God and things divine, a perception which to men can at best be hazy: *"Videmus nunc per speculum in aenigmate"* (I, ix, p. 16). As the author of *The Cloud* says, the perception is a "full knowing and feeling of his [God's] almighty-hood," or as much of a full knowing as is possible on earth, since a "clear sight shall never man have here in this life." [80] The knowledge may come from an understanding of Holy Writ given by the Holy Ghost or from a realization of unthought of or unconsidered secrets of the Divine (II, xliii).

Hilton writes of the secret revelations of the mystical experience in the last four chapters of Book II, explaining that the sights are those understood by the ghostly eye and briefly describing them as the beholding of Jesus, the seeing of angels, both damned and blessed, the understanding of the working of souls, the knowing of the Trinity, and the understanding of the Godhead. Dom Gerard Sitwell comments that Hilton's treatment of the mystical experience "is in the nature of a postscript" (as I have suggested, perhaps Hilton devoted little space to the mystical experience because he realized that while he could teach the lower levels of contemplation, he could not explain the ineffable). Sitwell writes, moreover, that "there is no theological difficulty" in Hilton's teachings on the material revealed, although the material revealed does not "in fact seem generally to form part of the experiences of other mystics." [81] Dom Sitwell is particularly interested in Hilton's relation of revealed truths and angels, referring also to Hilton's "Song of Angels," and he suggests that Hilton drew on Bernard, who separates the contemplation of God from that of angels and saints.[82] But the contemplation of angels is for Hilton a part of a larger perception of the Divine in the mystical experience, not a separate perception pertaining to a distinct level in it. "The sight of angels' kind" is indeed mentioned specifically (II, xlv, p. 457), but the list in which it occurs is set down for its cumulative effect as a hint of the ineffable. Also, in suggesting a particular relation between Bernard and Hilton because they both refer to the perception of angels in the mystical experience, Sitwell seems to overlook the author of *The Cloud*, who, when he is emphasizing the importance of a "blind stirring of love unto God for himself," specifically says that it is more important than the contemplation of angels and saints in their bliss.[83] It is the author of *The Cloud* who makes a distinction between the contemplation of God and that of angels and who is, therefore, close to Bernard. Hilton, on the other hand, lumps together the divine things perceived in the mystical experience.

Affection, the complement of cognition in the third part of contemplation, is not the same as the affection of the second part of contemplation, although the higher affection of the third part is partially the result of an intensification of the affection of the second part. The sweetness and fervor become a "ravishing" and consequent union in the third part, and this union, based essentially on charity, is what is known as the spiritual marriage, "the marriage made atwixt God and the soul, which shall never be broken" (I, viii, pp. 14–15). In Hilton the spiritual marriage must be distinguished from the avowed or "one-sided" spiritual marriages in many religions, like Catholicism, in which a nun or priest may be "married" to God since she is teaching children in a parochial school or since he devotes his life to caring for his parishioners. It is not a state indicated merely by a simple singleness of purpose, by any external token, like Margery Kempe's ring with *"Ihesus est amor meus"* engraved on it,[84] or by a voluntary emphasis on charity, like the *"Amor vincit omnia"* of Chaucer's Prioress. It is a state in which the soul, having rejected the physical, is by God's special grace "oned" with him and "conformed to the image of the Trinity," that is, to God in his essence rather than to the second person of the Trinity, Christ, in his manhood (I, viii, p. 14).

The spiritual marriage, as Helen Gardner points out, is not a favorite metaphor for union among the mediaeval English contemplatives,[85] although it is Biblically sanctioned in the *Song of Songs* and was emphasized by Bernard and especially by many of the fourteenth-century German contemplatives. Perhaps its most striking occurrence in the mediaeval English contemplatives is in the *Book of Margery Kempe,* in which God tells Margery she may fully embrace him:

Daughter, thou desirest greatly to see Me, and thou mayest boldly, when thou art in thy bed, take Me to thee as thy wedded husband, as thy dearworthy darling, and as thy sweet son, for I will be loved as a son should be loved by the mother, and I will that thou lovest Me, daughter, as a good wife ought to love her husband. Therefore thou mayest boldly take Me in the arms of thy soul and kiss My mouth, My head, and My feet, as sweetly as thou wilt.[86]

If Margery represents one extreme, Hilton represents the other. He does not intellectualize the union so that affection becomes another sort of cognition, for he constantly says that contemplation lies in the perfect love of God (II, xxi). He does, however, insist on the relation of the two qualities, a relation which is partially one of cause and effect and yet one in which the two qualities are interdependent. Charity, as will be explained, is the key means of achieving contemplation, and the mystical experience cannot be achieved without it. The union is the result of charity and it is based on charity, so that charity, or affection, is a prerequisite for and at the same time a quality of the union. Cognition is a result of the union, consequently co-existing with affection, though cognition itself cannot be a cause of the third part of contemplation. But within the third part of contemplation cognition can cause a heightening of affection, since further knowledge can intensify love. Cognition and affection are mixed in the mystical experience, each complementing the other, so that the union with God may be perfected.

Although the third part of contemplation, as "perfect as it may be here," consists of a special union based on love and of understanding with the ghostly eye, the full enjoyment of it cannot be had except in the "bliss of heaven" (I, viii, p. 14). What is experienced on earth is essentially what will be experienced in heaven, but the fullness of the experience varies greatly. The highest earthly contemplation is "verily a tasting, so little as it is, and an earnest of the sight of heavenly joy, not clearly, but half in murkness" because the soul is yet bound by "flesh deadly" (I, ix, pp. 16, 17), or, a bit more forcefully, bound by "an heavy lump of bodily corruption" which "mote aye be whilst it is here in this life" (II, xli, p. 433). Hilton is in accord with the author of *The Cloud*, who also says that the highest level of contemplation can be begun here by special grace but is to be fulfilled only in heaven.[87] Also, since the third part is indeed a tasting of the heavenly experience, the soul is partaking by the grace of God of that which it is not fully prepared for, so that it is working at a level above its capabilities and consequently cannot endure for a long time. As Gregory points out, even in the victory of the mystical experience, the soul is weakened:

In the wrestling of Jacob with the Angel, the Angel symbolizes the Lord, and Jacob, who contends with the Angel, represents the soul of each perfect man who exercises contemplation. Such a soul, when it strives to contemplate God, as if placed in a wrestle, now comes uppermost, because by understanding and feeling it tastes somewhat of the unencompassed Light; and now falls underneath, because in the very tasting it faints away.[88]

Simply, as James states, the mystical experience is transient.[89] Hilton writes that the ineffable sight in the mystical experience is "but shortly and little" (II, xxxii, p. 371), that the "sovereign feeling" must pass away, despite one's desire to retain it (II, xl, p. 424), and that the special grace of God which gives the mystical experience "changeably cometh and goeth" (II, xli, p. 433). In these matters he is in accord with his contemporaries, like the author of *The Cloud*,[90] and with the teachings of the contemplatives and mystics in general.

The value of the third part of contemplation is, of course, exceedingly great, far greater than that of the reasoned knowledge and affection of the first two parts, which are only silver and gold, as the author of *The Cloud* says.[91] Not only is the mystical experience given with a special grace, one which cannot be merited by man's own efforts, but the experience places the soul as close as possible to God before union after death. It is the "whole bread, meat for perfect souls," not the milk with which children are nourished (II, xxxi, p. 369); though the sight is in "murkness," it is yet so great that it is ineffable, and so strong that it cannot be sustained for a long time. Moreover, it cleanses the soul, subdues temptation in it, and leaves it rested, even though the experience proper is transient. Finally, it makes the soul one of God's "*carissimi*," one of those whom he will reward specially as well as generally with the wine at his table. For Hilton, "this is the state of perfection, and the way to heavenward" (II, xxxii, p. 373).

If a single quality were to be attributed to Walter Hilton's teachings on the three Christian lives and on the three levels of contemplation, it would be the one which some modern critics see in Hilton's work in general and which Hilton himself constantly emphasizes: moderation. In *The Scale* Hilton's moderation exists partially in his refusing to adhere to a plan at all costs, in his refusing to agree consistently with a tradition when he thinks parts of it unreasonable. His division of the three

Christian lives, for example, does not include regular, graphic starting and stopping points: where the active life ends and where the mixed life begins is not important, for the distinction between the two is one of proportion. Yet, when a precise distinction is necessary, he makes it clearly: the contemplative life is specifically the life of the solitary, the one who devotes his entire effort to contemplation and has no worldly cares to distract him. Between the two lower parts of contemplation he draws a relatively careful line, but he sees that reasoned knowledge can form the basis for devout meditations and fervor, so that the two parts may be mixed in the same person's religious life. Yet he makes it impossible to confuse or mix the lower parts of contemplation with the highest, though both the lowest parts and the highest part consist of kinds of loving and knowing. In his doctrine his moderation is his eclecticism: he will agree with his contemporaries that the solitary life is best and disregard Gregory's insistence that the mixed life gives greater merit, but he will devote a chapter to Rolle's *calor*, insisting that in spite of what Rolle says, *calor* is not sensible or literal, but metaphorical. In practical matters, his moderation allows him to insist that a man with worldly responsibilities should not leave the mixed life, even while he insists theoretically on the superiority of the contemplative one. Hilton's teachings on the three levels of contemplation and on the Christian lives are, then, clear and when necessary very careful and emphatic, but they are never artificial or "scholastic" in the pejorative sense. This moderation carries over into his teachings on the progress of the soul.

III

THE PROGRESS OF THE SOUL

𝕿he progress of the soul through the parts of contemplation is determined by a number of factors. For instance, one's external life will either limit or encourage his progress, depending on whether it is active or contemplative. One's ability to rid himself of temptations, to learn how to discipline his body moderately, and to avoid distractions in prayer and meditation will affect his progress, as will his patience and self-control in attempting to achieve the third part of contemplation, his humility or pride, or even his agility at getting rid of visiting gossips. There are, of course, hundreds of particular methods by which the soul can progress, methods which Hilton discusses in his teachings on asceticism and contemplation, but at the roots of these particular methods are a very few essential doctrines. These doctrines, which are not analyzed systematically in *The Scale* (as St. Thomas would have analyzed them) since *The Scale* is a guide to contemplation rather than a study of it, occur explicitly in many chapters of the work and implicitly in all that Hilton teaches. In aggregate, they illustrate the unity of Hilton's teachings, even in particular points, since the particular points stem from the few essential doctrines or their relationships.

The first of the essential doctrines is that the aspiring contemplative must have a strong desire for his goal, "for what is a man but his thoughts and his loves? These only make a man good or bad" (I, lxxxviii, p. 211). This desire must be inspected often by man, who is obliged to control its direction closely, for man's duty is dictated by his relative power or control. While we cannot blame one for not achieving the mystical experience, since it is a free gift of God, we can blame one for allowing his evil desires or worldly proclivities to reign in his internal life, since the control of desire is within man's power. Desire is so important that it is the key factor in determining whether one's soul has been reformed from the image of sin to the image of God:

Ransack thine own conscience and look what thy will is, for therein standeth all. If it be turned from all manner of deadly sin, that thou wouldest for nothing wittingly and wilfully break the commandment of God, and for that thou has misdone here before against His bidding, thou hast shriven thee thereof meekly, with full heart to leave it and with sorrow that thou didst it, I say then surely that thy soul is reformed in faith to the likeness of God. (II, ix, p. 254)

Desire, moreover, is the chief means by which a pilgrim keeps to the sole right road to Jerusalem (contemplation): whatever one hears or sees, no matter how he is beaten or robbed, and in spite of attempts to deceive him with lies or false joy, he will progress towards the "sight of peace" in contemplation, "for that thou covetest, that thou desirest, and nought else but that" (II, xxi, pp. 304, 305). Not only must the desire "be as it were made naked and bare from all earthly things," that is, free from all voluntary material distraction, if it is to be effective (I, xxv, p. 57); but the desire also must not be for even those pleasures of warmth or security which might occur with spiritual development, that is, the desire must be for the object and not for comforts or reliefs which might result from its possession (II, xli). Hilton's teaching on the necessity of a singleness of desire is, as Miss Underhill points out, in accord with the teaching of Augustine.[1] Augustine's *"Nihil aliud sumus quam voluntates,"* [2] in fact, is well translated by the passage from Hilton quoted above: "for what is a man but his thoughts and his loves?" (I, lxxxviii, p. 211). Hilton's teaching also corresponds strikingly to that of the author of *The Cloud,* who opens *The Cloud* with a prayer to God "for to cleanse the intent of mine heart" and who constantly insists that a "naked intent" is necessary for "the substance of this work," i.e., contemplation through love.[3] The author of *The Cloud* explains the "naked intent" just as Hilton explains desire, that is, as being free from a longing for a loss of pain or increase of pleasure due to the possession of the goal; moreover, in his explanation of the necessity of desire for progress in contemplation, his words remind one of Hilton's parable of the pilgrim seeking Jerusalem: "for the high and the nearest way thither is run by desires, and not by paces of feet."[4] The importance of desire may be partially attributable to God's knowing that man cannot do all the good that he desires and God's subsequent accepting of "every good will as for deed," as he tells Margery Kempe he does.[5] In *The Scale,* however, the importance of desire is more likely the result of Hilton's belief that all good is done more or less by God's grace, the grace being in proportion to the greatness of the good. Since the greatest good, contemplation, is completely a gift of God, man being receptive in the mystical experience, man must try "to do his share," so to speak, in the realm of lower good. If a strong desire is the most important active part man can assume in the process of contemplation, the possession of that desire, or even of the desire of that desire, will indicate to God that man is doing his utmost to ready himself for God's gift.

The objects of desire may be either primary or secondary, the secondary objects being not distinct or separate goals, but stages or means in the total process of contemplation which are relatively more advanced than the stage at which the contemplative actually finds himself.[6] A secondary object of desire is the next rung of the ladder, even though it is not the highest rung, since the next rung brings one closer to the highest one. Just as the beginner should hate sin, so should he desire "virtues and cleanness" "without stinting" (I, xxii, p. 52). The advancing contemplative should crave especially meekness and charity, for these virtues, more than others, purify and perfect the soul (I, lxxvi); indeed, if one guards his heart well, he will be able to develop "burning desires of virtues and of charity" (I, lxxxviii, p. 211). Devout prayer is a good secondary object of desire, especially since devout prayer, characteristic of the second part of contemplation, may help to purify the soul. Devout prayer itself contains and intensifies "the fire of desire," which, again, helps complete the soul's receptivity to God's gift (I, xxiv, p. 55). The secondary objects of desire, whether they be spiritual or physical workings or states, nourish the desire for the primary object: "For it fareth by works and by desire, as it doth by sticks and by a fire. For the more sticks are laid to the fire, the greater is the fire; right so the more divers ghostly working that a man hath in his thought for to keep whole his desire, the mightier and the more burning shall his desire be to God" (II, xxi, p. 309). And the secondary objects are valuable only as they intensify the desire or contribute to its fulfillment.

The primary object of desire is Jesus. The desire for Jesus fast in a heart is more important than "all bodily penance of all men living, or visions or revelations of angels appearing, songs and sounds, savours and smells, burnings and any pleasing bodily feeling, and shortly for to say, or all the joy of heaven and of earth which I might have without this desire to my Lord Jhesu" (I, xlvii, p. 114). Jesus is the Redeemer of mankind who will yet fight individually for a soul against the devil and drive sin from that soul if the soul will set the point of its thought upon him alone (I, xci); the desire for Jesus, consequently, encompasses a desire for a pure soul. Jesus, in fact, will himself further direct one's desire, leading the contemplative to the highest part of contemplation, so that desiring Jesus is desiring both the end of contemplation and a means to achieve it (II, xxiv). Eventually, as the desire for Jesus is graciously perfected, the soul will be able to center itself about that desire, so that "all worldly vanities and fleshly affections" will not only be driven out of the heart, but they will be beneath it (II, xxiv, p. 324). This desire, when in the second part of contemplation and intensified by grace, can lead to the ardent and singular devotion which critics usually associate with Rolle, but which Hilton recognizes also: "There dare no flesh fly rest upon the pot's brink boiling over the fire; right so may there no fleshly delight rest upon a clear soul that is happed [i.e., wrapped] and warmed all in fire of love, boiling and blowing psalms and laudings to Jhesu. This is very prayer" (II, xlii, p. 437). The singular desire for Jesus with the joy that accompanies it indicates, as Rolle says, that a man is truly "circumcised spiritually." [7]

That Jesus is the primary object of desire would seem to be a clear statement, but because of the cult of the Holy Name, the work of Hilton's contemporaries, and even the problem of ineffability in the mystical experience, the statement without qualification means almost nothing, or perhaps almost everything. Miss Allen notes that "the English medieval cult of the Holy Name began among the mystics, and therefore received primarily a spiritual expression." [8] The cult was not, apparently, the zealous one which would reduce all religious activity to the imagining of Christ's passion and which might develop the spiritual-marriage idea in its lowest or most material form, consequently seizing upon the name of Christ with an almost physical passion. Yet, the general appeal of the cult and its use of frequent and sometimes exclusive references to God in his manhood, references normally unexplained and often little more than pious ejaculations, would argue against an intellectual interpretation of the cult in its popular form.

Of the mediaeval English contemplatives, Rolle is most famous for his devotion to Christ, and in his works in general and especially in his lyrics the devotion to the Holy Name is strong. Miss Allen comments that "the devotion to the Holy Name of Jesus seems to be a prominent characteristic of the second degree" of love,[9] but this devotion continues in the third degree of love, most evidently in the constant use of "Christ" and "Jesus" in prayers and devotions.[10] Rolle's devotion to Christ and the

Holy Name is, however, not fully clear. The passage from the *Encomium* most often cited to illustrate his teachings on the Holy Name seems to suggest a rather unsophisticated fervor: "Hence many of the wretched worldly ones who think they will rejoice with Christ—because they do not love the name of Jesus —will suffer without end. Whatever you bear and though you give up all that you possess, unless you love the name of Jesus, you labor in vain." [11] Miss Allen, however, argues in the note in which she cites the passage that Rolle's meaning in his "various unguarded statements" on the Holy Name is really that we must desire the love of Jesus, or simply that we must desire salvation in order to get salvation. It is in a "rationalized sense" that the critic must regard Rolle's devotion to the Holy Name, she contends, a sense like Hilton's in *The Scale*. But Rolle does not labor to give the reader a key to his meaning, as Hilton does, and one going through Rolle's writings does not particularly feel that he ought to interpret Rolle's passionate outbursts in an intellectual way. And the critic who declines to read Rolle in a "rationalized sense" does not need to fear being attacked for presuming to say there is no meaning other than the literal one because he, a reader who is the product of a different society, does not see it; for Rolle's contemporaries, sharing his cultural milieu (so the argument for interpretation other than literal usually goes), would perceive the nonliteral meaning at once. Rolle's contemporaries did not perceive his "rationalized sense" either. Miss Allen refers to the "learned Carthusian" who "said that he had known more men to be ruined by Rolle's writings than to have profited," especially by Rolle's teaching of the "sensible fire of love," [12] which itself could be interpreted if one is to begin interpreting Rolle without cause. The author of *The Cloud* also writes about the problems caused by teachings which are apparently Rolle's; [13] moreover, when the author of *The Cloud* himself wishes to be understood spiritually, he warns the reader as Hilton does and he often gives his meaning in a "rationalized sense":

And therefore lean meekly to this blind stirring of love in thine heart. I mean not in thy bodily heart, but in thy ghostly heart, the which is thy will. And beware that thou conceive not bodily that which is said ghostly. For truly I tell thee, that the bodily and fleshly conceits of them that have curious and imaginative wits be cause of much error.

Ensample of this mayest thou see, where I bid thee hide thy desire from God so far as in thee is. For if, peradventure, I had bidden thee show thy desire unto God, thou shouldst have conceived it more bodily than thou dost now, when I bid thee hide it. For thou knowest well that all that thing that is wilfully hidden is cast into the depth of the spirit. And thus methinketh that there is great need to have much wariness in understanding of words that be spoken with ghostly intent, so that thou conceive them not bodily, but ghostly, as they be meant.[14]

The author of *The Cloud,* in other words, gives the reader specific directions to find another meaning in what he says. The author of *The Cloud,* however, "is almost unaffected by Devotion to the Holy Name," [15] so that unfortunately he gives no rationalized explanation of the name of Jesus. Margery Kempe, as Miss Allen points out, was not an enthusiastic member of the cult of the Holy Name,[16] and when Margery does refer to the Holy Name, her references seem very much like pious ejaculations with little intended specific meaning: ". . . Our Merciful Lord Jesus Christ, ever to be trusted, worshipped be His Name, never forsaking His servant in time of need, appeared." [17] The author of *The Cloud* and Margery, then, do not provide supplementary material which might help determine exactly the nature of the devotion to the Holy Name and to Jesus in Rolle. Yet by comparison with *The Cloud* and the *Book,* the critic can conclude at least that in Rolle the devotion is not obviously to be interpreted intellectually but that it certainly involves more than Margery's pious ejaculations. In Rolle the devotion to the Holy Name seems to be coupled with his sensible fire and his general teachings concerned with the fervent experiences of contemplation, so that the devotion is probably for the sake of the physical image which would aid in meditation.

However, if in Hilton the desire for Jesus or the name of Jesus is no more than part of the emotional and popular tendency towards the despiritualizing of religion for the purpose of intensifying sensible fervor by means of a more or less concrete object on which to focus attention, it is contradictory to all the rest of his teachings in *The Scale*. As shown, Hilton specifically relegates meditation, prayer based on the work of the imagination and utilizing especially scenes from the life of Christ, to the second part of contemplation, just as he specifically characterizes the third part of contemplation by a new knowledge, entirely different from and superior to the "knowledge" of the imagination. Hilton also says that the desire for Jesus is to be above or even to efface the desire for spiritual as well as earthly pleasures, spiritual pleasures which may come as the effects of progress. Consequently, if the desire for Jesus or devotion to the Holy Name is in Hilton to produce fervor in meditation, as its purpose seems to be in Rolle, Hilton has made the chief means of the progress of the soul, which ought to lead to the third part of contemplation, the same as the particular means for beginning contemplation or entering the second part of it, constantly emphasized as inferior to the third part.

But the problem is only a seeming one. It is true that Hilton makes much use of the name of Jesus in *The Scale*, a use partially explained by the desire for Jesus being the essential means of progress for the soul. He encourages meditation on the passion of Jesus in Book I, and in Book II, especially in the passages on the higher stages of contemplation, he refers to Jesus as the life of the soul (II, xli), as the end of contemplation (II, xliii), and as the "porter at the gate [of contemplation] ready to receive ilk a soul that will be reformed here in this life to His likeness" (II, ii, p. 231). If the Christo-centric passages are his, they suggest his concern for the second person of the Trinity, and the long passage on the Holy Name (I, xliv) indicates his interest specifically in the Holy Name. However, it is true also that

Hilton does not refer to Jesus always in the same way.[18] The key to understanding Hilton's references to Jesus—throughout *The Scale* and specifically concerning Jesus as the primary object of desire, without doing violence to Hilton's text or quibbling over words, and whether or not the Christo-centric expansions are his —is in recognizing that the meaning of Hilton's references is dependent upon the context in which they occur.

When Hilton is explaining that meditation is a means by which the second part of contemplation is achieved and one of the characteristics of the second part, he is most concerned with the passion of Christ as the second person of the Trinity who in physical form lived on earth. Simply, he is writing about "the manhood of Christ" (I, xxxv, p. 79). Jesus is seen in meditation "in a bodily likeness" so that one weeps or has compassion or rejoices in being saved by him.[19] By grace the meditation of the second part of contemplation becomes "an opening of the ghostly eye into Christ's manhood" (I, xxxv, p. 80), that is, a knowing "principally in imagination, and little in understanding," "the milk by which they [contemplatives] are tenderly nourished as children" (II, xxxi, p. 369). That "Jesus" in passages specifically concerning the second part of contemplation means "the manhood of Christ" is shown not only by Hilton's use of the word "manhood" in these passages, but by his elaborate efforts when discussing the third part of contemplation to emphasize that the cognition in the mystical experience has nothing to do with the imagination and that the sights in the mystical experience are ghostly. Distinguishing the ghostly sight of the mystical experience from that of the imagination in meditation would not be necessary if the sight in the imagination were not of a physical situation or person.

When Hilton is not writing about the second part of contemplation or the means of attaining it, he refers to Jesus not in his "manhood," but in his "Godhead," and he intentionally contrasts the two meanings: "For a man shall not come to ghostly delight in contemplation of Christ's Godhead, but he come first in imagination by bitterness and by compassion and by steadfast thinking of His manhood" (I, xxxv, pp. 80–81). Moreover, that Hilton normally uses the term "Jesus" to mean God is apparent in passages like the one in which he explains that God is heaven to man: "What is heaven to a reasonable soul? Soothly nought else but Jhesu God. For if that be heaven only that is above all things, then is God only heaven to man's soul. For He is only above the kind of a soul. Then if a soul may through grace have knowing of that blessed kind of Jhesu, soothly he seeth heaven, for he seeth God" (II, xxxiii, p. 375). This usage extends to the final chapter of *The Scale*, in which Hilton comments that "this knowing [of the mystical experience] only is worthiest and highest in itself of Jhesu God and man, if it be specially showed by the light of grace" (II, xlvi, p. 462). While such a juxtaposition of "God" and "man" might in isolation support a Christo-centric view of *The Scale*, in context it does the opposite. It occurs as an expansion of the statement that in the mystical experience "beginneth the soul for to perceive a little of the privities of the blessed Trinity" (pp. 461–62), that is, as an explanation of a perception of God as Father, Son, and Holy Spirit. In addition, even here specific passages occur in which "Jesus" must be construed as God. For example, when Hilton writes that the mystical experience brings a knowing "of our Lord Jhesu maker and keeper of all this fair university" (p. 463), he is obviously regarding "Jesus" as God the Creator rather than solely as Christ the Redeemer.

In case someone might wish to criticize him for his lack of precision in terminology, Hilton defends his seemingly loose terminology and his usage of "Jesus" in particular:

But perchance thou beginnest to wonder why I say one time that grace worketh all this, and another time I say that love worketh, or Jhesu worketh, or God worketh. Unto this I say thus, that when I say that grace worketh I mean love, Jhesu, and God: for all is one, and nought but one. Jhesu is love, Jhesu is grace, Jhesu is God; and for He worketh all in us by His grace for love as God, therefore may I

use what word of these four that me list, after my stirring in this
writing. (II, xlii, pp. 441–42)

Yet, when he writes of the primary object of desire, he is specific
enough often enough to make it clear that the intention one is to
have is a "whole intention to God" (I, xvi, p. 32), no matter what
word he uses to substitute for "God." Perhaps the difficulty in
understanding Hilton's usage is that it is exactly the opposite of
our own. Whereas we use "Jesus" primarily to refer to Christ in
his manhood and secondarily to refer to God, Hilton uses "Jesus"
generally to refer to God and only when he is involved with the
second part of contemplation to refer specifically to the manhood
of the Son. From his usage it appears that Hilton would
countenance the cult of the Holy Name, at least as it appears in
Rolle, only inasmuch as it would help the beginner in contemplation to meditate; and that in saying the primary object of desire
is Jesus, Hilton does not mean Christ in his manhood, but Christ
in his Godhead or God. Hilton's own most important explanation
of his usage corroborates this theory.

Included in Book I, xliv, is what is usually called the "passage
on the Holy Name," the textual problem of which has been
discussed in the first chapter. This passage deals with the
problem that "in some holy men's books" (p. 104) it is written
that he who cannot love the name of Jesus cannot be saved. The
books, which most critics regard as Rolle's, especially his *Encomium Nominis Jesu*,[20] have caused the hypothetical questioner of
Hilton to be astonished, since he had hoped that those who kept
the commandments and repented of their evil deeds would be
saved, though they "felt never ghostly sweetness nor inly savour
in the name of Jhesu" (p. 105). (Hilton has already made the
point in Book I, ii, that the active life, characterized by an
adherence to the commandments and the performance of the
works of mercy, is one of the lives which certainly can merit
salvation.) Hilton's justification or explanation of the devotion to
the Holy Name is at the same time a partial condescension to

those addicted to the cult in a passionate way and an explaining away of the cult in its popular form:

As unto this I may say as me thinketh, that their saying if it be well understood is sooth, and is not contrary to that that I have said. For this name Jhesu is nought else for to say upon English, but healer or health. Now every man that liveth in this wretched life is ghostly sick, for there is no man that liveth without sin, the which is ghostly sickness; as Saint John saith of himself and of other perfect men thus: *Si dixerimus quia peccatum non habemus, ipsi nos seducimus, et veritas in nobis non est*. If we say that we have no sin, we beguile ourselves and there is no soothfastness in us. And therefore he may never come to the joy of heaven until he be first made whole of this ghostly sickness. But this ghostly health may no man have that hath use of reason, but if he desire it and love it, and have delight therein, in as mickle as he hopeth for to get it. Now the name of Jhesu is nothing else but this ghostly health; wherefore it is sooth that they say that there may no man be saved but if he love and like in the name of Jhesu, for there may no man be ghostly whole but if he love and desire ghostly health. For right as if a man were bodily sick, there were none earthly thing so dear nor so needful to him, nor so mickle should be desired of him as bodily health, for though thou wouldest give him all the riches and worship of this world and not make him whole if thou mightest, thou pleasest him not. Right so it is to a man that is sick ghostly and feeleth the pain of ghostly sickness. Nothing is so dear nor so needful, nor so mickle coveted of him, as is ghostly health; and that is Jhesu, without which all the joys of heaven may not like him. (I, xliv, pp. 105–6)

The meaning of this passage is that one does not have to love the name of Jesus, but that he must love spiritual health and salvation, and consequently heaven; and as shown above, God is heaven to man (II, xxxiii). The point of the entire passage, or its essential logic, is that one can love or call on or desire whatever he wants in the spiritual world as long as he interprets his desired object in the right way. The logic is modern and very similar to the logic the Roman Catholic Church uses to justify praying to saints: a saint cannot be prayed to or desired as the final joy, but he can be prayed to as being encompassed in the final joy, the saint being an intercessor. By using Jesus to represent the object desired (God), Hilton makes a closer identification between the object desired and the word indicating it, since Jesus is the second person of the Trinity. This passage, moreover, gives the reader Hilton's instructions for interpreting the use of "Jesus" in *The Scale:* when "Jesus" is not obviously used to suggest a meditation or image, as in the second part of contemplation, and especially when it is used to indicate the primary object of desire, it must be interpreted as meaning God.

A few lines after Hilton has interpreted "Jesus" as meaning spiritual health, he adds a passage which seems to contradict all of his efforts to rationalize the devotion to the Holy Name:

Also I may say on that other part, that he that cannot love this blessed name Jhesu with ghostly mirth, nor enjoy in it with heavenly melody here, he shall never have nor feel in heaven that fullhead of sovereign joy the which he that might in this life by abundance of perfect charity enjoy in Jhesu shall feel and have: and so may their saying be understood. (I, xliv, p. 107)

If this passage referred to the second part of contemplation, there would be no problem, since the name "Jesus" could be used to suggest the image of Christ in meditation, but the words "fullhead of sovereign joy" and "perfect charity" indicate that Hilton is here writing of the third part of contemplation. If the primary object of desire is Jesus in his Godhead or simply God, a devotion to the "blessed name" in the third part of contemplation seems to present an incongruity: the mystical experience is different from the joy in heaven only in degree, not in nature, so that the perception of God in the two states is always a spiritual one, having nothing to do with knowledge in any physical way. Hilton, of course, expects the reader to interpret what is meant by a love of the name of Jesus. Again, Hilton in writing of the third part of contemplation explicitly defends his use of "Jesus," "God," "grace," and "love" interchangeably. Moreover, since the third part of contemplation is free from the working of the imagination, Jesus in his manhood, that is, the image of Christ, would not seem to be what is meant, so that a devotion to the Holy Name as such, implying a devotion to Christ in his manhood, would be even less likely to be Hilton's intention. However, a devotion to Jesus or the Holy Name with Jesus meaning God, grace, or love fits both Hilton's own explanation of the meaning of Jesus in the highest part of contemplation and his first goal of rationalizing the devotion to the Holy Name. Finally that the name of Jesus is to be enjoyed in "ghostly mirth" and that it is closely associated with "perfect charity" argue against "Jesus" in Hilton suggesting anything at all like the popular devotion to the Holy Name.

The Christo-centric passages do not invalidate my distinction, whether or not they are Hilton's. If they are not authentic, they do not affect Hilton's teachings; if they are authentic or if a critic wishes to consider them authentic, they must be read as Hilton intends them to be read. As I pointed out previously when discussing Miss Gardner's argument that the passages are later interpolations not by Hilton, the passages seem to provide a concrete or inspiring thought on which to base a recommended action, but they do not alter the action itself. If the expansions are specifically to provide an inspiring image and have to do with the lower parts of contemplation, they are in accord with Hilton's references to the manhood of Christ when he is teaching meditation, as, for example, in his explanation of the development of meekness. The words in brackets comprise the expansion: "And so by the grace of Jhesu Christ [through steadfast thinking on the meanness of His precious manhood] shalt thou mickle abate the stirrings of pride . . ." (I, xix, p. 41). If the expansions occur when Hilton is discussing the third part of contemplation, they must be interpreted according to Hilton's directions to interpret Jesus as meaning God, love, or grace. Whatever the case, the meaning of an expansion depends on its use in the passage in which it occurs, so that the expansions cannot be lumped indiscriminately to indicate an intensity in Hilton's devotion to the Holy Name, as Miss Underhill lumps them.[21]

Hilton's use of "Jesus" must be understood if one is to analyze correctly his teachings on contemplation. And most critics have failed to understand or distinguish. Miss Underhill not only lumps all the expansions to argue that Hilton wanted to add "a more warmly Christo-centric colour" to *The Scale,* but she writes of the "long and beautiful passage on the Holy Name of Jesus" as if it fervently advocated rather than rationalized and consequently derogated the popular devotion to the Name, though she realizes that the intellectual tone of the passage suggests the attitudes of the author of *The Cloud.*[22] The passage is "beautiful" only in that its dextrous manipulation of the meaning of Jesus, which makes the devotion to Jesus anything but the popular devotion to the Holy Name, is beautiful. Miss Underhill maintains that the final chapters of *The Scale* are "perhaps the most wonderful descriptions of Christo-centric contemplation that exist" and that Book II is generally Christo-centric:

We there get one of the most beautiful expressions in our literature of that peculiarly English devotion to the Holy Name of Jesus which appears in the earliest of our vernacular religious writings, *A Talking of the Love of God,* and illuminates all the works of Rolle and his school. In this worship of the Holy Name, with its penetrating intimacy, its spiritual realism, its poetic charm, we have perhaps the most precious treasure of mediaeval religion.[23]

Exactly in these final chapters is Hilton's identification of Jesus, God, love, and grace (II, xlii), so that what Hilton is writing about there is entirely different from the "poetic charm" of Rolle's work. Inge maintains that "Hylton, like Julian of Norwich . . . , knows that we can never get beyond the human Christ."[24] Failing to observe Hilton's distinction, Inge ignores not only the identification of Christ and God in the third part of contemplation, but Hilton's insistence, even early in *The Scale,* that the mystical experience consists "in knowing and in perfect loving of God" (I, viii, p. 14).[25] Dom Knowles seems to be aware of the problem of distinction when he says that Hilton frequently uses the name of Jesus "not only in place of 'Christ' in references to the sacred humanity, but also as a personal name for the Divine Son, where the author of *The Cloud* would have used the name of God." [26] But he does not develop the comment or its implications. Helen Gardner's interpretations often come very close to the point here. She fully sees the import of the passage on the Holy Name; and far from extolling it as "one of the most beautiful expressions" of the cult, as Miss Underhill does, she attributes the fact that it is missing in some manuscripts to the possibility that a "fanatical follower of the cult . . . disliked Hilton's moderation." [27] Even she concludes, however, that Hilton's devotion to Christ is like Rolle's and that "the *Scale* is throughout rooted and grounded in the love of Christ." [28]

It seems to me that Hilton's teachings concerning Christ and God, that is, his acceptance of the devotion to Christ in meditation and his insistence on Jesus as meaning God in the highest level of contemplation, can be explained in accordance with his general eclecticism. Just as obvious as Rolle's devotion to Jesus is the coolness of the author of *The Cloud* towards the use of Jesus in preference to God. As critics usually say, *The Cloud* is theocentric and intellectual in its view of God as the end of contemplation, even though it emphasizes nonintellectual means of gaining that end; and setting the works of Rolle against those of the author of *The Cloud* is a good way to make the theocentricity of the latter striking. But if the works of Rolle and those of the author of *The Cloud* are contradictory on this point, the suggestion that Hilton takes from each might lead the critic to expect contradictions in Hilton. But he does not find any. In Hilton's scheme (which must be the scheme in which the critic places the other mediaeval English contemplatives if he is to understand Hilton's attitude toward and relation with them), Rolle and the author of *The Cloud* are not contradictory in their teachings on Christ and God. The characteristics Rolle gives to contemplation, his *"canor," "calor,"* and *"dulcor,"* are not equivalent to Hilton's characteristics of the third part of contemplation, but to those of his second; moreover, Rolle's insistence especially on fervent love, which corresponds to Hilton's affection in the second part of contemplation, represents Rolle's view of the highest state, the "singular" one, as well as of the lower states. Thus, when Rolle advocates an intense love of Jesus, though Rolle may be writing about the highest state he knows, he does not seem to be writing about anything more than the fervor from gracious meditation based on the Passion or a like subject, which in Hilton is, again, proper to the second part of contemplation. The author of *The Cloud*, however, is barely concerned with the lower stages of contemplation, and his theocentric teachings apply to what he conceives of as the highest state, the state in which the soul is graciously given union and knowledge by God's sending a glimpse of light through the cloud of unknowing, which separates the Infinite from the finite. In Hilton's scheme, the author of *The Cloud* is writing of the third part of contemplation, the mystical experience proper, in which meditation specifically has no part. Since the devotion to the manhood of Christ is specifically suitable to meditation, the author of *The Cloud*, in devoting his work much more to the third part of contemplation than to the more elementary stages which lead to it, is naturally more concerned with God than with the humanity of Christ. Although Rolle and the author of *The Cloud* are opposed in that each describes the highest part of his own contemplation differently, they are not opposed in Hilton's scheme, in which what Rolle describes would be assigned to the second part of contemplation and what the author of *The Cloud* describes would be assigned to the third. Consequently, Hilton's eclecticism does not result in contradictions on this point. He can accept and encourage the devotion to Jesus in meditation and yet insist on God as the primary object of desire and the object of knowledge in the mystical experience.

Considering the problems caused by the popular cult of the Holy Name, basic problems which forced Hilton to insist on the obvious as when he says that "Jesus" is "not this word Jhesu painted upon the wall, or written with letters on the book, or formed by lips in sound of the mouth . . ." (I, xlvi, p. 111), one might wonder why Hilton involved himself in the turmoil. There are a number of possible answers. Unlike the author of *The Cloud*, who concentrates on the higher levels of contemplation, Hilton wanted his guide to lead the reader through the various steps of the entire process, so that he had to teach meditation for the second part of contemplation. Meditation requires images, images most easily drawn from the life of Christ. It may also be that the fear of heresy and criticism caused him to refer to Christ more than the theocentric works of the author of *The Cloud* refer to the Son,[29] although he teaches that the third level of contemplation is of God, not Jesus. Further, it may be that Hilton was sure that his reader would not be confused. The passage on the Holy Name is sufficiently explicit, and Hilton intersperses comments like "to God, to Jhesu—all is one" (I, xlvi, p. 112) frequently enough to prevent the reader's becoming fixed on the humanity of Christ alone. Hilton's reader would not be hurrying through *The Scale* but rather would be taking "it as it will come, and not all at once" (I, xciii, p. 222), so that he would be likely to read references to Jesus in light of the teachings of the entire chapter or section of material. But the primary reason for Hilton's use of the devotion to Jesus is, I think, that Hilton was not an iconoclast and saw no need to destroy something when it was merely abused. The cult of the Holy Name was popular, and Rolle's work certainly must have increased the devotion to Jesus. Many religious people may very well have been accustomed solely to a fervent devotion to Jesus and may well have objected to or not understood theocentric contemplation by itself. Moreover, "the idea of a Divine Man," as Bullett points out, bridges the "impassable gulf" between the finite and the Infinite,[30] so that a devotion to Jesus or, metonymically, to the Holy Name would appeal to the beginning contemplative. While the cult of the Holy Name may have degenerated to a level perhaps not much above that of superstition, it could be altered. By rationalizing the devotion to the Holy Name, Hilton could give his audience terminology it understood while he proceeded to present more advanced teachings. As in many of his methods, Hilton is here not adverse to expediency.

With God as the primary object of desire and with Jesus in his manhood, especially as the basis for prayer and meditation, as a secondary object of desire, the soul carries on its progress with the development of two important virtues, meekness and charity, both of which intensify the desire for God. In Hilton meekness is of two kinds, imperfect and perfect. Imperfect meekness is the result of an act of will based on reason (I, xix; lxviii). It comes from what is now called an examination of conscience: a man looks into his own soul, sees his sins and wretchedness, and "thinketh him because of his own sins that he is worse than the most sinner that liveth, and that every man doth better than he" (II, xxxvii, p. 397). This meekness is common to the beginner in contemplation, and though it is "boisterous and fleshly," it is also "soothfast and medicinable" (II, xxi, p. 306), helping the soul to purge itself of the desire to sin. Its opposite, perfect meekness, is "this meekness that the soul feeleth through grace, in sight and beholding of the endless being and the wonderful goodness of Jhesu" (II, xxi, p. 306). Since love also comes from knowing, the meekness felt at the sight of Jesus, in meditation or more perfectly in the mystical experience, is coupled with love, so that it is a meekness "in thine heart with affection" (I, xix, p. 41), inspired not by a regard of one's own wretchedness, but of God's superiority to all else that can be. This distinction between perfect and imperfect meekness, made also by the author of *The Cloud*, but with more precise analysis,[31] corresponds to that between the first and second parts of contemplation, and the relative values of imperfect and perfect meekness are also in proportion to the relative values of the first and second parts of contemplation.

The importance of meekness in the soul, whether imperfect or perfect, is great. Not only is meekness in the lowest of the Christian lives a requisite for salvation (I, xliv), but it retains its importance even to the highest. It is one of the first qualities necessary for beginning work in the spiritual life (I, xvi), and it prepares the soul for the reception of charity and determines the charity it will receive (I, lxviii). In practical and common matters, meekness, not excessive scrupulosity, will aid one to conquer gluttony and determine how much he should eat (I, lxxvi), and meekness will keep one from judging other men's actions (I, xvi; lxvi).[32] The meekness must range in duty from stifling the great pride which leads to heresy (I, lviii) to stifling the little pride which leads one to care "whether men blame him or praise him, worship him or despise him as for himself" (II, xxxvii, p. 401). About this last duty of meekness, the development of personal humility, Hilton is very insistent, both by his own example, as pointed out, and by instruction. In teaching that a contemplative must not care for the world's opinion, or care only enough to pray for the salvation of those who harm or despise him (II, xxxviii), he is setting a standard far above that which we find in Margery Kempe's expectation that she would be revered as a saint in her parish [33] or in Rolle's attack on his detractors as "scorpions." [34] The cultivation of meekness is so important to Hilton that, a bit ironically, it causes one of the very few passages in which there is a tendency to be harsh. Yet, he at once qualifies the harshness as a method of instruction:

Then thou that art so boisterous, so lewd, so fleshly, so blind in ghostly things, and namely of thine own soul which thee behoveth first know if thou shouldst come to knowing of God, how shouldst thou then feel thyself able or worthy for to have that state and likeness of contemplative life, the which life as I have said lieth principally in ghostly knowing and feeling of God? This I say to thee, not that thou shouldst forethink [read "forthink," MS Harl. 6579] thy purpose and be mis-paid [displeased] with thine enclosing, but that thou shouldst feel this lowness soothfastly in thine heart if thou might, for it is sooth and no lies. (I, xvi, p. 33)

The essence of meekness is for Hilton no more than the recognition of the true state of things: "For what is meekness but soothfastness? Soothly, nought else" (II, xx, p. 301). Whether one sees his own wretchedness or God's superiority, the sight should make him realize that by himself he is nothing. The recognition that causes meekness should result, with meekness, in the recognition of one's dependence on God and on his gift of grace. Consequently, in basic matters, like fighting for virtue, meekness will result in victory, while one's own efforts cannot, for meekness puts a soul "fully in God's hand" (II, xxxvi, p. 396). And in high matters, like the mystical experience, meekness and the subsequent recognition of one's dependence, again not one's efforts, will determine the degree of love possessed: "That is, these souls that are made so meek and so buxom to God that they work not of themselves, but suffer the Holy Ghost stir them and work in them the feelings of love with a full sweet accord to His stirrings, these are specially God's sons, most like unto Him" (II, xxxv, p. 389). The essence of meekness, then, recognition, eventually makes the soul receptive to God's gift by cultivating in the soul passivity, the quality James marks as usually found in the mystical state.[35]

As necessary for the progress of the soul as meekness is charity. In Hilton charity or love is an exceedingly important and somewhat complex subject, one requiring in analysis distinctions of kind, of degree, and of terminology, the last of which Hilton himself does not always maintain. First, charity is not the same as desire. While Miss Underhill says that love for the mystic is "the active, conative expression of his will and desire for the Absolute," [36] Hilton means by love a gracious affection of the soul for God, one that is not the result of man's willing. Desire is an act of will, sometimes gracious, based on reason and directed toward an object or goal, like the desire for virtue or God. Hilton often uses the verbs "desire" and "covet" interchangeably, as when he advises the contemplative not to "covet" bodily feelings, but to "desire" or "covet" ghostly ones and grace (II, xli). Also, that Hilton obviously distinguishes between loving and desiring is apparent from comments like "covet but only the love of God" (II, xxxiv, p. 380). Secondly, charity or love in Hilton is, of course, spiritual love. While this spiritual love will manifest itself in the physical world, especially in the loving of one's "even-christian" and consequent aiding of him (I, li, p. 124), it is, as Noetinger points out, entirely different from love between people in the natural sense: "Hilton opposes natural affection to charity. The first gives preference to those who are united to us by very close bonds; the second prefers those who are united to God. Charity, in effect, has God as a principal object, and extends to one's neighbor only inasmuch as he is united to or in relation with God." [37]

For Hilton there are two kinds of love, "love unformed" and "love formed," and the distinction between these two is of major importance:

Love unformed is God Himself, the third Person in the Trinity; that is, the Holy Ghost. He is love unformed and unmade, as Saint John saith thus: *Deus dilectio est.* God is love, that is, the Holy Ghost. Love formed is the affection of the soul, made by the Holy Ghost of the sight and the knowing of soothfastness, that is God only, stirred and set in him. This love is called formed, for it is made by the Holy Ghost. This love is not God in Himself, for it is made; but it is the love of the soul, felt of the sight of Jhesu and stirred to Him only. (II, xxxiv, p. 381)

Love unformed, since it is "God Himself," is a free gift of God, for it cannot be merited. That Hilton specifically means to identify love unformed, the gift, with God, and not merely an effect in the soul caused by God, is emphasized by his explanation of why love unformed is "the best and the worthiest" gift: "For there is no gift of God that is both the giver and the gift, but this gift of love" (II, xxxvi, p. 392). Hilton's identification of love unformed with God is consistent with, and explains with more precision, his identification of Jesus, God, love, and grace (II, xlii). Love unformed, as God or specifically the Holy Ghost, completes the Trinity in the preceding equation, while grace, the last element, represents the giving of God, in the three persons, of himself. The identification of love, Jesus, and God with the coexistent suggestion of the Trinity, corroborated interestingly by Hilton's specific inclusion in the mystical experience of an understanding of "the onehead in substance and distinction of persons in the blessed Trinity" (II, xlvi, p. 462), itself corroborates my previous argument that the object of contemplation and the primary object of desire is God, not specifically Jesus. The identification also explains Hilton's teaching that love unformed is the cause of all progress towards and knowing in the mystical experience (II, xxxiv), since love unformed, as God, is responsible for all things.

Less important than love unformed but far more common, since the perception of it is not peculiar to the mystical experience and it is not the prime cause, is love formed. Love formed, "the affection of the soul, made by the Holy Ghost" (II, xxxiv, p. 381), is what is normally understood by "love" or "charity" outside of the mystical experience proper. It, like love unformed, is a free gift of God, unattainable by man's own efforts, no matter how violent they may be (II, xxxv). However, unlike love unformed, which itself cannot vary since it is God but which is perceived or felt only partially in the mystical experience and fully in heaven, love formed itself varies greatly, being dependent upon God's grace for its foundation. The first level of love formed is based on faith, "without gracious imagination or ghostly knowing of God" (II, xxx, p. 358). It is the result of grace inasmuch as all good is the result of God's free giving, but it is more like the sort of love which might be based on the reasoned knowledge of the first part of contemplation, love, for example, which stems from seeing God's omnipotence or goodness in the order of the universe. Because reasoned knowledge is an inferior knowledge, the love based on it must be of a low form, according to Hilton's principle that "love cometh out of knowing" (II, xxxiv, p. 380). Indeed, this love "without gracious imagination or ghostly knowing of God," although adequate for salvation, is characteristic of a soul "in the lowest degree of charity" (II, xxx, p. 358). The second level of love formed comes from meditation, especially of "Jhesu in his manhood," as in the second part of contemplation. It is superior to the first level because of its basis, since inspired meditation does result in a sort of knowing in the imagination. As the source of knowledge of God becomes refined, so that it is neither finite man's reasoned knowledge nor even gracious knowing in the imagination, but rather the ghostly sight of the Godhead in the mystical experience, love formed becomes perfected, until it is eventually based on love unformed, or God. But since love unformed cannot be fully perceived except in heaven, love formed cannot reach its highest stage until then either.

Hilton's establishing love as one of the most essential factors for spiritual progress is, of course, quite in accord with Christian teaching in general. That one should love God above all things and love one's neighbor for the love of God are directives more or less applicable to all levels of Christian life. In the active or mixed lives, love for God is often best indicated by charity towards fellow Christians, and in the contemplative life, in which worldly cares do not figure, love is best indicated by constancy in devotion to God alone. The Church Fathers amplified the doctrine of love in Christianity and especially in contemplation. Gregory insists that "the greatness of contemplation can be given to none but them that love,"[38] and Bernard makes love a means to contemplation and one of the lasting effects of it.[39] Among the mediaeval English contemplatives the author of *The Cloud* says that the keeping of the laws and advice of the Bible, necessary for spiritual progress, is directly connected with love: "For if it be wisely looked, the ground and the strength of this working shall be seen nought else but the glorious gift of love, in the which by the teaching of the Apostle all the law is fulfilled: *Plenitudo legis est dilectio*, 'the fulness of the law is love.'"[40] The same author's recognition of the necessary interrelation between loving God and loving fellow Christians is apparent in his teaching that by sacrificing himself for his brothers, a good man accomplishes "the knitting of the soul to God (the life of it) by the heavenly food of charity." [41] Julian of Norwich, when she is explaining that spiritual light is God, who in turn is charity, distinguishes the kinds of love much as Hilton does, using, in fact, the terms "made" and "unmade" to modify "charity," although her explanation of the distinctions is brief and seems not to correspond exactly with Hilton's.[42] Richard Rolle, most famous for his teachings on love, perhaps because of the almost sensuous character love takes on in many of his descriptions, begins his "Ego Dormio" with an invitation which sounds like that of a court minstrel: "Ye that list to love, hold (hither) your ears, and hear of love." [43] He is, of course, writing of spiritual love, and he makes the point throughout "Ego Dormio" that love determines the soul's level of life here as in heaven. Rolle's concern with love, the desire for it, and the consequent anxiety over it, leads him in "The Form of Living" to explain seven tests which a Christian can use to decide whether he is in charity,[44] and in *The Mending of Life* in an apostrophe to charity, he identifies love as the means by which "we joy and ascend the heavenly ladder." [45] Hilton's emphasis on love as an essential factor for the soul's progress in contemplation is, then, as one would expect, not extraordinary. But the critic must be careful not to exaggerate love in Hilton in a sense that is not Hilton's.

"Love," like "Jesus," is a word which Hilton uses often, but also like "Jesus," it is a word which can mislead, since Hilton does not always mean by "love" what the word at once suggests to us, even in its spiritual sense. Father Pepler says that "the only certain 'machinery' [which will lead to heaven] is the love of God and a corresponding desire and generosity on man's part," and he calls Hilton the "Master of the love of God." [46] Such comments are acceptable only if the word "love" is qualified so that it does not mean primarily the affection of the soul developed by grace and man's efforts toward the Divine Being, but rather the Divine Being himself. As mentioned previously, Hilton says that love unformed, God, is the cause of all progress, not love formed; consequently, the meaning of desiring love as the "machinery" of progress is desiring God, and not the affection towards God:

Now may thou see that love formed is not cause why a soul cometh to the ghostly sight of Jhesu, as some men would think that they would love God so burningly as it were by their own might, that they were worthy for to have the ghostly knowing of Him. Nay, it is not so. But love unformed, that is, God Himself, is cause of all this knowing. For a blind wretched soul is so far from the clear knowing and the blessed feeling of His love through sin and frailty of the bodily kind, that it might never come to it were it not the endless mickleness of the love of God. But then because that He loveth us so mickle, therefore He giveth us His love, that is, the Holy Ghost. He is both the giver and the gift, and maketh us then by that gift for to know and love Him. Lo, this is the love that I spake of, that thou shouldest only covet and desire this unformed love that is the Holy Ghost. (II, xxxiv, pp. 381–82)

My explanation of desiring love in Hilton is not intended to suppress the importance of affection or love formed, but to set off Hilton's view of the superiority of love unformed, both as the Prime Cause and as the primary love one is to desire. As previously pointed out, Rolle's descriptions of advanced love fit at the second rather than the highest part of contemplation, at least according to Hilton's scheme. Rolle's idea of love, then, is comparable to Hilton's affection or love formed, and this divergence of views explains (with the differing personalities) Rolle's primary concern with the fervor of one's love toward God and Hilton's primary concern with love as God. The essential meaning of love in Hilton as God or love unformed corresponds with Hilton's meaning of "Jesus" as the primary object of desire, as set down previously: Jesus as God as the primary object of desire is the same as love unformed, which is the Prime Cause, the love which leads to advancement, and consequently which is to be desired over love formed. This correspondence further clarifies Hilton's identification of love, Jesus, God, and grace (II, xlii), an identification which would be impossible if the primary idea of love in Hilton were the affection of man's soul toward

God, i.e., love formed. Finally, that God as love unformed is primarily what causes progress and is to be desired is consistent with Hilton's teachings on grace, to be explained next, and with his teaching that the third part of contemplation consists of cognition and affection. The affection in the mystical experience is love formed as perfect as it may be on earth and caused by the ghostly sight or cognition of God, love unformed. Father Pepler's comments that Hilton is the "Master of the love of God" and that love is the "only certain 'machinery' " which will lead to heaven are indeed correct if "love" is defined as Hilton intends it to be.

Hilton's essential doctrines on the progress of the soul, concerning the desire for Jesus and meekness and charity, are very closely connected. He constantly mentions meekness and charity together, both as necessary qualities for progress whether one is in the lowest or highest level of contemplation and, as Dom Noetinger shows, as qualities which enable one another to grow.[47] Also, since charity in its highest form, love unformed, is identical with God, since love formed is the gracious affection of the soul towards God and based on a knowledge of God in its most perfect form, and since Jesus is God, the desire for Jesus is at once a desire for all of these. Meekness, since it is no more than a recognition of God's excellence and man's wretchedness, a recognition of truth, is bound up with the former as resulting from knowledge, which is also the basis of love formed and which, again, in the highest level of contemplation is of God himself. The coupling of all of these factors necessary for progress is apparent in Hilton's repeated suggestion that the contemplative keep in mind the following thought: "I am nought, I have nought, I covet nought, but one" (II, xxi, p. 305). "I am nought, I have nought" suggests meekness, and "I covet nought, but one" suggests the desire for Jesus, God, or love unformed. The center of all the factors necessary for progress is love unformed or God, which is the reason for Hilton's saying that the greatest gift is love unformed, since it is both giver and gift (II, xxxiv). But if the essence of progress is God and if finite man cannot by his own efforts achieve love unformed or God, man cannot attain the essence of progress by his own efforts. Such is Hilton's teaching.

Perhaps "Master of grace" is a better title for Hilton than "Master of love." It is true that *"Deus dilectio est,"* but it is also true that most important for the progress of the soul is that God gives his love, that is, that God bridges the gulf between the Infinite and the finite which man cannot bridge and that God does it freely, since man's efforts can never be great enough to merit God's action. I have referred many times to God's grace as essential for the means of the progress of the soul, for the attainment and holding of the parts of contemplation, and for the rewards of contemplation, but my references barely suggest the breadth of Hilton's teachings on grace. The doctrine of God's free giving or grace pervades *The Scale*. When explaining God's part in the progress of the soul, from his calling of a soul from worldly vanity to his final glorifying of it in heaven, Hilton says, "He doth all." Man is "nought else but a reasonable instrument wherein that He worketh" (II, xxiv, p. 318). Even the desire for the love of God—specifically the desire in the prayer "I am nought; I have nought; nought I seek nor covet but the love of Jhesu" (II, xxiii, p. 317), i.e., the very basic desire to please God —is the result of God's gift, of a "touching of His grace" (II, xxiv, p. 318). Prayer and meditation have been analyzed as specific means by which one comes to the second part of contemplation, but prayer merely prepares the soul to receive grace and "is not the cause for which our Lord giveth grace" (I, xxiv, p. 55), and meditation, even the most basic meditation in which a man regards his sins and asks mercy for them, is itself caused by grace put in men's hearts by God (I, xxxiv). Charity is a gift of God to those who are meek (I, lxviii), but meekness itself results from the working of a soul which "can feelably through grace nought himself" (II, xx, p. 301). Even the rather elementary meekness necessary to save a heretic must be sent by God (I, lviii). Hilton's same teachings on the doctrine of grace appear strikingly in his other works, especially in his interjected comments in his translation of the *Stimulus Amoris*, as Clare Kirchberger notes.[48]

The necessary results of a doctrine of grace which makes God responsible for all spiritual progress are that one should not presumptuously strain to achieve grace or the effects of grace and that since God freely gives grace, he can give it to whomever he wishes. When Hilton is advising the contemplative how to rid himself of the feeling of sins which might press upon him when he is trying to think of God, he tells him to "be not too heavy nor strive not too mickle, as though thou wouldest through mastery put them out of thy thought; for thou mayest not do so. But abide grace, suffer easily, and break not thyself too mickle" (II, xxiv, p. 323). If one enjoys God's grace and afterwards it is withdrawn, he should, according to Hilton's constant reminders, wait "with patient abiding till it come again" (I, vi, p. 11). When Hilton is describing the effects of love, he makes the point that indeed love does much, "but not in all His lovers alike full" (II, xxxvii, p. 403), and as one would expect, the highest part of contemplation is "a special gift only to chosen souls" (II, xxxiv, p. 384; see also I, ix), that is, God's grace freely given to whom he will.

In Hilton's contemporaries approximately the same teachings on grace are found, since the orthodox view of grace in the Roman Catholic Church is that it is a free gift of God. Margery Kempe says that "His will may not be constrained," that "it is in His Own free disposition," and consequently would maintain that God gives grace to whom he chooses.[49] Concerning tears and weeping, God tells Margery that he will sometimes withdraw them "so that thou shouldst have no vainglory, and that thou shouldst know well thou mayest not have tears or such dalliance, except when God will send them to thee, for they are the free gifts of God without thy merit, and He may give them to whom He will, and do thee no wrong." [50] Yet, though Margery repeats the doctrine of grace as it is in Hilton, in practical matters she seems to be able to accomplish very much by means of her own will, as when she easily summons God for a talk about her husband's desire that she either lie with him or eat and drink with him on Friday.[51] Julian of Norwich says that no man may enjoy the highest parts of contemplation in this life unless he is given them by a special grace, but she seems to suggest that the special grace can be merited: ". . . but faith and belief with charity deserve the meed, and so it is had by grace."[52] Rolle insists that the third degree of love is freely given by God to whom he chooses,[53] and his general teachings on the doctrine of grace are so consistent that Miss Allen is able to reject an alternate manuscript reading on the grounds that it is incongruous with them.[54] The author of *The Cloud*, as Miss Hodgson points out, "is much concerned with the burning question of grace,"[55] and his teachings are like Hilton's. If one has difficulty freeing himself from temptations, he should bow down like a coward overcome in battle and put himself in God's hands, and in any case he should not develop the "erring presumption" that by his own scholarship or intelligence he can advance his own contemplation, "God but suffering or only consenting."[56]

But Hilton's teachings on grace are more emphatic than those of his contemporaries, and they bring up some of the problems associated with the emphasis of the doctrine that God does all. In *The Scale* Hilton recognizes and treats, practically if not theologically, two of the major problems. The first of these is embodied in the well-known argument that if man cannot merit grace, if grace is necessary for spiritual advancement, and if God freely gives grace to whom he will, God predestines man's spiritual state. Dom Sitwell in a long note explains Hilton's handling of this problem in Hilton's statements that Christ died to save all men, even those who do not take advantage of the redemption, and that God wishes to damn no one (II, xxxiv); however, Sitwell also points out that Hilton tends to leave the center of the problem a mystery, especially in his attributing the beginning of a knowledge of how the evil are justly damned by God to the mystical experience, that is, to a special grace (II, xlv).[57] Hilton's lack of a real analysis of the problem is consistent with that seen in his other teachings. If the explanation of God's giving grace but his not predetermining man's salvation or damnation is to be understood only in the mystical experience, it is both ineffable knowledge and knowledge which cannot be attained by man's reason alone. Hilton would maintain, consequently, that such knowledge could not be properly conveyed in a book.

Associated with the problem of predestination and also resulting from the emphasis on the doctrine that God does all is quietism. Quietism, the teaching that man can do no more than remain perfectly passive and free from all disturbance if he wishes to have union with God, is in Christianity based on the belief that since God's grace is given freely, we should do no more than make ourselves receptive to it by putting all else from our minds. Among the pagan neo-Platonists quietism took its form in the belief that the simple "negation of all that is not God is followed inevitably by the inflowing of the divine." [58] Among the mediaeval contemplatives quietism is a special problem because of the extension of the doctrine of grace which discourages great personal efforts to progress spiritually as presumptuous and even dangerous: "the devil hath his contemplatives," the author of *The Cloud* says, and they are those who strive too hard to gain contemplation by their own efforts.[59] If one cannot get grace by his own power and if an attempt to is presumptuous, perhaps the only reasonable thing to do is to cultivate passivity or receptivity. Then if God does give grace or, in the highest level of contemplation, mystical union, the soul will receive it as fully as it can. Miss Underhill treats quietism as one of the chief dangers of contemplation and differentiates it from the quiet or peace which the contemplative receives with union and the active state of freedom from externals which he cultivates as a prerequisite to the third part of contemplation.[60] The Roman Catholic Church views quietism as an abuse of contemplation and as heresy.

The problems stemming from quietism can be extreme. One group of quietists decided that passivity free from temptation and disturbance is best achieved by giving in to all temptations at once, with the corollary that illicit carnal pleasures did not stain the soul as long as one's will remained with God. The Spanish contemplative Molinos, condemned as a quietist in the seventeenth century, taught that images must never be a part of prayer and that passivity and contemplation had nothing to do with the externals of religion, like confession or penance. Master Eckhart, some of whose principles were condemned as quietistic in 1329, taught that good cannot come from external actions, which cannot make one good, but only from God's work in the soul.[61] But the problems of quietism can be very practical ones too. Inge, when he points out that many of the dangers mystics and contemplatives have encountered are due to a desire to achieve the highest levels of contemplation without the preliminary "toilsome preparation" necessary,[62] comes close to touching the practical question of the relation between man's effort, grace, and quietism. Hilton fully recognizes that a difficulty exists, for he sets up a hypothetical questioner to introduce it:

Whereto should I travail? Whereto should I pray or think, wake or fast, or any other bodily penance do for to come to such grace, since it may not be gotten nor had, but only of the free gift of Jhesu? Therefore I will abide in fleshliness as I am, and right nought do of such works bodily nor ghostly until He give it; for if He will give it, He asketh no working of me. What so that I do, and how little I do, I shall have it. And if He will not give it, travail I never so fast therefore, I get it never the sooner. (II, xx, p. 302)

And as an extension of this question, why should a contemplative not begin at once to clear his mind of all so that God will have a blank to work on, and to wait patiently, as Hilton often suggests he should do, but without action of any sort?

Theologians and scholars have means of explaining the doctrine of grace so that it does not result in quietism. Dom Cuthbert Butler, after a discussion of the controversy over whether acquired contemplation (contemplation achieved by the efforts of the soul rather than primarily by grace) exists, makes the point that even in infused contemplation (contemplation as a gift of grace, in Hilton's sense) "there is an element of effort on the part of the will, in placing the mind in the state of recollection and attention, and in keeping the attention fixed on God by recalling it when it wanders, or reviving it when it fades away." [63] Dom Knowles gives the scholastic explanation "that God suits His gifts to the various degrees of advancement that souls have reached" and that the capacity of the receiver determines in part what is received: "In other words, it is the imperfect human organism that receives perceptibly, but inadequately, the divine gift to the soul, and it receives it in such a way as to scale it down to its own capacity." [64] Making this view, which is also essentially Noetinger's,[65] coincide exactly with Hilton's is difficult because of the suggestions in Knowles' statements that God will automatically give grace of a certain intensity if the soul by its own efforts makes itself capable of receiving such grace. Grace begins to be a gift which is merited, acquired, or deserved, whereas in Hilton it is none of these. Moreover, Hilton makes grace responsible even for one's primary desire for God, for one's most basic good actions, so that even developing a capacity for receiving grace is in Hilton the result of grace. James says that although in the mystical experience proper "the mystic feels as if his own will were in abeyance," the mystic can help bring on a mystical state "by preliminary voluntary operations, as by fixing the attention, or going through certain bodily performances, or in other ways which manuals of mysticism prescribe." [66] While James is here not treating specifically the relation between grace and man's efforts in Christian contemplation, his argument corresponds with Butler's argument above, and as a generalization, it describes the teachings of most contemplatives and mystics, though it may not answer specific questions.

Hilton's contemporaries recognized some seeming relation between grace in contemplation and man's efforts, although they specifically maintain that grace is a gift. When God is speaking to Margery Kempe, he says definitely that many of Margery's experiences are given by his grace, though his words perhaps suggest that she gained others by her own merits:

And, daughter, in Heaven shall it be known to thee how many days thou hast had of high contemplation, through My gift, on earth, and although it be so, that they are My gifts and My graces that I have given thee, yet shalt thou have the same grace and reward in Heaven, as if they were of thine own merits, for freely have I given them unto thee.

But highly I thank thee, daughter, that thou hast suffered Me to work My will in thee, and that thou wouldst let Me be so homely with thee. . . .[67]

In the experiences which God gives by his grace, Margery merely allows him to work in her, so that she would be no more than Hilton's "reasonable instrument," and in the experiences which she perhaps merits, she seems to be the controlling factor. In the latter, however, the experience itself may yet be a gift, and Margery's actions may merely be her preparing herself to receive the gift. Rolle qualifies his statement that gracious contemplation cannot be merited, but his qualification poses problems: "Therefore I trow this is given to none meedfully, but freely to whom Christ will; nevertheless I trow no man receives it unless he specially love the Name of Jesu, and in so mickle honours It that he never lets It pass from his mind except in sleep." [68] If love in Rolle is a gift, as it is in Hilton, then the means of being receptive to God's grace is a gift also, so that man's active part is yet unexplained. If love here means desire or voluntary fervor, it explains Rolle's position, especially since the contemplation Rolle is writing of is the second part of contemplation in Hilton's scheme, but it still does not explain Hilton's, since even a fervent desire for God is in *The Scale* the result of grace. The author of *The Cloud* deals with the problem as a scholastic might and argues that God gives grace only to a soul able to receive it, but he also says that no soul without the gift is able to have it, so that the capability to receive comes with the gift:

The condition of this work is such that the presence thereof enableth a soul to have it and to feel it. And that ableness may no soul have without it. The ableness to this work is oned to the work itself, without separation; so that whoso feeleth this work is able thereto, and none else. Insomuch, that without this work a soul is as it were dead, and cannot covet it or desire it. Forasmuch as thou willest it and desirest it, so much hast thou of it, and no more and no less: and yet it is no will, nor desire, but a thing thou knowest never what, that stirreth thee to will and desire thou knowest never what. Reck thee never if thou knowest no more, I pray thee; but do forth ever more and more, so that thou be ever doing.[69]

While the theoretical discussion of the author of *The Cloud* about the relation between the gift and one's ability to receive it solves little and does not eliminate the quietistic question, the implication in his final comment, "do forth ever more and more," is that somehow one can advance towards or prepare for the reception of the grace. In practice, of course, the author of *The Cloud* teaches that an aspiring contemplative can prepare to receive the grace by rejecting the world, desiring God, and thinking of him, but the final problem caused by God's being responsible even for the contemplative's desire remains.

Hilton's answer to the hypothetical quietist who asks, "Whereto should I travail?", is that "inward" and "outward working" make one able to receive grace and keep his desire strong (II, xx, p. 302). Prayer, for example, cleanses (I, xxiv), but prayer is still a gift itself, and one can only "suffer our Lord give what [as much prayer as] He will, and ken Him not" (I, xxxiii, p. 75). Hilton seems to realize that all arguments lead back to the doctrine of grace, for the hypothetical questioner appears more than once to ask about it. Hilton's answer is never satisfactory in that it does not clarify the relation between God's doing all good and man's active role in contemplation:

> But now say some of them thus: "I would fain love God, and be a good man and forsake the love of the world if that I might; but I have no grace thereto. If I had the same grace that a good man hath, I should do as he doeth; but for I have it not, therefore I may not, and so it is not me to wit, but I am excused." Unto these men I say thus: Sooth it is as they say, that they have no grace and therefore they lie still in their sin and may not rise out. But that availeth them not, nor excuseth them not against God, for it is their own default. They unable them by divers ways so mickle, that the light of grace may not shine to them nor rest in their hearts. (II, xv, p. 280)

The relation has to do with man's will and God's gift: "He formeth only by Himself, but He reformeth us with us; for grace given, and applying of our will to grace, worketh all this" (II, xxviii, p. 346). But when Hilton is explaining the simple desire for Jesus and says, "I expect that it shall bring thee to perfect love of our Lord Jhesu" (II, xxiii, p. 317), he seems to suggest that man's spiritual activity might naturally lead to grace and that consequently one who wants grace will have it. Such an interpretation is very close to maintaining that one does, after all, have control over his attaining grace, a doctrine incompatible with Hilton's explicit statements that God does all in the process of contemplation.

A critic might explain the doctrine of grace and its relation to man's activity and quietism in *The Scale* by distinguishing actual from sanctifying grace. Actual grace is given to all men in a quantity sufficient for man's rejecting temptation, doing good, and attaining salvation. Actual grace would be the grace which enables one to desire Jesus, pray, or meditate, while sanctifying grace would be a special grace God gives to a man who chooses to use rather than reject actual grace and who may even devote himself to the most intensive development of good based on actual grace. Such an explanation is consistent with Dom Sitwell's view of Hilton's third part of contemplation as a union with God based on sanctifying grace,[70] and it is perhaps suggested in Hilton's statement that while Christ died for all men, even Jews and Saracens and false Christians, the gift of love "is not common, but it is a special gift only to chosen souls" (II, xxxiv, p. 384). Also, when Hilton discusses affection, he remarks that affection based on reason, for example, on seeing God's glory in the universe, is good since it is the result of "the general grace that He giveth to all His chosen souls," but it is not at all equal to the affection based on a "special grace" in his perfect lovers (II, xxxv, p. 390). Yet, it must be admitted that while the "special grace" would seem to correspond to sanctifying grace and to the grace of the gift of love to "chosen souls," the "general grace" does not seem to correspond to actual grace or the grace common to all through Christ's redemption since the "general grace" is also for "chosen souls" and not for mankind. My explanation in terms of actual and sanctifying grace of the relation in *The Scale* between the doctrine that God does all and the duty of man to strive to perfect himself must remain conjectural. Hilton never makes the particular distinction in graces himself; he seldom distinguishes types of grace at all, and when he does, he does not use consistent terminology; and he never satisfactorily and precisely explains the fundamental relation between grace and man's duty.

While Hilton does not clarify the problem of quietism theoretically, practically he indicates the relation between grace and man's efforts very clearly and makes impossible a quietistic interpretation of his teachings. Although he constantly refers to contemplation, love, and grace as gifts, according to his doctrine and to his wish to make a contemplative meek, he just as constantly emphasizes the lower levels of prayer, contemplation, and spiritual activity, like the reading of the Bible and of religious books (I, xv). He gives specific means to begin active and voluntary meditation on the Passion and devotes much time to basic prayer, and far from encouraging imageless contemplation or passivity by means of mere negation, he warns the contemplative not to give up the common vocal prayers of the Church too soon (I, xxviii). As for the passivity which precedes the mystical experience, as Dom Sitwell points out, Hilton suggests that it will come when God gives it; he does not, like the author of *The Cloud,* insist on the contemplative's voluntary attempt to stop prayer and meditation based on images or reasoning.[71] Most important, Hilton's inclusion of major elements from the ascetic or religious-handbook tradition in *The Scale,* like his discussion of the deadly sins and the means one uses to rid himself of them, encourages individual action and discourages quietism. His moderation in his advocating ascetic practices, like fasting, would indicate a further consciousness of the relation between the doctrine of grace and the necessity for personal effort: immoderate ascetic practices may lead to the presumption that one can merit grace, while moderate ones carried out meekly can prepare the soul to receive the gift of grace necessary for spiritual advancement. Hilton's inclusion of major elements from the religious-handbook tradition may be, in fact, the result of a deliberate attempt to avoid quietism in his guide, in which he may have thought that practical example and advice would be more appropriate and effective than a theoretical discussion, the latter being the concern of dialecticians rather than contemplatives.[72]

Hilton's doctrines on the means of the progress of the soul correspond essentially with those of Catholic theology. Grace from God in effect accomplishes all, since man, because of Adam's sin, cannot save himself. Yet, the grace must be co-operated with by man, so that eventually man can make his soul meek and receptive to more intensive grace in the form of more love, and this love with yet more grace and the desire for God leads toward perfect charity or love. In Hilton the several means of progress function together to advance the soul. The means are distinct from the levels of contemplation, and they are not rungs on a ladder which one utilizes and then forgets. Rather, they are interrelated from the first upward movement of the soul to the mystical experience itself, in which the desire for God only in the meek soul is rewarded with the greatest gift of grace, love unformed, or God himself. The proportionate relation between these means may vary in particular situations: the very great sinner or heretic may be first turned towards God primarily by the gift of meekness (I, lviii), though unless he acts on this gift by desiring the love of Jesus, he will not benefit from it. The more advanced meek soul may best strive for progress by concentrating on his desire for God or love, though God's grace is necessary before actual progress. But again, it is by the constant interplay of all the means—meekness and charity, a strong desire for Jesus or God, and God's gift of grace—that the soul perfects itself and advances through the various levels of contemplation.

The beginning of the soul's progress comes with its realization of its own nature. Comprised of mind, reason, and will, the soul is like the Trinity, but it is a made trinity, unlike the divine Trinity, which is an unmade one (I, xliii, xlv). The image of the soul as a trinity, used also by Julian of Norwich,[73] suggests the excellence of the soul because of its likeness to God, an excellence and worthiness which must be recognized if man is to realize the necessity of reforming the soul from the image of sin to the image of God (II, xiv). The image of sin, which destroys the image of God proper to the soul because of the soul's higher nature, is the result of the inordinate rule of sensuality, the lower part of the soul, the part which man shares with beasts (II, xiii). This division of the soul into higher and lower parts, going back to Plotinus but known in the Middle Ages through the Church Fathers,[74] must also be recognized so that the lower part, sensuality, may be subordinated to the higher. If the recognition and proper subordination of the two parts are not made, the soul will seek "meat from without" instead of "angels' food" (I, lxxix, p. 192) or, more colorfully, "swine's meat of fleshly savours" instead of the "ghostly savour of heavenly joy" (I, lxxxix, p. 213), for it will not be fully aware of the deserts of its superior part.

It is interesting that a knowledge of the nature of the soul, a knowledge like that one might associate with scholastic theology rather than contemplation, is of great importance to the contemplative; it is also interesting that Hilton's definitions and to a certain extent his terminology on this point are generally in accord with the definitions and terminology of scholastic theology, as Dom Sitwell and especially Dom Noetinger point out.[75] Although Hilton's discussion of the nature of the soul is not nearly so long or so detailed as the corresponding discussion by the author of *The Cloud*,[76] Hilton's discussion is adequate for the goal of his practical guide, and it indicates his willingness to use scholastic knowledge when it serves his purpose. His teachings on self-knowledge, while they correspond in general with the teachings of mystics and contemplatives, correspond in particular with his own view that reasoned knowledge can be a factor in contemplation, as shown in his description of the first part of contemplation. Further, they reveal his general attitude toward scholasticism, an attitude which, as pointed out previously, is not the hate or disdain of the man of the heart for the man of the head. Finally, Hilton's insistence on knowledge as a starting point for the reform and perfection of the soul strengthens my contention—as apparent in my explanation of "Jesus" and "love" as meaning God, rather than Christ and affection, when the words are used in conjunction with the essential progress of the soul or the third part of contemplation—that Hilton intended *The Scale* to be read on a rational or even somewhat intellectual level rather than on a passionate, devotional, or poetic one.

After the soul has realized its own nature, its likeness to the divine Trinity, and its ideal subordination of lower to upper parts, it looks at itself as it is in reality. "In this inward beholding" the soul sees the "wretchedness and the mischief" it has fallen into because of sin (I, xlii, p. 96); that is, the soul sees the "image of the first Adam," an image of sin caused by self-love (I, liv, p. 130). As Dom Noetinger points out, this self-inspection is really an examination of conscience,[77] but in Hilton the examination of conscience is not merely a systematic sorting of sins into their respective categories. While Hilton devotes a number of chapters to the deadly sins and to their parts in the total image of sin, his emphasis is always on the contrast between the image of sin and the image of God rather than on the evil of the sins themselves. His inclination is always towards the positive rather than the negative. A man who comes home, that is, looks into his soul, and finds there only "stinking smoke and a chiding wife" runs out of his house, but he is repelled not so much by what he finds as by the horror of what he finds in contrast to the goodness he should have found, the image of Jesus (I, liii, p. 128). When one finds in his soul "a false image, that men call an idol" (I, lxxxiv, p. 203), he cries for mercy and wants to repent because he knows he should find a likeness of the Trinity. The structure of Book I, xliii, which precedes the chapters on the deadly sins and in which Hilton likens the soul to the Trinity, is based on the element of contrast. The explanation of the dignity of the soul is followed by a contrasting explanation of the soul in sin; moreover, the latter explanation itself is developed by contrast, so that the contemplative is told to "see now then the wretchedness of thy soul" by setting its ideal "love" and "sweetness" against its actual "foul beastly lust and liking" (p. 101). The last sentence of the chapter makes a final contrast, one which significantly ends on a positive point when it explains that the image of sin can be reformed by the merits of Christ's passion. For Hilton, then, the examination of conscience, rather than a technical analysis of sin, is a recognition of the image of sin so that the soul will be driven to reform itself to the image of God, the image which its highest part possesses at least potentially.

After the recognition of the disparity between the image of sin and the image of God comes the desire of the soul to resemble the divine Trinity and to restrain its lower part, sensuality. This desire with its basis is the characteristic of the fundamental reformation of the soul, called by Hilton a "reforming in faith" (II, v, p. 241). By a reforming in faith Hilton means specifically believing in the Catholic Church, a "secure troth in all articles of the faith, and the sacraments of Holy Kirk, trowing them steadfastly with all the will in thine heart" (I, xxi, p. 47). This faith, encompassing a faith in Jesus, the powers of the redemption, and God's mercy and grace, is one of the three things, with meekness and desire, necessary for the "secure ground" on which a soul builds its spiritual state (I, xvi, p. 32). The reform in faith, however, is not a mere state of acceptance of doctrine and realization of the disparity between the image of sin and the image of God, a state that might support the dictum that faith alone is necessary for salvation. Part of the reforming in faith is based on the soul's not assenting to "stirrings of sin and fleshly desires" (II, v, p. 241). In fact, one reformed in faith "may not be idle nor reckless, for the image of sin is so near fastened to him and so continually presseth upon him by diverse stirrings of sin, that but if he be right wary he shall full lightly through assent fall again thereto" (II, xi, p. 260). Reformation in faith is achieved by the positive action on the soul by either baptism or penance, baptism to reform the soul from original sin and penance to reform it from actual sin (II, vi). Baptism so reforms the soul that a Jew or Saracen baptized immediately before his death will go straight to heaven, while a newborn baby without it is "nought but an image of the fiend and a brand of hell" (II, vi, p. 243). Penance both reforms the soul as it brings God's forgiveness and gives to the soul a "warrant of forgiveness against all his enemies," like a charter which a king gives to a forgiven man, so that the soul can be confident of its reform in spite of temptation (II, vii, p. 246). For strong temptations yet bother the soul reformed in faith:

Fair is then a man's soul, and foul is a man's soul. Fair in as mickle as it is reformed in faith to the likeness of God. But it is foul in as mickle as it is yet meddled with fleshly feelings and unreasonable stirrings of this foul image of sin. Foul without as it were a beast, fair within like to an angel. Foul in feeling of the sensuality, fair in trowth of the reason. Foul for the fleshly appetite, fair for the good will. (II, xii, p. 267)

In Hilton the reformation in faith corresponds generally with purgation in the usual triad of purgation, illumination, and union. But it involves only the very beginning of purgation, the state in which the newly converted or recalled soul struggles with very basic temptations and tries to act according to the common principles in orthodox teaching. The reform in faith does not require the personal power to suppress all temptation, but only the constant desire to suppress it. This reform of the soul, however, is adequate for salvation, and it is the reform common to beginning contemplatives and to actives in general (II, v).

The reformation in faith is also important as a necessary development within the soul striving for more perfect reform and contemplation. But since temptations are so very strong in the soul reformed in faith only, so strong that they may destroy the reform by turning the desire from God and re-erecting the image of sin, the soul reformed in faith must beware of its precarious position, which it must endeavor not merely to maintain, but to improve:

For it fareth by him [one reformed in faith only], as it doth by a man that were drawn out of a pit, and when he were up, he would no further go than the pit's brink. Soothly he were a mickle fool, for a little puff of wind or one unwarily stirring of himself should soon cast him down again worse than he was before. Nevertheless if he flee from the brink as far as he may, and go forth on the earth, then though there come a great storm he is the more secure, for he falleth not in the pit. (II, xviii, pp. 291–92)

A worldly man, though he possesses much, is never heard to say, "Ho! I have enough, I will no more of this," and in the same way the contemplative must ever desire and "travail all his wits and his mights" in an effort to gain more grace (II, xviii, pp. 292–93). Hilton's practical emphasis on action and forward motion at this point is consistent with his teaching that will and grace work together and with the general nonquietistic tone of *The Scale*. Moreover, his teaching that the reform in faith is adequate for salvation and common to actives, with his encouragement of contemplatives to advance, is a further illustration of his moderation, which involves his unwillingness to disparage or slight the active life in order to extol the contemplative one. Finally, his very treatment of this exceedingly basic material in Book II especially, which many critics regard as the product of a more mature and advanced contemplative than Book I,[78] suggests his adherence to the idea that one must ascend the scale to perfection rung by rung, even when he evidently is most interested in teaching the higher parts of contemplation to a soul already somewhat advanced spiritually.

The advancement of the soul from this very basic reform in faith first leads, by the means previously discussed, not to an easier suppression of temptation, but to an attempt to reject the pleasure of the worldly vanities which cause temptation. To begin to break the image of sin, one must reject "fleshly lusts and worldly likings, which are but as wormwood" (I, lxxx, p. 193), "cast out full cleanly all loves and likings, sorrows and dreads of all earthly things" (I, xlvii, p. 115), and ignore money and possessions and the pleasure they can offer (II, xiv). This working is painful for the soul, since the soul must reject material goods as possible objects of pleasure, but the final reward will compensate for the pain (I, lxxxix). The rejection of "all bodily thing, for all that is without, and his own body" is necessary for the soul seeking God in contemplation (II, xxxiii, p. 377). The rejection is indeed a dying to the world: "*Michi mundus crucifixus est, et ego mundo*" (II, xxvii, p. 340). The purpose of this rejection of the world, a rejection which is, of course, mental as well as physical, is to enable the soul to withdraw its thought from "all bodily thing outward" and thus give itself to spiritual work (II, xxx, p. 357).

Hilton's teaching that a contemplative should reject worldly loves by dying to or rejecting the goods of the world is basic Christian teaching, corresponding directly with Christ's command that to follow him, one must give up what one has. Hilton intends his teaching to be accepted in a literal rather than a modern sense, that is, he expects the contemplative to reject the goods themselves rather than only the temptations which might occur with the use of the goods. He is teaching abstinence and not temperate pleasure, and his teaching on this point coincides with his view that the full enjoyment of contemplation is the prerogative of the recluse. Explaining "the business of Poverty," Miss Underhill says that the detachment from worldly things is the "Negative aspect" of purgation,[79] and she seems to feel that the rejection of the world is very important only in the early stages of contemplation. Hilton's view of the rejection of the world is more in accord, however, with Waite's suggestion that detachment is a primary quality of the whole process of contemplation rather than of a single part of it.[80] Hilton does not praise the rejection of the world for itself, that is, as a mere ascetic practice which is meritorious because it is painful, but for its preparatory qualities. In his discussion of Platonism and mysticism, Inge, using, interestingly, the "dying" metaphor, explains the principle of rejection as it seems to me to appear in *The Scale:* "We are first impelled to seek the Infinite by the limitations of the finite, which appear to the soul as bonds and prison walls. It is natural first to think of the Infinite as that in which these barriers are done away. And in practice we must die daily, if our inward man is to be daily renewed."[81] Hilton's view that the rejection of the world and the consequent rejection of all sensuous enjoyment are necessary to produce a state in which the soul is receptive to contemplation resembles Platonic and especially neo-Platonic doctrine,[82] but it also, of course, appears in the Church Fathers. Gregory, for example, teaches that sensuous enjoyment must be rejected so completely that the mind can remain without distraction by physical images.[83] Among Hilton's contemporaries, the author of *The Cloud* says that one must leave his "outward bodily wits" to prepare for contemplation,[84] implying that what causes the senses to function must be rejected, and he specifically tells the contemplative to "put a *cloud of forgetting* beneath thee, betwixt thee and all the creatures that ever be made." [85]

Rejecting the pleasures of the world and not merely sin, the abuse of those pleasures, the soul may begin to free itself from the outward desires which prohibit its withdrawing into itself.[86] This withdrawing of the soul into itself begins with what is usually called "recollection," the centering of the mind on itself, or, more precisely, on its highest part, which is the image of God. The development of this state is natural, since while seeking God an aspiring contemplative continues to reject unsuccessful approaches and to try to devise effective ones, a process which Augustine has carefully and extensively marked out.[87] During the rejection of the world and recollection the soul enjoys the second part of contemplation, fervent prayer and meditation, but as recollection becomes perfect, the fervors of the second part of contemplation, especially as they stem from images in meditation, begin to decrease. The soul enters into itself to use "reason," the "lantern of the soul," to try to know itself (I, xlviii, p. 117), and this action is called introversion. The purpose of introversion is not merely to see that the soul should be like the image of God rather than the image of sin, but to work within the image of sin to seek the image of God. This working of the soul within itself is difficult, for the image of sin obscures (I, xlviii), but the work eventually becomes more and more positive, the soul concentrating more on finding Jesus than on rejecting the world. For Jesus is lost in the soul: "Thou hast lost Him, but where? Soothly in thine house, that is in thy soul. If thou haddest lost Him out of thine house, that is to say, if thou haddest lost all the reason of thy soul by the first sin, thy soul should never have found Him again; but He left to thee reason, and so He is in thy soul and never shall be lost out of it" (I, xlix, p. 119). Hilton maintains that this inward seeking is necessary for the contemplative, referring to Augustine's teaching that one must know his soul to know God (I, xl), and he emphasizes that one must delve deep into his heart to find God (I, xlvii). One need not "run to Rome nor to Jerusalem for to seek Him there" (I, xlix, p. 119), Hilton says, perhaps at once referring to the state of pilgrimages of the day and encouraging the ghostly sister in her solitude, solitude which facilitates introversion.

Introversion, as Gregory says, is a medial state, one sought not to be enjoyed, but to be used:

When the soul, stript of bodily images, is the object of its own thought, it has passed through the first door. But the way leads from this door to the other, that somewhat of the nature of the Almighty God may be contemplated. And so, the soul in the body is the life of the flesh; but God, who gives life to all, is the life of souls. And if life that is communicated (vita vivificata) is of such greatness that it cannot be comprehended, who will be able to comprehend by his intellect of how great majesty is the Life that gives life (vita vivificans)? But to consider and to grasp this fact is already in some measure to enter the second door; because the soul from its estimate of itself gathers what it should think concerning the unencompassed Spirit, who incomprehensibly governs what He has incomprehensibly created.[88]

Gregory's explanation is basically Hilton's, though, of course, Hilton is primarily concerned with directing the process, not analyzing it. But Hilton does analyze somewhat, as when he explains how God is within the soul:

Upon this self manner shall this word within be understood. It is commonly said that a soul shall see our Lord within all things and within itself. Sooth it is our Lord is within all creatures, but not on that manner as a kernel is hid within the shell of a nut, or as a little bodily thing is holden within another mickle. But He is within all creatures as holding and keeping them in their being, through subtlety and through might of His own blessed kind and cleanness unseeable. (II, xxxiii, p. 376)

The purpose of introversion and man's regarding of his own soul is often explained by the mirror image, early used by Paul to suggest how man shares with the Divine, as Fairweather points out.[89] The Middle-English translator of *Benjamin Minor* writes that the soul "is like a mirror in which, when it is clean, all things are clearly seen," [90] and as Inge points out, the teaching that one ascends towards God through his own soul, that is, that the purged soul can reflect God, is insisted upon by the Victorines.[91] That this teaching is the basis for Hilton's emphasis on the rejection of the world, recollection, and introversion is apparent in his comment that one must cleanse his soul and enter into it to inspect it because "thy soul is but a mirror, in the which thou shalt see God ghostly" (II, xxx, p. 358). The soul, then, achieves introversion to bring itself nearer to the primary object of its desire, God, and in Hilton introversion is negative in that the soul is not greatly distracted by objects of the world or desires for them and positive in that the soul strives for or intensely desires God.

The state which the soul advances to after introversion is variously called by Hilton "night," "murkness," or "nought" (II, xxvii, pp. 336–45). Except for the mystical experience proper, it is the most important state in contemplation. This nought or murkness following introversion must be differentiated from the "murkness of conscience and this nought" which are perceived by the soul when it first recognizes in itself the image of sin. The first "murkness of conscience" or nought is the image of "false misruled love" for one's self (I, liv, pp. 130–31), while the nought following introversion (for which I shall reserve the word "nought," although Hilton's own terminology is not consistent) is a "rich nought," one to be desired (II, xl, p. 416). This nought is in nature the same as introversion, but it is introversion perfected so that its negative action, the rejecting of desires for worldly pleasures, is eliminated from the consciousness because of the strength of its positive action, the desire for the love of God, now unimpeded:

And that is when thy soul through grace is made so free and so mighty and so gathered into itself, that it lust not to think on right nought, and that it may without letting of any bodily thing think of right nought: then is it in a good murkness.

This nought I mean thus. That a soul may through grace be gathered into itself and stand still in itself freely and wholly, and not be driven against the will nor drawn down by mastery for to think or like or love with cleaving of affection to any sin, or vain or earthly thing. Then thinketh the soul right nought; for then thinketh it of none earthly thing cleavingly. This is a rich nought. And this nought and this night is a great ease for the soul that desireth the love of Jhesu. It is in ease as for thought of any earthly thing, but not as for Jhesu; for though the soul think not of any earthly thing, nevertheless it is full busy for to think on Him.

What thing then maketh this murkness? Soothly nought else but a gracious desire for to have the love of Jhesu. (II, xxiv, pp. 323–24)

Hilton's nought is not like the result of what is often referred to, but not by Hilton, as the *via negativa*. The latter leads to God also by means of rejection, recollection, and introversion, but usually concludes introversion with complete negativity and passivity or even, as Fairweather says, with "a Buddhistic nihilism." [92] As Inge says, Hilton "strikes off the fetters of the time-honoured Dionysian tradition, the paralysing creed which blurs all distinctions, and the 'negative road' which leads to darkness and not light." [93] Hilton accomplishes this goal in the same way that he prevents his teachings on grace from being interpreted as quietistic: he emphasizes the action of desire in the "rich nought," not a passive absorption into a world soul or a mere negation of all accompanied by a patient waiting for grace. But Hilton just as emphatically teaches that nought comprises only the desire for Jesus and nothing else, not even any other good. In it the imagination ceases to function and consequently meditation must cease (II, xxx), and in it the soul is isolated from all, "both good deeds and bad," as it seeks God (II, xxi, p. 307). Moreover, nought in Hilton is to be understood on a rational, not a poetic, level. It is like the "dark night of the senses" of *The Cloud*, which, as Miss Hodgson says, exists "when the 'cloud of forgetting' hides all customary objects of consciousness and the 'cloud of unknowing' hides God." [94] In fact, although Dom Knowles sees a major difference between the dark night of *The Cloud* and Hilton's nought,[95] the two states are in their major qualities alike, since the author of *The Cloud* also maintains that introversion begins with the negative action of "treading down of the thought of all the creatures that ever God made" and the positive action of "the stirring of love," [96] and that it is perfected into an undistracted thinking of one's "naked being—the which is thy God and thine intent." [97] Finally, nought is a state which only the advanced contemplative enjoys, and it must be regarded in the light of Hilton's emphasis, like that of the author of *The Cloud,* that he is writing for contemplatives, not actives. In view of the selected audience of the two writers, a criticism like that which Rufus Jones makes of *The Cloud* (a criticism which, if valid, would apply equally to *The Scale*) seems somewhat naïve: "But it is a very bad start on the journey to say that we must begin by 'forsaking' and 'turning away' from everything that has been created, every divine light that glimmers in the world of things, every heavenly word that has been uttered in human love and sacrifice." [98] For both Hilton and the author of *The Cloud,* the state of nought is important to the contemplative precisely because it eliminates all that is made, whether good or bad, that is, all that the active must be concerned with. The soul can then desire only that which is unmade and obviously superior to "everything that has been created." Seeing God and his qualities in nature is the work of the scholastic or even the poet. Seeing God is the work of the contemplative.

A discussion of the state of murk or nought or Divine dark is common to writings on mysticism or contemplation, but the descriptions of the state, as Miss Underhill says in her chapter entitled "The Dark Night of the Soul," vary greatly: "As in other departments of mystical activity, so here, we must beware of any generalization which tempts us to look upon the 'Dark Night' as a uniform experience, a neatly-defined state which appears under the same conditions, and attended by the same symptoms, in all the selves who have passed through its pains." [99] And with the various descriptions of the state come various estimations of its worth and various selections of its major qualities. In Hilton the emphasis on the value of nought is that it is the final stage of the soul before the mystical experience and that it is itself a state of grace, coming from a "gracious desire for to have the love of Jhesu" (II, xxiv, p. 324). Since the nought dispels the desire for the use of the bodily wits, "it is a stopping out of the false love of this world, and it is a nighing to the true day," that is, "the true day of the love of Jhesu." Also, since the soul in nought is hid "from noise and din of fleshly affections," the soul is in a peaceful state (II, xxiv, pp. 321–22): it is a soul rewarded a hundredfold with rest and peace and love (II, xxvii). The soul in nought, however, despite the graciousness of the state and the peace it offers, is not yet at its goal, the third part of contemplation: "For wit thou well, though that thy soul be in this restful murkness without troubling of worldly vanities, it is not yet there it should be, it is not yet clothed all in light, nor turned all into fire of love; but it feeleth well that there is somewhat above itself that it knoweth not nor hath not yet, but it would have it, and burningly yearneth it" (II, xxv, p. 328). The nought is still completely void except for the desire of the soul. Yet, though the nought must be distinguished from the goal of the soul, it is necessary as a final step to the goal: "This dying to the world is this murkness, and it is the gate to contemplation and to reforming in feeling, and none other than this"; and if a soul "will come by any other gate, he is but a thief and a breaker of the wall, and therefore as unworthy he shall be cast out" (II, xxvii, p. 341). Finally, as a necessary last step the state of nought insures the soul that it will not be misled by the fiend, for, as Hilton explains, "I expect after true murkness before cometh never feigned light" (II, xxvi, p. 335).

Nought, the void of all that is not God with a desire for the love of God, is altered by grace to produce in the soul the most perfect state it can achieve while in the body, a reforming in faith and feeling, which leads to the mystical experience. The reform in feeling must not be interpreted in a physical or sensible way, as Rolle's sensible feelings are to be; rather, it is to be understood as a fulfillment "in knowing of God's will, in all understanding and in all manner ghostly wisdom" (II, xxxi, p. 367). The reform in feeling is based on a perception of God, on, as Father Pepler says, "true Christian 'gnosis.'" [100] "Feeling," then, must be understood as experimental knowing. The soul in the state of nought desires God in contemplation, or Jerusalem, but he does not have it until he sees "small sudden lightings that glide out through small crannies from that city" (II, xxv, p. 328). Again using the imagery of light, Hilton likens a man reformed in faith to a blind man who knows that he is in the sun only when an honest man tells him so, and a man reformed in feeling to one who sees the sun fully, so that he no longer needs to believe it is there on someone else's word. However, since man's perception and knowledge of God cannot be complete until he reaches heaven, he is until then not fully reformed in feeling, but rather he is like a man whose sight of the sun is only partial: "That other man seeth a light of the sun, but he seeth it not clearly, what it is, nor as it is; for the lid of his eyes letteth him that he may not see. But he seeth through the lid of his eyes a glimmering of great light; and he betokeneth a soul that is reformed in faith and in feeling, and so is contemplative" (II, xxxii, p. 372). This teaching is consistent with Hilton's explanation that the third part of contemplation can be completed only in heaven and with his view that when the soul is magnified, that is, brought to the highest state it can attain while in the body, it is "reformed in feeling in party" and must wait to be glorified and "fully reformed in the bliss of heaven" (II, xxviii, p. 349). The state of the soul after nought and based on a gracious experimental knowing of God is, then, specifically a reform in faith and feeling.

It is difficult to determine exactly the chronological and other relations between the reform of the soul and the mystical experience. It seems that the two are concurrent in some of the passages in which they are mentioned together, as in the passage in which Hilton explains the state of those who are beginning to have "gracious touchings" in understanding and in love but who cannot maintain them: "And therefore they are not yet reformed in feeling, nor they have not yet the full gift of contemplation" (II, xxix, p. 355). It would not be unreasonable for Hilton to maintain that the reform and the mystical experience are concurrent, since both are based on a new and special knowledge and, apparently, the same knowledge: the reform, following nought, must be based on a knowledge not like reasoned knowledge, for the discursive faculties are silenced in nought. Also, if mere reasoned knowledge were the basis for the reform, the states of rejection, recollection, introversion, and nought would not necessarily have to precede the reform in faith and feeling, and Hilton says they must. The special knowledge or cognition of the third part of contemplation, already discussed, is also not reasoned knowledge. It is, in fact, a spiritual sight which seems to be equal to the "feeling" or experimental perception of the reform. Moreover, the knowing at the basis of the reform in faith and feeling is explained as a knowing "felt in understanding" and is called "whole bread, meat for perfect souls" in contrast to milk for a child (II, xxxi, p. 369); similarly, the cognition of the third part of contemplation is explained as "sweeter to the ghostly feeling" and is called "whole meat for perfect men," again in contrast to milk for children (I, ix, pp. 16–17). If the basic knowledge for reform in faith and feeling and for the third part of contemplation is the same and if the two states are mentioned as existing concurrently, one might make the obvious suggestion that we merely have different terms for the same thing. While such a suggestion would be justifiable according to Hilton's generally casual attitude towards terminology, it ignores Hilton's use of "contemplation" terminology to explain the spiritual levels themselves and his use of "image" and "reform" terminology to explain specifically the conditions within the soul as it progresses. Of course, one would expect overlapping in a discussion of the levels of spirituality in the abstract and of the various conditions of the soul in its real progress, but if the overlapping were so complete that it obliterated distinctions, separate terminology would hardly be necessary. But Hilton does use separate terminology.

On the other hand, although the reform in faith and feeling and the third part of contemplation are based on the same knowledge perceived in the same way and although they seem to be concurrent in some passages, Hilton at other times suggests at least a chronological relation between them. When he is explaining the importance of reform, Hilton says that "no man may come to the contemplation of the Godhead, but he be first reformed by fullhead of meekness and charity to the likeness of Jhesu in His manhood" (I, xcii, p. 221). Contemplation here, the mystical experience, must come after the reform in faith and feeling, for the reform "by fullhead of meekness and charity to the likeness of Jhesu" occurs only after the soul has found Jesus, that is, after the desire for Jesus in the state of nought has been partially fulfilled. Later in *The Scale* Hilton suggests the same chronological relation between the reform and the mystical experience, only more specifically: "This ghostly opening of the inner eye into knowing of the Godhead I call reforming in faith and in feeling. For then the soul somewhat feeleth in understanding of that thing that it had before in naked trowing. And that is the beginning of contemplation . . ." (II, xxxiii, p. 378). In this passage Hilton identifies the highest reform man can achieve in this life with the very beginning of the mystical experience; consequently, the mystical experience a mature contemplative may receive, one more advanced than that of the "beginning of contemplation," would follow the highest reform possible on earth. This latter explanation of the relation between the reform in faith and feeling and the mystical experience seems to me the most acceptable. It is consistent with Hilton's general teaching that the image of sin must be destroyed, that is, that the soul must be reformed, before it can enjoy contemplation. Also, according to the doctrine of grace, a soul receives grace in proportion to its capacity to receive it, so that a capacity for the mystical experience, a great gift of grace, would have to precede the mystical experience itself, and the capacity to receive the mystical experience is only in a soul reformed in faith and feeling. Perhaps the chronology of the relation is that the soul is first reformed by a gracious sight, which is the very beginning of the mystical experience, and then progresses to more perfect contemplation after the reform, the knowledge necessary for the reform being essentially that of the mystical experience but differing in degree. The essential sameness of the knowledge of the reform and the mystical experience would account for Hilton's sometimes mentioning the two as if they were concurrent, and the varying degrees of the knowledge of the two would account for his indicating at other times that the reform precedes the mystical experience. Hilton, however, never carefully explains the relation between the two states, perhaps because he is not concerned with such theoretical problems or because he feels the ineffability of the mystical experience will make his attempts futile. My explanation, therefore, must remain a conjecture.

The separate treatment of the progress of the soul in this chapter is, of course, ideal or theoretical. The soul in its internal progress must constantly relate to the levels of contemplation, to the first level as well as to the mystical experience; moreover, the relation, while on the surface explicable by simple charting, encompasses more than a chronological statement can suggest.

In their relation to the soul in progress the parts of contemplation act as producers of pleasure, and the interims between the parts act as producers of pain, so that the whole relation between the parts and the soul in progress is based on the alternation of the feelings of pleasure and pain in the soul. The feelings, of course, are spiritual ones, and the alternation is a gradual one, not an abrupt one from black to white to black. The first pain the soul feels is in rejection and recollection, in the casting off of the false pleasures of the world. One must "swink and sweat" if he wishes to withdraw his thoughts from bodily loves, and he must suffer pain in his effort to seek Jesus in his soul (I, liv, p. 129). The breaking of the image of sin is difficult and necessitates pain, but the soul can suffer the pain with an expectation of comfort: "Nevertheless, I expect whoso would suffer this pain awhile, steadfastly cleaving upon that naked mind of Jhesu Christ and upon desire that he would nought have but his Lord, and fall not lightly therefrom nor seek no comfort outward for a time, for it lasteth not long, our Lord is near and soon shall ease thy heart" (I, lxxxix, p. 214). The pain the soul is suffering is that resulting from purgation, but the soul need not wait until purgation is complete before it is rewarded with pleasure. Sometime during the process of introversion, but before the soul reaches the state of nought, the soul achieves the first necessary part of contemplation, fervent prayer and meditation.[101] Meditation makes the heart "melt into wonderful sweetness of Jhesu Christ" (I, v, p. 10), offering "a little tasting of the sweetness of the love of God" (I, vi, p. 11), and prayer turns into "ghostly mirth and sweet song" (I, vii, p. 12). This gracious pleasure is comfortable to the soul which has worked, though its fervor may pass away (I, v); the pleasure is so comfortable, in fact, that Hilton must advise the soul not to relax completely in it, but to remember to desire the third part of contemplation (I, vii). For the progressing soul the pleasures of the second part of contemplation must wane, for meditation is brought about through the imagination, and the imagination must cease to function in the necessary nought which precedes the third part of contemplation (I, xxxvi). The pleasures of meditation, moreover, come before the process of introversion is complete, so that a perfecting of introversion, a part of purgation, must precede the mystical experience. But as the pleasures of meditation decrease, pain increases, pain from the continuation of purgation and from the very loss of the pleasures of meditation.

The height of pain in the interim between the second and third parts of contemplation is perhaps best described with the words "spiritual dryness," words made well known to literary critics by Sister M. Madeleva's work on the *Pearl*.[102] Spiritual dryness or "aridity" or "interior desolation" occurs when the soul, having lost the pleasures of meditation, "feels that God has abandoned him" and is "bewildered, desolate, downcast, and discouraged."[103] The devil, perceiving that devotion is withdrawn from the soul, "that the soul is left as it were naked for a time," sends great temptation of all kinds to men: he "vexeth them so that hardly may they have any rest" (I, xxxvii, pp. 84, 85). The temptations are "speedful and profitable" (I, xxxix, p. 90), even though the soul feels "dread and doubts and perplexities" and seems "as it were forsaken of God and left all in the hands of the fiend" (II, xxviii, p. 348). The painful interim of spiritual dryness is, as Miss Underhill says, "the final purification of the will or stronghold of personality."[104] In it one learns that he will be tried until he "will put all his trust in Him fully" (I, xxxix, p. 90). In emphasizing trust as a necessity here, Hilton is giving one of what Sister Madeleva calls "the ordinary antidotes which spiritual directors have prescribed at all times against this visitation [spiritual dryness]."[105] Also, he is especially close to the teachings of the author of *The Cloud*, who says that during the "storms and temptations" of this interim one should not be overly afraid, but merely "have a lovely trust in our Lord."[106] The great pains of spiritual dryness can be borne because they are temporary and because the soul knows, as the author of *The Cloud* says, that each time God returns, he returns "more worthlier and merrylier" than before,[107] or more specifically, as Hilton says, because the pleasures of meditation are gone so that "the heart might be set and fixed more busily in ghostly desire and seeking of His Godhead" (I, xxxvi, p. 83).

The pains of spiritual dryness decrease as the soul perfects its introversion, and when the soul has entered the state of nought and temptations have ceased, it begins to enjoy the pleasures of peace and the feeling that its next step will involve the supreme pleasure for man, the mystical experience. The knowing which is the basis of the reform in faith and feeling and of the mystical experience, together with the affection based on it and resulting in the soul's union with God, represents a peak of pleasure in the alternation of pleasure and pain. Yet, the alternation does not cease at this peak. The transiency of the mystical experience, due to the "changeability" of grace "as well in state of perfection as in state of beginning," causes a continuation of the pleasure-pain alternation, a continuation which the contemplative will perceive unless "he is either full perfect or full blind" (II, xli, pp. 429, 430). Since a complete reform in feeling and perfect contemplation may be had only in heaven, the alternation must continue at least in some degree until that time, except in the case of a "special spouse"; however, as one becomes more perfect and acquires more stability in grace, the frequency of the alternation decreases (II, xli, p. 430). The pain in this continuous alternation, Hilton says, must be accepted, not fought: "A wise lover is he, and a well taught, that soberly and reverently hath him in His presence, and lovely beholdeth Him without dissolute lightness, and patiently and easily beareth him in His absence without venomous despair and over painful bitterness" (II, xli, p. 429).

Hilton never refers to the principle of alternation either by the name I have given it or any other. However, the effects of the applied principle exist throughout *The Scale* and are discernible in every movement of the soul. Suggestions of this principle are found in most of the teachings on contemplation and mysticism, but Hilton's emphasis on a continuous alternation (rather than, for example, on the single alternation between purgation and illumination or between spiritual dryness and the mystical experience) perhaps indicates that he thought of the pleasure-pain principle as a binding force for the whole of *The Scale*. Theologically the principle would be acceptable: while one of the attributes of God is that he is not changeable, one of the attributes of man is that he is, so that man would not expect to find constancy even in his union with God until God glorified him in heaven. While Hilton's recognition of the alternation may have come from the books by holy men to which he refers (II, xxxii *et passim*), from his training in the schools, or from his own experience in contemplation, his extended use of it may have been to provide a constant relation between man's first rejection of sin and the culmination of his spiritual life in heaven, that is, to make strikingly clear in *The Scale* itself the scale idea: that a painful effort is necessary to go from rung to rung, but that each achieved rung brings greater satisfaction. Also, the alternation of pleasure and pain provides a number of logical and closely related divisions of material which the contemplative can study one at a time, so that the practical effects of the principle are consistent with Hilton's general technique of teaching bit by bit. Moreover, the alternation of pleasure and pain is good psychology. Much pain, though the reward sought is very great, will cause fatigue and possibly despair, but when the pain is alleviated at certain points with minor rewards, the contemplative can progress towards his ultimate goal with renewed freshness. Finally, for the contemplative as well as the soldier, "Sweet is pleasure after pain." The interims of pain themselves make the parts of contemplation more pleasurable when they are at last achieved: the tasting of heavenly sweetness in meditation, for example, is intensified in proportion to the lack of sweetness the soul feels in its work of rejection. The implicit principle of the alternation of pleasure and pain, as indicating the basic relations in *The Scale* between the soul in its progress and the parts of contemplation, must be understood, I think, if the critic wishes to see Hilton's art. The recognition of the applied principle not only helps to reveal Hilton's techniques as a director, but begins to explain the relation among the parts which make up the constitution of *The Scale*.

These teachings on the progress of the soul, though not presented analytically in *The Scale,* reveal a plan which is ultimately based on the perfect contemplation of God but which in every detail is related specifically to the progressing contemplative, a plan, therefore, theoretically unified and practically serviceable.

ORTHODOXY, MODERATION, AND PSEUDOCONTEMPLATIVE PHENOMENA

$\mathfrak{I}$n a work on contemplation the fundamental teachings, that is, the teachings on points commonly discussed by contemplatives, are those which concern the spiritual process itself and whatever is directly pertinent to achieving the goal of the process. In *The Scale* the Christian lives are important as they allow one to devote himself to the parts of contemplation, and the parts of contemplation are important as goals for the soul as it develops spiritually with the means Hilton specifies. The contemplative's treatment of these fundamental points, his relative emphasis on them, and his presentation of them—whether passionate and poetic, cold and analytical, or temperate and persuasive—establish his position among writers on or directors of contemplation. But elements in his work other than his fundamental teachings, elements not necessarily common to the writings of contemplatives in general, can often reveal more exactly or make more striking his particular place among contemplatives. The elements may be pervasive ones apparent throughout his teachings and qualifying all of them, or they may be added detailed points of concentration of interest outside of the spiritual process but related specifically to contemplation. Both kinds of elements further reveal Hilton's position. Pervading his work are a great concern for orthodoxy and a flexible moderation, and specifically added to it is an interest in pseudocontemplative phenomena.

Orthodoxy, the first of these differentiating elements, might reasonably be an expected or an unexpected characteristic of the writings of a contemplative. As a member of the Church, the contemplative should follow Catholic doctrine unhesitatingly, but as one partaking of a special union with God based on nonreasoned and ineffable knowledge, he might perceive a truth not recognized, thought of, or accepted by the Church, that is, a truth revealed only to chosen souls. The contemplative's experimental perception should lead him to alter his life according to the truth perceived, but on the other hand, his duty to the organization which led him towards contemplation stresses conformity. Which way one goes depends upon an individual decision. For every sensational instinctive action of a Joan of Arc, there are probably many desires or feelings for action suppressed by the faithful humbling themselves to the Church, though, as Miss Underhill says, "the loud voices and strange declarations" of the contemplatives and mystics who do not comform, the heretics, often "have drowned the quieter accents of the orthodox." [1] As I have previously said, principles from the contemplative writings of Eckhart were proscribed in 1329, and the Spanish contemplative Molinos was condemned as a heretic in the seventeenth century. But most critics agree with Waite's general contention that the mediaeval contemplatives especially were firmly orthodox.[2]

This orthodoxy provided a guiding line or perhaps a shelter for the fourteenth-century English contemplatives, and Bullett, discussing Rolle, the author of *The Cloud*, Hilton, and Julian, writes that "their orthodoxy, so far as I know, has never been questioned." [3] Miss Allen, commenting on the following prayer to Jesus to keep the contemplative free from error, a prayer from Rolle's *Meditations on the Passion*, says that it "well renders the faith in his own orthodoxy which is always implicit in Rolle, though not part of his most characteristic and continual message": [4] "Fasten me in belief to Thee, sweet Jesus, so that neither evil lore, nor error, nor heresy may turn me from my belief; and grant me, sweet Jesus, that my belief be in measure, not too broad, believing what should not be believed, nor too narrow, rejecting what should be believed; and, sweet Jesus, make me believe in all the sacraments and ordinances of Holy Church, and trust to God for my salvation." [5] In another note Miss Allen attributes to Rolle's orthodoxy some of his inconsistency, suggesting that he sometimes moderates earlier striking and enthusiastic comments to rid them of any unorthodox tone.[6] Since Rolle is primarily concerned with a fervent love for Jesus and not very much interested in the theoretical or refined aspects of contemplation and since he is convinced of his own orthodoxy, he does not show any special or defensive concern for his position in the Church, so that his orthodoxy does not distinguish him.

But the author of *The Cloud,* although his teachings are just as orthodox as Rolle's, feels forced to emphasize his orthodoxy, since he is treating the highest part of contemplation and many of its refined characteristics. He emphasizes it, as Miss Hodgson points out, by repeating that traditional Christian teachings must underlie a contemplative's work.[7] The author of *The Cloud* makes submission to and correction by the Church necessary for one who wishes to begin work at contemplation,[8] with the result that he would agree with Hilton's teaching that a reform in faith is a necessary first stage in the progress of the soul. And in the final chapter of *The Cloud,* in his instructions to those who feel moved or whose progress is aided by his book, the author of *The Cloud* lays down as the first means of determining the graciousness of any "stirring" in the work of contemplation a checking to determine whether all is done with a pure conscience "according to the law of Holy Church and the advice of their counsel." [9] For the author of *The Cloud,* then, orthodoxy is necessary as a basis for contemplation and as a guard against being misled in contemplation itself. Yet, the stress of the author of *The Cloud* on orthodoxy is only in proportion to the height of the matters he deals with, so that while it is greater than Rolle's, it is neither striking nor differentiating. Rather, it is the assurance one might reasonably expect from a cautious member of the Church.

Julian of Norwich in her *Revelations* seems perfectly orthodox without being overly concerned with orthodoxy itself, and comments like "I know by the common teaching of Holy Church, and by my own feeling" [10] are probably simple statements of fact and not attempts to emphasize the accordance of her teachings with doctrine. But Margery Kempe is certainly very much concerned with insisting on her orthodoxy, and understandably so, since it was questioned. Miss Allen says that Margery's stress on the Divine inspiration of her pilgrimages "may make one element in her propaganda for orthodoxy," [11] propaganda which seems to permeate the *Book*. For example, in a long passage God explains to Margery what he knows that she believes and comments on her beliefs as correct ones given by him. The tone and theological matter of some of the points in this passage, as of the following ones, indicate a specially motivated regard for the orthodox:

And thou thinkest that the Holy Ghost hath the same properties, equal with the Father and the Son, proceeding from Them both.

Also thou thinkest that each of the Three Persons in the Trinity hath what the other hath, in Their Godhead; and so thou believest verily, daughter, in thy soul that there be three divers Persons and one God in substance, and that each knoweth what the others knoweth, and each may do what the others may do, and each wills what the others will. And, daughter, this is a very faith and a right faith, and this faith hast thou only of My gift.[12]

Throughout her career Margery fails to show a very humble submission to members of the hierarchy of the Church. In fact, she seems often to teach and expose rather than listen and confess, alienating many. She may want, consequently, to make her orthodox position very clear partially to avoid criticism by those whose advice she flouts. Whatever the case, Margery's emphasis on her orthodoxy is not astonishing, but merely in proportion to her patent need for security.

Hilton's concern for orthodoxy and submission to the Church is, on its most apparent level, much like that of his contemporaries, that is, reasonably in proportion to the matters he treats. Dom Knowles comments that "Hilton throughout *The Scale* so clearly presupposes a background and daily life of Catholic piety and practice that it is unnecessary to labour the point," [13] and the orthodoxy of this background is often expressed by simple references to the guardianship of the Church. As I have indicated, Hilton makes "sure faith" one of the necessities for beginning contemplation, "sure faith" being specifically a loving and worshiping of "all the laws and ordinances made by prelates and rulers of Holy Kirk, either in declaring of the faith, or of the sacraments or in general governance of all Christian men" (I, xxi, pp. 47–48). And throughout *The Scale* Hilton reminds the reader that being orthodox is the way to be saved and to develop spiritually, for the road to Jerusalem (contemplation) is "grounded meekly in the faith and in the laws of Holy Kirk" (II, xxi, p. 305). All one's actions or attempts to progress should be made to conform to the rules of the Church (I, xxiii): if one wishes to live as a recluse, he cannot merely run from the world (as Rolle did), but he must secure permission from the authorities of the Church or enter "any religion approved" (I, lxi, p. 146); if one feels inspired to preach and humbly carries out God's will, he will receive a special reward, provided that he acts with the approval of the Church (I, lxvi). For the soul in its progress the importance of the Church extends from the first reform from the image of sin, the reform in faith, to the cognition in the mystical experience, in which there is "a little beholding of Holy Kirk whilst it is travailling in this life" (II, xlv, p. 456). These references and others like them interspersed throughout *The Scale*, though added obviously to emphasize submission to the Church and orthodoxy, do not particularly distinguish Hilton. Again, they are reasonably in proportion to the delicacy of the matters he treats; moreover, their impact is general and encompassing rather than specific; and their matter-of-fact content and tone suggest stability and calm rather than insecurity or anxiety.

In addition to these references, however, there is in *The Scale* evidence of a great concern about the orthodoxy of particular teachings. The teachings are not those peculiarities which might disturb the modern reader but which Hilton evidently readily accepts, like the unquestionable damnation of all Jews and pagans (II, iii) or the view that an unbaptized child is "nought but an image of the fiend and a brand of hell" and must be damned (II, vi, p. 243), with the subsequent implication that Hilton belongs with Augustine among the *"tortores parvulorum."* [14] Rather, the concern which Hilton shows is over teachings which should not normally have caused problems for him, like the doctrine about the sacrament of penance. As Waite points out, the mediaeval contemplatives accept the sacraments generally "without evasion, equivocation, or mental reservation of any kind." [15] Father Pepler makes a similar but qualified statement: "They [the contemplatives] seem to have forgotten the full significance of the sacramental life of the Church. Indeed such things always seem to fade in a mystic era; or rather they are taken for granted, as the foundations performing their essential function unseen." [16] Father Pepler's statement generally describes Hilton's attitude towards the sacraments. Hilton maintains that baptism and penance, for example, are necessary means to reform a soul (II, vi), but he also does seem to view the sacraments as pertinent especially to a subcontemplative Christian state, while never suggesting they are unnecessary: "By great are understood souls that are profiting in grace, or else perfect in the love of God, the which are reformed in ghostly feeling. By small are understood souls unperfect, of worldly men and women and other, that have but a child's knowing of God and full little feeling of Him, but are brought forth in the bosom of Holy Kirk and nourished with the sacraments as children are fed with milk" (II, x, p. 258). When, however, he focuses his attention on penance, Hilton takes a defensive or at least a particularly emphatic stand. Penance is not only a desirable guarantee that one is free from sin, but it is a necessity according to the law of the Church "that every man and woman should once in the year at the least be shriven of all their sins that come to their mind to their ghostly father, though they have had never so mickle contrition beforetime" (II, vii, p. 248). Hilton apparently knew exactly the decision of the Fourth Lateran Council that annual confession is necessary, for his words "every man and woman" translate the opening words of Canon xxi, "*omnis utriusque sexus.*" [17] Although the decision was made in 1215, so that the teaching should have been quietly and traditionally accepted by Hilton's generation, Hilton seems at the same time both anxious that the law be followed and yet a bit hesitant about accepting theoretically the necessity of penance for perfect men or contemplatives. The following passage, which continues Hilton's explanation that every man and woman must confess annually, reveals the paradox:

Nevertheless, I expect well that if all men had been as busy about the keeping of themselves in fleeing of all manner of sin, and had come to as great knowing and feeling of God as some men have, that Holy Kirk should not have ordained the token of confession as for needful bond, for it had not needed. But for all men are not so perfect, and peradventure mickle of the more part of Christian men is unperfect, therefore Holy Kirk ordained confession by way of general bond to all Christian men that will know Holy Kirk as their mother and will be buxom to her bidding. If this be sooth, as I expect it is, then errs he greatly that generally says that confession of sins for to show a priest is neither needful to a sinner nor behoveable, and that no man is bound thereto. (II, vii, p. 248)

Hilton's concern for the acceptance of penance as necessary is evident in the last lines of the passage, and the easiest explanation for his concern is that he wanted to warn the reader against the heresy of the Lollards, who attacked confession as unnecessary and even dangerous for the soul, as Noetinger points out.[18] Hilton's concern, however, might also be from his recognition that the soul specially inspired by God and graciously partaking of the mystical experience may feel that it can safely lay aside fundamental observances. Indeed, one might reasonably assume that being treated with "whole meat for perfect men," the third part of contemplation (I, ix, p. 17), the soul might at times find insipid the milk children are fed with, the sacraments (II, x). If the latter is the case, the concern would imply a very orthodox view of the sacraments by Hilton. And in fact, though Hilton does not generally stress the sacraments, his teachings could easily and without conflict underlie a more sacramental spirituality, as Dom Gerard Sitwell has argued.[19]

More important than Hilton's emphasis that contemplatives must accept the doctrine of penance, however, is his explanation in the same passage of why annual confession is necessary for them. The explanation implies that penance is not naturally necessary for contemplatives, but artificially necessary because of the Church's decree. The Church passed the law because "all men are not so perfect" (II, vii, p. 248); consequently, when contemplatives conform to the law, they are doing so simply because it is the law, for as men concerned with keeping themselves pure, they merely happen to be included in the "general bond." For pure contemplatives, in fact, annual penance may be no more than an acknowledgment that they are "buxom" to the Church. Achille Luchaire points out that a result of the canon requiring annual confession is that penance becomes a law and not "a matter of the individual conscience," [20] and it is interesting to see how Hilton maintains the law while preserving the integrity of the advanced contemplative's conscience. The very fact that penance is not naturally necessary for the advanced contemplative seems to me to be the cause of Hilton's insistence on conformity to the law. What is a law and naturally necessary at the same time would hardly have to be insisted upon. Hilton's reasoning in this passage is much like that in the passage on the Holy Name, for in both he distinguishes internal truth from external observance or technique.

Besides in the specific emphasis on the necessity of penance, Hilton's great concern over orthodoxy appears in his general teachings against what is called, but not by Hilton, antinomianism. Antinomianism, as Inge defines it, is the belief that "he who is led by the Spirit can do no wrong,"[21] a belief which, as Fairweather states, goes back in Christianity to Paul's "Where the Spirit of the Lord is there is liberty" (2 Cor. 3:17).[22] Colledge has suggested that the phrase "liberty of spirit" would have meant to a mediaeval European not "any kind of religious or intellectual tolerance," but a "liberty of spirit from flesh."[23] Such a view is difficult to accept first of all in the light of Patristic commentaries on the passage.[24] Also, antinomianism as reflected specifically by the phrase *"Ubi spiritus Domini, ibi libertas"* was known to the mediaeval English contemplatives: in "An Epistle of Discretion in Stirrings of the Soul" the contemplative is warned not to bind himself to any "singularities, as it were under colour of holiness," by calling on Paul's witness.[25] Especially for the contemplative is such a doctrine important, for the cognition in contemplation is given by God and indicates a close relation with him, so that it should be believed. But antinomianism can easily lead to heresy.

In *The Scale* Hilton seems to say that antinomianism is the cause of all heresy, and he consequently exhorts the contemplative to submit all his actions to the judgment of the Church. This exhortation is different from the expected and common order to submit, for it aims specifically at a contemplative who is sufficiently advanced to be inspired or to believe he is inspired. Contemplatives who achieve a knowledge not sanctioned by the Church and who pursue its practical application are, Hilton says, inspired by the fiend and driven by pride: "They ween that the following of their own will were freedom of spirit, and therefore they begin to rain as black clouds water of errors and heresies, for the words that they show by preaching resound all to backbiting and to striving, and to discord-making reproving of states and of persons; and yet they say that all this is charity and zeal of righteousness" (II, xxvi, p. 333). The heretic who feels he can interpret Holy Writ and will not submit is also driven by pride (II, xliii), and it is significant that Hilton so often connects antinomianism, the following of one's inspiration against the law of the Church and the basis of heresies, with pride, the basis of all sins.[26] One's rejection of personal inspiration must be so complete that any "imagining" not supported by the Church (an inspiration not supported seems automatically to become an "imagining") must be thrown off in favor of the Church's ordinance, even though the ordinance may seem unreasonable (I, xxi, p. 48).

An easy explanation for Hilton's exhortations against antinomianism is, again, the temper of the times. As Miss Allen says, "the Lollards had put every man on the defence for his orthodoxy,"[27] so that a careful writer would emphasize the orthodoxy not only of doctrines which heretics attacked, like the necessity of penance, but of his teachings in general in order to establish clearly at least a firm intention to conform. Hilton's emphasis on meekness as one of the necessary means for the progress of the soul, though traditional, may have a second purpose: besides preparing the soul to receive further grace, it suggests in *The Scale* a constant and entire submission to the authority of the Church by the contemplative. Another major and obvious reason for Hilton's exhortations against antinomianism could be his firm belief in the Church's authority and doctrines. As Waite points out, belief rather than a fear of being accused of heresy may be a more plausible cause for the orthodoxy of the contemplatives: "The *via prudentiae* which they studied had no relation to any time-serving and material discretion. They less than any, as the heroes of a strange enterprise of sanctity, would have been actuated by a mere question of personal safety."[28] A third cause for Hilton's great concern for submission might stem from the comprehensiveness of *The Scale*. Although Hilton insists that *The Scale* is for contemplatives only (I, xciii), the subject matter of the book extends from the explanation of the characteristics of the active life to a description of the mystical experience, and the purpose of the work is to guide one through the entire process of contemplation. Beginners with little or no intellectual foundation in doctrine or weak spiritual backgrounds might read the book (and *The Scale* quickly became popular with people other than contemplatives), and especially these might begin interpreting their states enthusiastically but incorrectly. Exhortations against following one's own feelings and towards submission to the Church might keep abuses minimal. All of these causes may be responsible in some degree for Hilton's teachings against antinomianism, but there might be a fourth cause more important than any of them.

Just as Hilton's emphasis on the necessity of annual penance may be the result of his belief that such penance is not naturally necessary for the advanced and pure contemplative but that it is necessary to show submission to the authority of the Church, his exhortations against antinomianism could be the result of his belief that the contemplative might generally follow his inspirations, but that he should submit to avoid possible abuses based on false inspiration or even external problems which may distract him from his work. Delacroix has shown freedom in spiritual things to be one of the outstanding characteristics of mystics and contemplatives,[29] and it seems strange that Hilton's great concern for orthodoxy should oppose him diametrically to this characteristic. *The Scale* is generally in accord with other contemplative writings in its teachings on the levels of contemplation, the transiency and ineffability of the mystical experience, the special cognition of the advanced soul, etc. Perhaps Hilton as a contemplative found that the Church is to be followed as a governing body, but also that a man at home, i.e., in his own soul, has more freedom than a man in the street, one explaining his views to others. This is not to suggest that Hilton is a heretic in disguise, but only that he made distinctions between one's spiritual life in itself and his spiritual life in relation to the Church. His emphasis on orthodoxy would come from his desire to maintain a balance between spiritual freedom and submission.

Throughout *The Scale* Hilton teaches that the lower levels of contemplation and their characteristics should not be confused with the primary object of desire, God; and the scale idea itself makes all means to God rungs to be used. The second part of contemplation is gracious and joyful, but the contemplative must always look towards the third part and be ready to reject meditation for cognition as God gives his grace (I, vii). Likewise, the lowest form of prayer, which is for a "boisterous and rude and fleshly" man who has not enough grace for meditation (I, xxvii, p. 61), should be used until a contemplative by grace is lifted to a higher prayer and then should be rejected, unless the contemplative has an external duty to the Church: "As to this manner of prayer, which is called vocal, me thinketh unto thee that art religious, and by custom and by rule art bound for to say matins and hours, I hold it most speedful for to say them as devoutly as thou might" (p. 60). The emphasis on submission to the Church here in the contemplative's continuation of vocal prayer is in direct contrast to the freedom which a soul would naturally have to follow grace to a higher form of prayer. The same distinction is made when Hilton is explaining that spiritual customs voluntarily held can hinder a contemplative if he does not readily dispense with them when he is called or led by a higher grace. Hilton concludes, logically, that such customs should be dropped when necessary: "But the custom of another thing that letteth a better is for to leave when time is, where a man may. As thus, if a man have in custom for to say thus many beads, or for to think this manner of thought thus long time, or for to wake or kneel thus long, or any other such bodily deed, this custom is for to leave sometimes when reasonable cause letteth, or else if more grace come in other way" (II, xxi, p. 310). But he qualifies one's following God's grace and his dropping such customs not only with the words "where a man may," but specifically by explaining that his directions are for one who is "free," that is, "not bound but under the common law" (pp. 309–10). Again, one obviously has a freedom in his spiritual life to follow God's grace, but again, Hilton emphasizes that the freedom is not so great that it may controvert the authority of the Church. Like his solution to the problem of quietism, Hilton's solution to the problem of antinomianism is practical rather than theoretical. Also like his solution to the problem of quietism, it is effective.

Besides a great concern for orthodoxy, pervading *The Scale* is a flexible moderation or, as Hilton calls it, discretion. I have referred to particular instances of Hilton's moderation, as in his treatment of the active life, which he never disparages to extol the contemplative life and to which he consistently gives just rewards. Moreover, Hilton's balancing of the freedom of the spirit led by God with an emphasis on orthodoxy is based on and reflects his moderation. The moderation pervading *The Scale* is not subtle; it is at the basis of all its teachings and at the same time explicitly and emphatically one of them, despite the incongruity that an emphasis on moderation might suggest. The moderation encompasses all things, the teachings of the religious-handbook tradition as well as of the contemplative one: the going towards Jerusalem (contemplation) "is nought else but ghostly working, and bodily also when need is; which thou shalt use by discretion . . ." (II, xxi, p. 308). In eating and drinking and praying and in the lower levels of contemplation, a man, unless he feels the grace of God leading him on, should "keep discretion, for the mean is best." In fact, Hilton tells the contemplative, only in desiring the love of Jesus and what it entails, that is, only concerning the primary object of desire, "hold thou no mean, for the more that it [sic] is of this [desire], the better it is" (I, xxii, pp. 51, 52).

Particular manifestations of Hilton's moderation in his teachings on asceticism and contemplation begin to suggest the comprehensiveness of his concern for balance. While Miss Underhill—referring especially to contemplatives like Madame

Guyon, who held wormwood in her mouth, wore a hair shirt, and walked only with stones in her shoes—concludes that "pain, therefore, the mystics often court,"[30] Hilton even in his basic exhortations to the active or beginning contemplative to mortify himself for the purging of his soul seems unable to mention mortification and pain without commenting on discretion:

Also a part of active life lieth in great bodily deeds, which a man doth to himself, as great fasting, mickle waking, and other sharp penance-doing; for to chastise the flesh with discretion for trespass before done, and by such penances for to refrain lusts and likings of it, and make it buxom and ready to the will of the Spirit. These works, though they be active, they help mickle and ordain a man in the beginning to come to contemplative life, if they be used by discretion. (I, ii, p. 4)

In his most specific directions his moderation is yet apparent, sometimes so much so that it makes what seems to be a specific direction not specific at all. When he is explaining how love slays gluttony and instructing the contemplative in his choice of food, Hilton recommends ale and bread or fish or flesh or even "the best meat that is good in the own kind," "out-taking meat that through craft of curiosity is only made for lust" (II, xxxix, pp. 412–13). The contemplative should eat what least disturbs him in his work, so that Hilton's moderation ends in this case not in an arbitrary rule allotting a daily pound of bread, but in a principle of temperance, a principle to be applied by each contemplative according to his relative state. Hilton's moderation is flexible, then, or it is a true moderation.

In his teachings on contemplation Hilton's moderation continues with the same flexibility. A soul on the way to Jerusalem is beset by enemies, one of which, scrupulosity, plants doubts that the soul was "not shriven aright" or that it has forgotten "some old sin" hidden in the heart. The soul should merely ignore these enemies and proceed "with discretion after counsel of thy sovereign or of thy ghostly father" (II, xxii, pp. 312, 313). But if scrupulosity persists, especially for a man reformed only in faith, and if "his conscience be greatly grieved" over temptations which he does not know whether he assented to, he should confess and "dispute no more about them that are passed and forgiven whether they were deadly or venial" (II, xi, pp. 264, 265). Again, Hilton's moderation does not harden into a rule, but it is moderation for the sake of expediency. For the advanced contemplative who has achieved the state of nought, Hilton's moderation is yet important. Hilton stresses that time is necessary to pass from the false light of the world to the true light of Jesus, so that the contemplative must wait patiently (II, xxiv). And in the last chapters of *The Scale* when he is discussing the mystical union, Hilton says that Jesus does not make a soul "a true perfect spouse to Him" "suddenly" (II, xliv, p. 453). Even in the third part of contemplation, then, the soul must conduct itself moderately, according to the intensity of grace God gives.

Moderation or discretion, as a virtue of reasonable men, would be expected to qualify the teachings of these men. In Christianity the early Desert Fathers have left sayings which sometimes correspond exactly with Hilton's teachings, both specifically and generally. Concerning the diet, "Abba Antony said: 'Some wear down their bodies by fasting. But because they have no discretion, it puts them further from God.' "[31] Even the flexibility of Hilton's moderation is tersely expressed in Christian sayings which preceded his work by at least a thousand years: "Abba Mark asked Abba Arsenius: 'Is it good not to have any comfort in one's cell? I saw a brother who had a few cabbages, and he was rooting them out.' And Abba Arsenius said: 'It is good. But each man should do what is right for his own discipline. If he has not strength to endure that, he will plant them again.' "[32] Among Hilton's English contemporaries such a moderation is most evident in the works of the author of *The Cloud*. His basic teachings on discretion correspond exactly with Hilton's, even to his contrasting admonition to the contemplative to be discreet in all things except the desire for God.[33] Concerning the emphasis of the author of *The Cloud* on moderation in ascetic practices,

Miss Hodgson notes that he is like Rolle and Hilton, and she adds that his emphasis continues in his minor works.[34] The moderation of the author of *The Cloud*, however, seems to be not as pervading or as constantly evident as Hilton's, perhaps because in his specialization in the higher levels of contemplation the author of *The Cloud* feels that he does not need to concentrate on fundamentals. In Rolle is found the same contrasting admonition to be moderate in all things except the love of Jesus, though the proportions of the contrast are reversed to emphasize the love:

Lord Jesu, I ask Thee, give unto me movement in Thy love withouten measure; desire withouten limit; longing withouten order; burning without discretion. Truly the better the love of Thee is, the greedier it is; for neither by reason is it restrained, nor by dread thronged [distressed], nor by doom tempted. No man shall ever be more blest than he that for greatness of love can die. No creature truly can love too mickle. In all other things all that is too mickle turns to vice, but the more the strength of love surpasses the more glorious it shall be.[35]

Rolle elaborates his belief that discretion is important to prevent virtue from becoming vice when he warns the contemplative against the dangers of extreme abstinence,[36] and throughout his works he comments on the value of discretion. However, whether because of his own frequent passionate excesses or of the extremes of violent criticism and brotherly love in his work, one feels that Rolle pays lip service to moderation but is not especially affected by it. In fact, Rolle's very personality, revealed throughout his writings, perhaps makes any concern of his for moderation either a defensive or self-correcting one or an incongruity. Margery Kempe's energetic actions usually seem not to be qualified by moderation, and at one point she is "slandered and reproved by many people, because she kept so strict a life." [37] Although Miss Allen, commenting on this passage, says that "Margery gradually relaxed her early rigours," [38] nowhere in the *Book* is there an implied or explicit concern for moderation which reminds one of Hilton. Moderation is mentioned in the *Book*, as in God's telling Margery that "discreet penance" is good,[39] but it seems to be a real qualifying factor for her even less than it is for Rolle. Hilton's contemporaries, then, either mention or stress moderation in some degree, but in none of them is moderation as basically pervading and influential or as specifically emphasized as it is in *The Scale*.

Hilton's striking and flexible moderation may have a number of causes. It may stem naturally from his personality, just as Rolle's lack of discretion seems to stem from his. Hilton's humility would keep him from insisting on extremes or unchangeable rules, for he would recognize that his advice might not in every case be applicable to his reader and would want to give the reader as wide a path as possible for his road to Jerusalem. The quiet tone of *The Scale* coupled with Hilton's humility seems to reveal a personality which could be only moderate: "I speak further than I do, but I pray thee do thou as I say by the grace of God, if thou mayest, or any other man whoso will; for that were a comfort to mine heart, that though I may not have it in myself as I say, that I might have it in thee, or in another creature which hath received of our Lord more plenty of His grace than I" (I, lxxi, p. 175). His moderation might also be the result of his consciousness of teaching techniques: allowing flexibility in private applications of directions makes *The Scale* valuable to more people and makes unnecessary detailed and intricate explanations of how much to sleep or pray or drink. Moderate teachings seem to make goals more easily attainable than unflexible or extreme ones, encouraging the contemplative, as Hilton's advice to "be not adread too mickle of thy blackness" does (II, xii, p. 271), or giving him trust and responsibility, as Hilton's direction to eat what least hinders work does (II, xxxix). Thirdly, Hilton might stress moderation as the necessary result of his doctrine of grace: since God does all, any immoderate efforts on man's part alone might be presumptuous and lead man away from, rather than towards, his goal. "Too mickle fasting" will hinder a man's progress, Hilton says, quickly adding, "unless he have the more grace" (I, lxxv, p. 186). Finally, and what seems to me most important, Hilton stresses moderation in all things except the love of God to maintain constantly the subordination of the means to the end.[40] When Hilton is explaining why a contemplative should eat fish or flesh or bread and ale, whatever least hinders him in his work, he clearly refers to this subordination: "For all the business of the soul is aye for to think on Jhesu with reverent love, without letting of anything, if that it might. And therefore since that it must needs somewhat be letted and hindered, the less it is letted and hindered by meat or drink or any other thing the liefer it is" (II, xxxix, p. 412). Any extreme in the means, of course, might draw attention to the means themselves. Moderation for the sake of subordination coincides with the scale idea of Hilton's work. Just as the rungs of the ladder are important only as they are useful to bear one upwards, so the secondary objects of desire and the lower levels of spiritual life and their characteristic actions are valuable only as they allow the contemplative to achieve the primary object of his desire, God. And that Hilton intends his moderation to result in a subordination of all specifically to the primary object of desire is evident in his advice to the contemplative to work physically and spiritually "by discretion upon this wise. What work that it be that thou should do, after the degree and the state that thou standest in bodily or ghostly, if it help this gracious desire that thou hast for to love Jhesu, and make it more whole, more easy, and more mighty to all virtues and to all goodness, that work hold I best . . ." (II, xxi, pp. 308–9). The flexibility of Hilton's moderation is equally the result of his desire for subordination. People in particular situations must determine the particular degree of fasting or praying which best intensifies their desire for God, for moderation hardened into a pound-of-bread rule might itself distract the contemplative from his primary object of desire. The most important cause for Hilton's moderation, then, seems to be his wish to focus all the contemplative's attention on God by making the specific means of progress towards God definite only as they are expedient.

Besides his great concern for orthodoxy and his flexible moderation, distinguishing *The Scale*—but as a specific addition rather than an influencing factor—is Hilton's interest in pseudo-contemplative phenomena. Pseudocontemplative phenomena are those which are not a necessary part of the spiritual process of contemplation but which can accompany it or are associated with it. They are, as Butler calls them, "the accidental accessories" which unfortunately are now often identified with contemplation and which, especially when exaggerated, represent the "undesirable side of mysticism." [41] In *The Scale* these phenomena are both mental and physical:

By this that I have said mayst thou somewhat understand that visions or revelations of any manner spirit, in bodily appearing or in imagining, sleeping or waking, or else any other feeling in bodily wits made as it were ghostly; either in sounding of ear, or savouring in the mouth, or smelling at the nose, or else any sensible heat as it were fire glowing and warming the breast, or any other part of the body, or anything that may be felt by bodily wit, though it be never so comfortable and liking, are not very contemplation. . . . (I, x, p. 19)

The mental phenomena, visions, are different from the cognition of the third part of contemplation, for the cognition is an ineffable and spiritual knowing, while visions are closely associated with the action of the senses or the lower parts of the soul. Concerning the causes and validity of mental phenomena, the critics vary greatly. While C. H. Hamilton maintains that these phenomena and even the mystical experience are no more than the products of a sensible nature led to act in a certain way by its environment,[42] Miss Underhill seems to be defending the Divine inspiration of mental phenomena when she places the discussion of them above the reach of most critics: "We forget, whilst arguing industriously on these matters, that it is really as impossible for those who have never experienced a voice or vision to discuss it with intelligence, as it is for stay-at-homes to discuss the passions of the battle-field on the materials supplied by war correspondents." [43] In any case, the phenomena are not common to all contemplatives. Dom Butler says that a distinguishing quality of the contemplation of Augustine, Gregory, and Bernard is "the entire absence of any such element of vision, locution, revelation," and he contrasts these three with the women who, perhaps because of their "psychic make-up," comprise "the line of great seers of visions and hearers of revelations." [44] And Inge, observing that visions seem to be rewards for beginners in contemplation, adds that "the spiritual guides of the Middle Ages were well aware that such experiences often come of disordered nerves and weakened digestion; they believed also that they [such experiences] are sometimes delusions of Satan." [45]

In fourteenth-century England some of the most interesting examples of pseudocontemplative mental phenomena occur in Julian's *Revelations,* and Julian's reaction to them is most important. When Julian comes to consciousness after her revelations and speaks to "a religious person" about them, she says, "I had raved today," [46] implying that she did not accept the Divine inspiration of her visions. Even after she recognizes their validity, she does not make the visions indicative of her status as a contemplative or even spiritual goals of special worth: "For the shewing I am not good but if I love God the better; and inasmuch as ye love God the better, it is more to you than to me." [47] Her subordination of her visions to a higher goal resembles Hilton's treatment of visions very closely, especially since the higher goal is the same as Hilton's primary object of desire. The subordination is so complete in the *Revelations* that Dom Knowles says it is one of the major characteristics distinguishing Julian from other "visionaries who have described the Passion or some of its incidents." [48] As cautious as Julian about accepting visions unhesitatingly is Rolle, who tells the story of a recluse visited by a spirit who said he would lead her to heaven. On the advice of her confessor, the recluse asked the spirit at its next appearance to show her the Virgin, and when the spirit could not and tried to deceive her with the image of another woman, the recluse knew it was the fiend tempting her.[49] Such a story, while it generally questions the validity of visions, seems to establish a means for determining whether they are from God. Rolle, however, is not so naïve that he believes that certain "loaded questions" will automatically determine the source of a vision or revelation, for, as in his discussion of the six kinds of dreams,[50] he often seems hesitant about accepting any visions because of the great possibility of error. Margery Kempe is in contrast to Julian and Rolle in her quick acceptance of visions. When St. Jerome appears to her while she is praying in Rome, blesses her because she weeps for people's sins, and praises God for putting so much grace in Margery's soul, Margery does not hesitate to accept the vision as valid,[51] though such a vision might be something like what one would expect a fiend to present to a proud soul. At times, however, Margery has a vision followed by God's confirmation that the vision is valid, so that she evidently need not be anxious. Praying at an altar, Margery falls into "a little slumber" and sees an angel clothed in white bearing the "Book of Life": "Then said she to the child:—'Where is my name?' The child answered and said:—'Here is thy name, written at the Trinity's foot,' and therewith he was gone, she knew not how. And anon, afterwards, Our Lord Jesus Christ spake unto her and said:—'Daughter, look that thou be now true and steadfast, and have a good faith, for thy name is written in Heaven in the Book of Life; and this was an angel that gave thee comfort.' "[52]

Hilton's interest in mental pseudocontemplative phenomena begins early in *The Scale,* and beginning concurrently is an insistence that visions and revelations must be distinguished as authentic and unauthentic or good and evil. Hilton implies doubt about the authenticity of such phenomena when he describes them as "made as it were ghostly," and he explains the basis of his doubt by quoting St. John: *"Nolite credere omni spiritui, sed probate si ex Deo sint*" (I, x, pp. 19, 20). But since doubting the authenticity of a vision would keep the soul in an indefinite state and perhaps cause anxiety, Hilton gives a means by which the authenticity of a vision can be determined, a means not at all based on trick questions or theological analysis. If a vision is good, it will, after the initial amazement of the soul, increase the contemplative's desire for God or for that which will increase his love for God (I, xi). Thus, a vision of Christ in his manhood is good and from God if "answering thereto" is a "devout affection," that is, if resulting from it is a nearing in some way to the primary object of desire (I, xxxv, p. 80). If visions are good only as they aid the contemplative's love of God, they must be subordinate to that love. And Hilton teaches not only that such visions are entirely different from "very [true] contemplation" (I, x, p. 19), but specifically that all "visions or revelations" are inferior to a desire for the love of God (I, xlvii, p. 114). Hilton also subordinates such mental phenomena by a logical argument: unlike the love of God, visions can be good or evil, so that they cannot be "best" (I, x, p. 20), for what is "best" would have to be unchangeable good.

When a vision is inspired by a fiend, it may be easy to recognize as evil by its very nature, as a temptation is (I, xxxvii), but the most dangerous vision, inspired by "the midday fiend," consists of feigned light (II, xxvi, p. 330). Feigned light comes to a man when he is not trying to perfect himself "through lasting desire to Jhesu," but rather is driven by pride (II, xxvi, p. 331). In a proud man the start of such a vision might be in an indiscreet working of his wits (I, xxviii), but the development of the vision seems to be dependent upon the pride of man plus the work of the devil, as Hilton explains in the "Song of Angels": "For if a man have any presumption in his fantasies and in his workings, and thereby falleth in to indiscreet imagination, as it were in a frenzy, and is not ordered nor ruled of grace, nor comforted by ghostly strength, the devil entereth in, and by his false illuminations, and by his false sounds, and by his false sweetnesses, he deceiveth a man's soul." [53] That an evil vision is at least partially the result of pride is consistent with Hilton's teaching that a good vision intensifies the desire for the love of God. Pride, as self-love, is the opposite of the soul's love of God, or the primary object of desire. Hilton's interest in visions and his practical solution to the problem of their authenticity distinguish *The Scale* because of the comprehensiveness of view which they suggest. Hilton warns against unhesitatingly accepting visions as vigorously as Rolle does, but if a vision is good, he teaches the contemplative to accept and use it as completely as Margery Kempe accepts and uses her visions; moreover, his insistence on subordination is as great as that of Julian and perhaps greater, for Hilton argues for subordination logically as well as spiritually. Hilton's treatment also suggests a more intellectual and less reverential attitude toward the mental nonessentials of contemplation than Miss Underhill wishes to allow. Such an attitude distinguishes Hilton from the visionaries who are partially responsible for the pejorative connotation of "mysticism" but does not, on the other hand, reduce his contemplation to a level of scholasticism.

Often more intriguing and revealing than comments on visions or revelations are the attitudes of various authors towards physical pseudocontemplative phenomena. Again, the critics vary greatly. While Riley suggests these phenomena are "pathological symptoms" "created, we suspect, by hypnotic suggestions from the confessional," [54] Miss Underhill maintains her cautious stand of not judging "whilst psycho-physical relations remain so little understood." [55] Father Thurston in *The Physical Phenomena of Mysticism,* following the official practice of the Roman Catholic Church, seems generally reluctant to accept physical phenomena as Divinely inspired unless other proofs of sanctity are available.[56] Inge's comment in an early essay on Hilton that "we may almost say that the worth of a mystical treatise varies inversely with the importance which it attaches to these experiences, which, of course, were formerly ascribed to supernatural agencies"[57] seems to me to be an accurate and careful statement based on the teachings of many contemplatives; in his work of half a century later, however, Inge discredits physical phenomena almost entirely and avows a "tendency" to be "very sceptical."[58] Dom Butler, while never indicating definitely his belief about the authenticity of "psycho-physical phenomena," does insist that "they find no place in the descriptions given of their experiences by our three Doctors; there is no suggestion of anything more than a deep absorption of mind in prayer, such that consciousness is lost of external things and of the operations of the mind itself."[59] There is, then, no agreed-upon opinion about physical pseudocontemplative phenomena, though the inclination of the critics seems to be towards a hesitancy in accepting rather than a belief in a relation between the phenomena and contemplation.

The importance given to these phenomena by Hilton's contemporaries also varies greatly. Rolle's insistence that the *"calor"* he felt was physical distinguishes his works,[60] forming, in fact, "a part of Rolle's influence which the later mystics sought to correct," as Miss Allen notes.[61] In contrast to Rolle is Julian with her almost complete disregard of physical phenomena. In fact, when Julian does mention physical phenomena, they are part of a diabolical torture: "The fiende came again with his heat, and with his stench, and made me full busie. The stench was so vile and so painful, and bodily heat also dreadful and travellous."[62] The contrast between the teachings concerning physical phenomena in Rolle and Julian exists also between Hilton's two other contemporaries, though far more markedly and though the views are reversed in relation to sex.

The author of *The Cloud,* in accord with the general intellectual tone of his work, scorns physical phenomena in proportion to their deviation from normal activity. Contemplatives misunderstand teachings, he says, so that "they travail their imagination so indiscreetly that at the last they turn their brain in their heads. And then as fast the devil hath power to feign some false light or sounds, sweet smells in their noses, wonderful tastes in their mouths, and many quaint heats and burnings in their bodily breasts or in their bowels, in their backs and in their reins, and in their privy members." [63] In theory the author of *The Cloud* recognizes that physical phenomena can be both good and evil, though he tells the contemplative to find the means for distinguishing them in "another man's work." [64] In practice, however, he condemns such phenomena vehemently, as if they were necessarily evil. Men who "hang their heads on one side, as if a worm were in their ears" and who whine and cry are like hypocrites or heretics, driven by "presumption and curiosity of wit," [65] and it is the devil who causes the action of those who, thinking that they are eating sweet angels' food which is falling softly from heaven, "have it in custom to sit gaping as though they would catch flies." [66] The author of *The Cloud* says not only that such phenomena are not valid indications of an advanced state in the soul, but that one addicted to them is not a contemplative: "they be very tokens of unstableness of heart and unrestfulness of mind, and especially of the lacking of the work of this book." [67]

A number of the actions which the author of *The Cloud* scorns can be found as indications of holiness in the *Book of Margery Kempe*. Margery's "dalliance" with the saints is often so sweet that she falls on the ground, weeps, and twists her body,[68] and as evidence of God's frequent visitations it is revealed that once Margery had fourteen crying spells in one day.[69] The fire of love particularly affected Margery, causing what she probably thought of as one of the great proofs of her sanctity: "When she came into the churchyard of Saint Stephen's, she cried, she roared, she wept, she fell to the ground, so fervently the fire of love burned in her heart." [70] Margery defends the physical phenomena which accompany her contemplation, especially her crying spells, by citing miracles God worked on others to convince them of the holiness of the phenomena and by referring to treatises like the "Prick of Love" and the *Incendio Amoris*, which support her actions.[71] But even she sometimes wondered whether she was interpreting bodily what was meant spiritually and whether the phenomena might be "deceits and illusions." [72] The importance of physical phenomena in the *Book* is measured interestingly by annotations in the manuscript, annotations in red which Professor Meech says "are of no authority in textual matters." [73] For example, to the sentence in which God thanks Margery for sheltering him and the Virgin in her bed, the annotator has added "gostly," [74] obviously fearing a physical interpretation, an interpretation which in this case would be likely only because of the tone of the *Book* resulting from Margery's constant emphasis on physical phenomena.

Hilton's teachings on physical pseudocontemplative phenomena are first revealed in his insistence on metaphorical interpretations of many phrases. The fire of love, for example, "is not bodily, for it is only in the ghostly desire of the soul" (I, xxvi, p. 59), and "that God is fire" does not mean he is "fire elementary" (which might burn when perceived), but that he is "love and charity" (II, xxxiii, p. 378). Hilton does, however, accept a number of physical phenomena as such, that is, not as mere misunderstandings of what should be interpreted metaphorically, and as good. "Sweet tears" are the result of the enjoyment of the second part of contemplation (I, v, p. 10), and "great weepings and many tears of the eye" naturally accompany the looking of the soul into itself and its recognition of the sins within (I, xxxiv, p. 77). It is possible, in fact, if God's grace leads that way, that one might legitimately spend the rest of his life weeping for his sins, though Hilton distinguishes a life spent this way from the contemplative life (I, xli). Bodily fervors in general can be a sign of much grace, since often they are given as nourishment to a soul, as meat is given to a pilgrim, to aid him on his way (II, xxix). The basis for distinguishing good from evil physical phenomena is like that for distinguishing mental phenomena. If the phenomena aid one to increase his desire for God or to progress towards God, they are good. If they distract one from the love of Jesus by calling his attention to themselves or to the pleasures they offer, they must be suspect, whether they consist of "any merry sounding with thy bodily ear, or in thy mouth any sweet sudden savour, other than of kind, or any heat in thy breast as it were fire, or any manner delight in any part of thy body . . ." (I, xi, p. 21).[75]

Hilton's acceptance of some physical phenomena as good is accompanied by a coldness towards them. This coldness is in part the logical result of his teaching that physical phenomena are inferior to mental ones and, consequently, also to contemplation. They are not "very contemplation" (I, x, p. 19), and they are of much less value than "a soothfast desire and a clean in mine heart to my Lord Jhesu Christ" (I, xlvii, p. 114). Even when the feelings are "graciously given of God," they are characteristic of souls "not yet reformed in feeling" and not yet possessed of a spiritual love of God (II, xxix, p. 352). Those who have such gifts should not "rest in such feelings too mickle; but in as mickle as they help the soul to more stableness of thought in God, and to more love," since resting in the feeling may aid the devil's work (II, xxx, p. 365). Besides being inferior to true contemplation, physical phenomena are for Hilton inferior even to secondary objects of desire. While a contemplative can desire prayer and meditation as rungs which lead towards perfection, "bodily feelings, be they never so comfortable, we should not covet" (II, xli, p. 431). Physical phenomena, then, are in *The Scale* completely extracontemplative, and their position in Hilton's scheme is the first factor contributing to Hilton's coldness towards them.

A second factor is Hilton's temperament. He is practical and intellectual rather than passionate or poetic, and external shows would probably be very offensive to him. The results of his temperament on this point are seen not only in his insistence on figurative interpretations of phrases like "fire of love," but in particular additions and renderings in *The Scale*, like his expanded translation of St. Paul:

In caritate radicati, et fundati, ut possitis comprehendere cum omnibus sanctis, quae sit longitudo, et latitudo, sublimitas, et profundum. Be ye rooted and grounded in charity, that ye might know, he saith, neither sound of ear nor sweet savour in the mouth, nor none such bodily thing, but that ye might know and feel with all holy, which is the length of the endless being of God, the breadth of the wonderful charity and the goodness of God, the height of the almighty majesty of Him, and the groundless deepness of the wisdom of God. (I, xii, p. 26)

Hilton's exclusion of physical phenomena as a part of contemplation, an exclusion not in his source, stems here, I suspect, as much from the bent of his personality as from a conscious emphasis on the inferiority of the physical. This same bent or temperament is seen in Hilton's explanation that a great showing of physical phenomena might be the result not of men's greatness of love, but of the "littleness and weakness of their souls, that may not bear a little touching of God":

Right as a costrel that is old, when it receiveth new wine that is fresh and mighty, the costrel swelleth out and is in point for to cleave and burst, until the wine have boiled and purged out all uncleanness. But as soon as the wine is fined and cleared, then standeth it still, and the costrel whole. Right so a soul that is old through sin, when it receiveth a little of the love of God, that is so fresh and so mighty that the body is in point for to cleave and for to break, were it not that God keepeth it whole. But yet it bursteth out at the eyes by weeping and at the mouth by speaking, and that is more for weakness and feebleness of the soul than for mickleness of love. For afterward, when love hath boiled out all the uncleanness of the soul by such great fervours, then is the love clear and standeth still; and then is both the body and the soul mickle more in peace, and yet hath the self soul mickle more love than it had before, though it shew less outward. (II, xxix, pp. 352, 353)

It is a man's abuse of his nature, not his nature itself, which causes these phenomena, and, in fact, Hilton says specifically that one who was never very foul with sin will come to a reform in feeling "without great fervour shewed outward" (II, xxix, p. 354).

It is difficult to separate exactly in Hilton the logical subordination of physical phenomena from the natural feeling against them, for the major quality of both the subordination and Hilton's temperament is a moderate intellectualism. But one gets the feeling that it is temperament which leads Hilton to view these phenomena with disfavor as much as it is temperament which leads Margery Kempe to favor them. Finally, Hilton's coldness on this point is consistent with his moderation. The coldness never becomes the vitriol of the author of *The Cloud,* and it is always set against his explicit statement that some physical pseudocontemplative phenomena may be good.

These three final elements in Hilton's teachings on contemplation, his great pervading concern for orthodoxy and flexible moderation and his specific interest in pseudocontemplative phenomena, cumulatively make more striking the intellectual as opposed to the devotional and poetic quality of *The Scale.* They reveal, moreover, the practical balance in Hilton's teachings which keeps *The Scale* from becoming a scholastic or theological treatise while on the other hand never letting it countenance caprice or heresy. Finally, they show Hilton's interest in developing a guide which is clear and definite enough to be effective but which does not imply or necessitate stereotyped action.

THE SCALE OF PERFECTION
AND THE RELIGIOUS-HANDBOOK
TRADITION

$\mathcal{B}$esides Hilton's teachings on contemplation, *The Scale* contains material which suggests a tradition very different from the contemplative one. In preceding chapters I have called this the "religious-handbook tradition," which I have treated as characterized by instructions on asceticism but which in its least restrictive meaning suggests all works that are religious or devotional but specifically neither contemplative nor speculatively theological. The works of Rolle, the author of *The Cloud,* Hilton, and Julian do not belong to the religious-handbook tradition, just as a work like Aquinas' *Summa Theologica* does not. The materials from the religious-handbook tradition, then, are those which instruct practically and which, charted in the spiritual hierarchy, precede teachings on contemplation. In Hilton's case, however, the treatment of the materials can be understood best, or perhaps only, in the light of his contemplative teachings.

The religious-handbook tradition, of course, might be subdivided a number of ways: penitentials containing detailed instructions for priests hearing confessions are different in intention and development from general guides to the ascetic life, like the *Ancrene Riwle;* and general guides are different from popular presentations like *Handlyng Synne,* which attempts to make morality vivid for the uneducated layman. The religious-handbook tradition as I shall refer to it, however, will be the encompassing one: "Some of these manuals are the work of prelates, others of parish priests. Some are written by regulars for the use of regulars only, such as monks, canons, friars, or nuns. Some are written for the educated layman, who may read these books either as a duty or as a pleasure to enlighten his way to salvation. A great many are to be used by the priest in his contact with laymen, either in preaching or in performing the Sacraments, be he bishop or vicar, canon, monk, or friar." [1] Again, the works within it will be similar positively in that they are religious or devotional and negatively in that they are not intended to teach contemplation or to discuss academic points.

The distinction between the religious-handbook tradition and the contemplative one is not always maintained, and either confusion or a vagueness of meaning pervades, or results from, much of the scholarship which touches on works from both traditions. In his essay *On the Continuity of English Prose from Alfred to More and His School*, R. W. Chambers writes of the works of the contemplatives as "devotional literature," and he comments that "at the time when Rolle and Hilton first set to work to write their books of contemplation addressed to dedicated women, the *Ancren Riwle* was the most popular and widely known book of that type. . . ." [2] Chambers' calling the *Ancrene Riwle* a contemplative work does not, naturally, affect the quality of his discussion, but it does suggest the looseness of definition which many fine scholars seem willing to accept. Helen Gardner, explaining that *The Scale* is a spiritual guide, says that "it is in the tradition of the *Ancren Riwle* and it is often nearer in spirit to the *Riwle* than to Rolle and the *Cloud*." [3] Miss Gardner does not mean, however, that *The Scale* is in the religious-handbook tradition or that the *Ancrene Riwle* is contemplative, since she goes on to say that the similarity between the two is the result of "a kinship of temper and style" [4] and since she prefaces her essay with a comment that *The Scale* develops out of the fourteenth-century contemplative movement and can be "properly understood" only with reference to Rolle and the author of

The Cloud, that is, to contemplatives.[5] Evelyn Underhill, whose extensive work on contemplation might have warned her of the possibility of confusion, calls *The Scale* a "devotional work" when she evidently means a contemplative one.[6] And on the same page Miss Allen refers to *The Scale* first as "Walter Hilton's long classic of mystical literature" and then as a "highly influential monument of mediaeval English piety."[7] In the work of each of these influential critics, the lack of distinction in terminology could abet the confusing of a treatise which guides the soul towards mystical union, with one which simply edifies morally or presents systematic, formal prayer.

The distinction between the two traditions is, however, clear enough in the works of many writers. As early as the first part of the fifth century, Cassian, having previously written his *Institutes,* an ascetic work, makes the distinction in the preface to his *Conferences:*

Just as I have taken my little boat into harbour and decided not to write any more, I see an ocean opening out in front of me. It is evidently my duty that I should, however rashly, set down on paper something about the way of life and the teaching of those great Egyptian saints before it is forgotten. And my little boat has now to venture out among the perils of much deeper water than before: for life in a hermitage is a finer life than that in a monastic community, and the contemplation of God (which is the continual aim of the hermits) is a loftier life than the pursuit of the daily virtues which is the purpose of life in a monastic community. It is therefore your duty to help me with your prayers. . . .

I pass now from the outward and visible life of the monk (the subject of my earlier book) to the invisible life of the inner man; from the vocal prayers of the canonical office to the unceasing prayer which St. Paul commanded. If anyone, through reading my earlier work, has won the allegorical name Jacob got for himself by "supplanting" the sins of his flesh, he may now learn the rules of the perfect life and win (if I may so put it) the merit and the name of Israel (which means, the man who sees God).[8]

Among recent critics, Dom Knowles has made the distinction, for in his 1961 revision of *The English Mystics* (1928) he excludes his early chapter on the *Ancrene Riwle*, partly because it "is not in any real sense of the term a *mystical* book." [9] Moreover, he distinguishes the contemplative from the religious-handbook tradition in his chapter on Hilton when he argues that "in the first book Hilton is concerned almost entirely with the preparatory ascetic life," while in Book II he treats of contemplation.[10] Yet Dom Knowles, in his final comments on Hilton, says in the same paragraph that there is a "deep mystical appeal of the whole work" and that *The Scale* is a "devotional classic" because of Hilton's "sane and methodical presentation of the ascetic life." [11] But what is most important is that Hilton makes the distinction in *The Scale*. When he is explaining that sins must be put down if one wishes perfection, he says that virtue must be cultivated:

And this may not be done by one manner of work, but by divers works and many, after sundry dispositions of men. As now praying, now thinking, now working some good work, now assaying himself in diverse wises; in hunger, in thirst, in cold, in suffering of shame and despite if need be, and in other bodily distresses for love of virtue and soothfastness. This knowest thou well, for this readest thou in every book that teacheth of good living. (II, xx, p. 298)

The books that teach good living, like the *Benedictine Rule*, the *Ancrene Riwle*, *The Book of Vices and Virtues*, or *Handlyng Synne*, are those in the religious-handbook tradition, and Hilton's principle of distinction here, it should be noticed, is that the intention or goal of the book classifies it. *The Scale of Perfection* teaches perfection in contemplation, as *The Cloud* does, while the *Ancrene Riwle* and *Handlyng Synne*, though on different levels, are intended to teach good living only.

After laboring to emphasize the distinction between the religious-handbook and the contemplative traditions, I must immediately add that some overlapping is common. While each tradition has its major and particular characteristics, minor elements and vestiges of major elements often fade from one tradition into the other, with no exact boundaries. One would expect a recluse who had perfected himself in the ascetic life to begin to desire contemplation, but one would not expect him to reject all of the ascetic practices which led him towards contemplation immediately after his first enjoyment of the most basic kind of contemplation. Father Garrigou-Lagrange, analyzing the distinction between ascetical and mystical theology, concludes that "practically two excesses must be avoided in the direction of souls": a rejection of ascetic practices at once might lead to quietism, and no rejection of such practices might result in boredom in a soul no longer satisfied with the lower life or merely "good living" and desiring contemplation.[12] And in practice, the excesses are avoided by the fading of some of the elements of one tradition into the other.

The major elements of the religious-handbook tradition can indicate what Hilton is referring to as contained in the books that teach "good living." The works in which these elements appear will be cited not as possible sources of *The Scale* or as bases for the existence of particular elements in the tradition. As Pfander points out in his treatment of the *Parson's Tale*, the elements are part of a "stream that flows to Chaucer,"[13] that is, they are part of a tradition so well known and so comprehensive that it often cannot be analyzed in terms of particular sources or influences. Moreover, individual characteristics common to the tradition are not necessarily peculiar to it: animal imagery, for example, occurs in much other literature as well as in the visual arts of the Middle Ages. But in aggregate the characteristics differentiate the tradition. No attempt will be made to discuss any facet of the religious-handbook tradition fully or to draw up a complete list of the elements in it. The resulting simplification will stress the major elements of the tradition according to their relative importance as background materials contributing to a fuller understanding of *The Scale*. Finally, the major elements discussed will be those enumerated in the *Constitutions of Lambeth* of 1281 as fundamental matters in which all Christians should be instructed: the fourteen articles of faith; the ten

commandments; the two commandments of love; the seven
works of mercy; the seven capital sins, with their offspring; the
seven principal virtues; and the seven sacraments.[14] While Arch-
bishop Peckham's directions in the *Constitutions* were specifically for preachers, the elements listed are those which appear
consistently in the religious-handbook tradition, although not all
of them necessarily appear in each work and the enumeration
and explanations in the *Constitutions* in no way represent a
source for the whole of the tradition.

An explanation of the articles of faith, the first element
mentioned in the order of Peckham's *Constitutions*, might be
most expected from the pulpit. A basic knowledge of Christian
consistently in the religious-handbook tradition, although not all
Christians, while teachings on specific duties, more likely to be
conveyed privately and by means of a handbook, would be
effective only after the articles of faith were subscribed to. In
The Book of Vices and Virtues, translated in the fourteenth
century from Friar Lorens' *Somme le Roi,* the articles of faith
are listed and explained.[15] Though brief, the treatment is clear,
and the separate points are numbered, so that the treatment is in
no way like a mere general exhortation to submit to the Church.
The commandments are also treated in *The Book of Vices and
Virtues,* again briefly but very clearly, and the discussion is
followed by a note on the Decalogue as a whole; the note explains who is to obey the Decalogue and the sanctions attached
to it, and it relates the Decalogue to the two greatest commandments.[16] In *Handlyng Synne* Robert Mannyng of Brunne does not
translate the explanation of the twelve articles of faith which
occurs in his original, William of Waddington's *Manuel des Pe-
chiez,*[17] but he treats the commandments at length, adding exempla not in Waddington, like the story of the bloody child maimed
by oaths (Christ), used to illustrate the evil of swearing.[18] His
treatment of the commandments, since it is avowedly for the
uneducated,[19] is popular and exceedingly explicit; it stands in
strong contrast to the brief treatment in *The Book of Vices and*

Virtues, and the two distinct treatments of the commandments illustrate the great range in the levels of the audiences addressed by the handbooks. The seven works of mercy are treated in *The Book of Vices and Virtues,* and in dealing with them the author adds to and illustrates his clear and brief explanations (like his explanations of the commandments and the articles of faith) with Biblical stories or exempla: to emphasize the necessity of caring for the sick, he tells the story of a man who was "squeamish" about sick bodies but who nevertheless washed a sick man's feet and afterwards drank the dirty water to cleanse his own soul.[20] In the *Ancrene Riwle* the works of mercy are treated, sometimes negatively. The recluse, because she is poor, cannot be liberal, especially with other men's alms, and the author of the *Riwle* makes his point with a typical homely metaphor: "It is not proper for an anchoress to be liberal with other people's alms. Would not a beggar be loudly laughed to scorn if he invited people to a feast?" [21]

Of more interest than the treatments of the articles of faith, the decalogue, and the works of mercy are those of the sacraments, especially of penance, for, as Pfander points out, Peckham's decrees drew especial attention to penance.[22] Attention would also be directed to penance, however, by the doctrine of annual confession affirmed in 1215 and by the tradition of penitential manuals, guides for priests hearing confessions and assigning penances. In *Handlyng Synne* all of the sacraments are treated in order, with penance treated proportionately and receiving no outstanding emphasis; however, immediately following the treatment of the last sacrament is a section on confession alone, which is more than two-thirds the length of the entire section on the sacraments.[23] This section on confession, explaining the twelve points and the eight graces of shrift, provides part of the basis for Professor D. W. Robertson's argument that the whole of *Handlyng Synne* is a "confessional manual" in the "tradition of penitential literature." [24] Again illustrated by exempla intended for the uneducated, the section on confession in *Handlyng Synne* is far less erudite, though at the same time far more vigorous, than the treatment of confession in Chaucer's *Parson's Tale*, which Pfander argues is also a kind of penitential manual.[25] While in *The Book of Vices and Virtues* there is no systematic treatment of all of the sacraments, penance is by itself analyzed fully. An explanation of the various reasons for confessing is followed by an analysis of the five things that disturb true confession, an analysis popular rather than formal in tone: "the second thing is a wicked fear of having to do great penance, which the devil puts into the heart of a sinner: 'You cannot do these sharp penances and live the life you are accustomed to.' Such men fare as does a horse that is shy, that is afraid of his own shadow; and indeed, all the penance that men must do in this world, in comparison to what is in hell or purgatory, is but a shadow." [26] The *Ancrene Riwle*, like *The Book of Vices and Virtues*, does not explain all of the sacraments systematically, but it explains confession in even greater detail than *The Book of Vices and Virtues* does. The entire fifth part or distinction of the *Riwle* is devoted, for example, to details on the circumstances of a sin which must be included in confession, how often one should confess, and to whom one should confess.[27]

Often more important than the sacraments generally, but not more important than penance particularly, are the virtues and their development in the religious-handbook tradition. In *The Book of Vices and Virtues* the theological and natural virtues are treated consecutively with their subdivisions and illustrated with Biblical and popular stories.[28] The treatment is on a persuasive rather than an intellectual level, though the elaborate breaking down of some of the virtues into their components suggests an ultimately careful plan. In *Handlyng Synne* the virtues are not systematically treated; also, most of the tales illustrate evil states rather than good ones, though a few, like "The Tale of St. Macaire and the Two Good Married Women," are positive in their presentation of virtue.[29] In the *Ancrene Riwle* the virtues are treated together and in the order in which they oppose the deadly sins: "Brotherly love," for example, opposes envy, as patience opposes wrath.[30] In the *Parson's Tale* the virtues are treated in the "*Remedium*" following the discussion of each sin: "Now wol I speke of remedie agayns this foule synne of Envye. First is the love of God principal, and lovyng of his neighebor as hymself; for soothly, that oon ne may nat been withoute that oother." [31] Chaucer's treatment is practical and heavily dependent upon Biblical materials, and it illustrates the exceedingly common mediaeval view that tends to regard the virtues only in relation to the vices and that consequently makes the virtues, certainly in a literary way and probably in a religious way, dependent on the deadly sins.

But of all the subjects listed for instruction in the *Constitutions* and occurring in the religious-handbook tradition, the most important directly concerns evil rather than good. The capital or deadly sins provided a favorite topic for the Middle Ages, and some critics have interpreted them as the bases of literature of that period. Morton W. Bloomfield has carefully studied the sins, especially as they appear in mediaeval literature, and has explained many of their subtle variations as well as their background and development.[32] The sins became common to theological discussions especially through the influence of Gregory,[33] and they often appear at the basis of the structure of early penitentials, like the *Penitential of Cummean* and the *Penitential Ascribed to Bede*.[34] They are passed into later mediaeval literature by important treatises like Guillielmus Peraldus' *Summa de Vitiis et Virtutibus* and Friar Lorens' *Somme le Roi*.[35] Invariably the treatment of the deadly sins in works of the religious-handbook tradition is, proportionately, long. In *The Book of Vices and Virtues*, sloth, listed as the fourth deadly sin, is analyzed according to the seven causes which keep one from beginning good work, the seven causes which keep one from amending, and the six causes which keep one from concluding his good works.[36] Less formal than the treatment of the sins in *The Book of Vices and Virtues* is that in the *Ancrene*

Riwle, in which the results of the sins are made very striking: "The greedy glutton is the devil's manciple, but he is always about the cellar or the kitchen. His heart is in the dishes, his thought all on the cups, his life in the casks, his soul in the pitcher. He comes before his lord besmutted and besmeared, a dish in one hand, a bowl in the other." [37] That the section on the deadly sins was considered by contemporaries as one of the most important in the *Riwle* is evident from the short manuscripts of the work, like MS Caius 234/120, in which only the sections on penance and the deadly sins with their opposing virtues are transcribed.[38] The treatment of the sins in *Handlyng Synne,* as one would expect, is both very full and very popular, according to Mannyng's intention to teach the uneducated. The exempla illustrate the sins as they might occur in common or at least actual situations, and Mannyng's interpolated exhortations, like the one to judges after the story of the judge who would not be merciful and who consequently was shown no mercy by God,[39] indicate his desire to be as specific and persuasive as possible. The treatment of the sins in the religious-handbook tradition, then, is generally proportionately long, often complex, as in the explanations of subdivisions, and usually illustrated by either Biblical or homely and very specific examples, depending on the intended audience of the work.

An important literary characteristic in the treatment of the sins in the religious-handbook tradition, besides exempla, is the use of metaphorical language. Especially common in explanations of the subdivisions of the sins is root and branch imagery. In *The Book of Vices and Virtues* the author says that while pride manifests itself in many ways, "there are seven principal branches . . . that come out of a wicked root." [40] In the *Parson's Tale* the same imagery occurs, but in a form even more extended:

Now is it bihovely thyng to telle whiche been the sevene deedly synnes, this is to seyn, chieftaynes of synnes. Alle they renne in o lees, but in diverse manneres. Now been they cleped chieftaynes, for as muche as they been chief and spryng of alle othere synnes. Of the roote of thise sevene synnes, thanne, is Pride the general roote of alle harmes. For of this roote spryngen certein braunches, as Ire, Envye, Accidie or Slewthe, Avarice or Coveitise (to commune understondynge), Glotonye, and Lecherye. And everich of thise chief synnes hath his braunches and his twigges, as shal be declared in hire chapitres folwynge.[41]

More common than root and branch imagery in the treatments of the sins is beast imagery, the extended use of which is apparent in Bloomfield's appendix entitled "The Association of Animals and Sins." [42] In *The Book of Vices and Virtues* John's vision of the seven-headed beast (Rev. 13:1–3) is recounted, and the author comments that the seven heads represent the capital sins, which the devil uses to seduce the world.[43] In the *Ancrene Riwle* pride is identified with the lion, envy with the serpent, wrath with the unicorn, sloth with the bear, covetousness with the fox, gluttony with the pig, and lechery with the scorpion, and following the identification is an explanation of each of the sins in terms of the appropriate beast and its offspring.[44] While, of course, other imagery is used, root and branch and beast imagery seems to be the most popular in the treatment of the deadly sins, the last and the most important element in the religious-handbook tradition.

In *The Scale of Perfection* each of the major elements of the religious-handbook tradition occurs, at least in a very slight way, but the most obvious, most important, and most distinguishing occurrence is that of the deadly sins. Brief references to the sins are interspersed throughout *The Scale*. When the contemplative first looks at his soul, he sees the deadly sins rather than the love of Jesus (I, xv), and that the soul "is all blinded in pride, fretted in envy, overlaid with covetise and defouled with lechery and other great sin" is precisely what keeps it from reform and consequently from contemplation (II, xiii, p. 273). The themes of the image of sin and the reform to the likeness of Jesus which run through *The Scale* are respectively based positively and negatively on the deadly sins; moreover, necessary for the reform itself is a recognition of one's corruption by the sins (I, lxxxix). In the interims in which "the devil perceiveth devotion mickle withdrawn, that the soul is left as it were naked for a time," the devil uses the sins as the basis for "burning" temptations to try to keep the contemplative from advancing (I, xxxvii, p. 84). And the problems caused by the very existence of the sins can be both practical and irritating: as pointed out previously, the contemplative wishing to avoid gluttony but having to eat is given no rule to follow and must assume the responsibility of determining by discretion what meat and drink to take (II, xxxix).

Besides the references to the sins interspersed throughout *The Scale,* in Book I there is an extensive and careful treatment of all of the sins. The treatment (chapter lii through chapter xci) encompasses forty of the ninety-three chapters of Book I. Except for two, all of these forty chapters pertain either to the deadly sins, their actual appearance in life, the means for avoiding them, or the reforming of the soul specifically from them. Chapters lxi and lxii, the exceptions, explain the various states in the Church and the various rewards of heaven. The structure of the treatment of the sins is based first on the sins themselves in the order of pride, wrath, envy, covetousness, gluttony, sloth, and lechery (lv–lxxvii), and secondly on an explanation of the senses and their relation to the image of sin in contrast to an explanation of the image of Jesus (lxxviii–xci). The development of the first part of this structure, though the structure itself is most common in the religious-handbook tradition, is in a major way very different from typical developments of the sins in the religious-handbook tradition. Hilton makes no attempt to show equally the subtleties or difficulties of each sin; rather he analyzes each sin in proportion to its bearing on contemplation. While Chaucer, for example, devotes almost as many lines to covetousness as to pride in the *Parson's Tale,*[45] Hilton devotes one chapter to covetousness (lxxi) and eight to pride (lv–lx; lxii–lxiii). This proportional development begins to reveal Hilton's use of the sins as a major element from the religious-handbook tradition, and it is consistent with and emphasizes his general eclecticism. The second part of the structure of Hilton's treatment, based on the senses and their relation to the image of sin in contrast to the image of Jesus, continues the development of the sins as they relate to contemplation, since they are viewed as comprising the negation of the state necessary for contemplation.

Although Hilton's proportional development distinguishes his long treatment of the sins in Book I, some of the minor characteristics of the treatments in the religious-handbook tradition appear without alteration in *The Scale*. Bloomfield has pointed out that many of the works of the fourteenth-century contemplatives "show a dissatisfaction with the over-classification of sin" and "an independent attitude and a carelessness about detailed enumeration and analysis which are refreshing if unusual." [46] But classification and subdivision, though informal, do appear in *The Scale*, as in Hilton's first chapter on wrath and envy:

The branches of ire and envy are these: hatred, evil suspicion, false and unreasonable deeming, melancholy rising of heart against them, despising, mis-saying, unreasonable blaming, unkindness, backbiting, misliking, angriness, and heaviness against them that despise thee or speak evil of thee or against thee, a gladness of their trouble, and a fury against sinful men, and other that will not do as thee thinketh they should do, with a great desire of thine heart under colour of charity and righteousness that they were well punished and chastised for their sin. (I, lxiv, p. 154)

Hilton's subdivision of these two sins is not much like the treatment of envy in *The Book of Vices and Virtues*, which is organized to the point of artificiality with its discussion of the three branches of envy, the three ways in which an envious heart sins, the three kinds of envious words, and the three kinds of envious deeds,[47] but it has a close parallel in the list of offspring of the serpent of envy in the *Ancrene Riwle*.[48] To illustrate his treatment of the sins, Hilton also uses a number of examples, but not popular exempla like those in *Handlyng Synne*. When he is explaining that wrath and envy should not be allowed to affect one's charity, he expands fully the implications of Christ's behavior towards Judas:

Learn for to love thine enemies and sinful men, for all these are thine even-christians. Look and bethink thee how Christ loved Judas, that was both His deadly enemy, and a sinful caitiff. How goodly Christ was to him, how benign, how courteous, and how lowly to him that He knew damnable. And nevertheless He chose him to His Apostle, and sent him for to preach with other Apostles. He gave him power to work miracles, He showed to him the same good cheer in word and in deed as He did to other Apostles, He washed his feet and fed him with His precious body, and preached to him as He did to other Apostles; He bewrayed him not openly, nor mis-said him not, nor despised him nor spake never evil of him; and yet though he had done all these he had said but sooth. And over more, when Judas took him He kissed him and called him His friend. And all this charity showed Christ to Judas which He knew for damnable; in no manner feigning nor flattering, but in soothfastness of good love and clean charity. (I, lxx, p. 168)

But the most striking of the minor similarities between the treatments of the sins in the religious-handbook tradition and in *The Scale* is not that of subdivision and classification or of the use of extended examples, but the similarity of imagery. Among the various images Hilton uses in connection with the deadly sins, like the image of the well or spring from which temptation and sin flow (I, xv, lv, xc) and the image of the deadly sins as "black stinking clothes" (I, lii, p. 126), is the branch image common to the religious-handbook tradition: "Turn this image [of sin] upside down and look well therein, and thou shalt find two members of envy and ire fastened thereto, with many branches springing out of them, the which let the love and charity that thou shouldest have to thine even-christian" (I, lxiv, p. 154). Besides the branch image, and used much more in *The Scale,* is the beast image. The deadly sins and the image of sin they make up turn man into a "beast's likeness" (I, liii, p. 127; II, iii, p. 236), and especially the sins of the flesh, gluttony, sloth, and lechery, "make a man well beastly" (I, lxxii, p. 177). Also, Hilton likens the sins to specific beasts:

The proud man is turned into a lion for pride, for he would be dreaded and worshipped of all men, and that no man withstood the fulfilling of his fleshly will, neither in word nor in deed; and if any man would let his misproud will, he waxeth fell and wrath, and will be wreaked of him as a lion wreaketh him on a little beast. This man that doth thus is no man, for he doth unreasonably against the kind of man, and so is he turned and transformed into a lion. Envious and angry men are turned into hounds through wrath and envy, that bark against their even-christian, and bite them by wicked and malicious words, and grieve them that have not trespassed with wrongful deeds, harming them in body and in soul against God's bidding. Some men are forshapen into asses, that are slow in the service of God, and evil willed for to do any good deed to their even-christian. They are ready enough for to run to Rome for worldly profit and for earthly worship, or for pleasaunce of an earthly man. But for ghostly meed, for help of their own souls, or for worship of God, they are soon irked. They will not thereof, and if they aught do they go but a pace and with a froward will. Some are turned into swine, for they are so blind in will and so beastly in manners, that they have no dread of God, but follow only the lusts and likings of their flesh, and have no regard to the honesty of man, for to rule them after the bidding of reason, nor for to restrain the unreasonable stirrings of the fleshly kind; but as soon as a fleshly stirring of sin cometh, they are ready for to fall thereto, and follow it as swine doth. Some men are turned into wolves that live by raven as false covetous men do, that through mastery and oppression robbeth their even-christian of their worldly goods. Some men are turned into foxes, as false men and deceitful that live in treachery, and in guile. (II, xiv, pp. 276–77)

These theriomorphic metaphors,[49] with the Biblical exempla and the subdivision of the deadly sins, show Hilton's knowledge of and willingness to use materials from another tradition if they are expedient, much as his use of the devotion to the Holy Name shows his eclecticism. The characteristics, however, are really little more than minor techniques of presentation, so that they cannot indicate how Hilton is adapting his treatment of the sins to his contemplative purpose, as his proportional development of the sins indicates. But emphasizing how Hilton adapts the treatment of the sins from the religious-handbook tradition to *The Scale* is the third and most important aspect of his discussion of the sins, his remedy for them.

To be able to appreciate fully Hilton's remedy, a reader must recognize two distinguishing marks in his attitude toward the sins. In the first place, he makes certain that the reader understands the difference between mortal and venial sins. One is guilty of a deadly sin when he commits an action which his conscience tells him is a deadly sin or when he knowingly commits an action forbidden by God and the Holy Church (II, xli). Stirrings or temptations "of pride or of envy, of ire or of lechery, or of any other head sin" without consent are not deadly sins (II, x, p. 255), except for Jews and Saracens who do not believe in Christ and for whom all is sin (I, lvi). For the good man, in fact, even some enjoyment of these stirrings or temptations does not necessarily constitute a deadly sin:

Nevertheless a man or a woman which disposeth him to life contemplative, if it be so that he forsake himself as in his will and offer him wholly to God with a full general will that he would not sin in pride wittingly, nor have no vain joy in himself wilfully, but only in God if he could and might, and after this full will offered to God he feeleth many stirrings of vain glory and delighteth in them for the time, for he perceiveth it not: this liking is but venial sin. And namely if it be so that when he cometh to himself he perceiveth this vain liking, and he reproveth himself and against-standeth this stirring with displeasing of will, and asketh mercy and help of God, then the liking which before was sin our Lord of His mercy soon forgiveth it. (I, lx, p. 143)

Hilton says that one should flee all sins (I, lxxii) and that a good man, realizing that all sins keep him from God, does not ask what is venial and what is mortal (I, lxxxi). Yet, his differentiating the sins seems the result of his desire to keep the contemplative always advancing. A contemplative has vowed to live without sin; but occasional minor faults, really against his desired goal, should not discourage him, especially since God will readily forgive them.

The second distinguishing mark in Hilton's attitude toward the sins is his explanation of why they are wrong for the contemplative specifically. "What is sin but a wanting and a forbearing of God?" Hilton asks; consequently, for anyone who has God for his primary object of desire, whatever "letteth him from the love of God is great sin" (I, lxxxi, p. 196). The sins keep one from the nought and peace necessary for the highest part of contemplation (II, xxvii), and they must be burned out by the love of God if the soul is to be truly illumined (II, xxvi). Even venial sins are evil because they affect the contemplative's progress: though they "break not charity, soothly they let the fervour and the ghostly feeling of charity" (II, lxxxii, p. 199). For the contemplative who might momentarily succumb, "grouchings or fleshly angrinesses" are not deadly sins, "but I say that they let cleanness of heart and peace of conscience, that thou mayest not have full charity, by the which thou shouldest come to life contemplative" (I, lxix, p. 165). The deadly sins and the temptations to them, then, are in *The Scale* emphasized as evil primarily because they hinder contemplation, and not because they lead to damnation. Hilton here qualifies basic Christian teaching for the contemplative reader, though his very reliance on basic teaching at the same time helps explain the general popularity of *The Scale*. Contemplation never becomes a goal restricted to perfect men who do not need to be warned of sin.

Hilton's remedy for the deadly sins is consistent with and partially explained by the two distinguishing marks in his attitude toward them. If mortal and venial sins are differentiated so that the contemplative will not be discouraged by minor faults and if the deadly sins and the temptations to them are evil because they hinder contemplation, a critic might reasonably expect the remedy for the sins to be in terms of the contemplative's goal also. It is true that in *The Scale* Hilton sometimes opposes various virtues to the deadly sins, as they are opposed in many of the works of the religious-handbook tradition: "Slay then and break down pride and set up meekness; also break down ire and envy and raise up love and charity to thine even-christian; also in stead of covetise have poverty in spirit, in stead of accidie fervour of devotion with a glad readiness to all good deeds, and in the stead of gluttony and lechery sobriety and chastity in body and in soul" (I, lxxxvii, pp. 209–10).[50] And it is also true, as Noetinger points out, that in chapters xxxvii–xxxix of Book II Hilton, following a well-known tradition, opposes the capital sins to the virtues which are the gifts of the Holy Ghost.[51] However, these oppositions and Noetinger's comment must be understood in the light of Hilton's own subordination of all virtues, even as they contrast to the vices, to the means for the progress of the soul, a subordination obvious in the very chapters Noetinger is referring to. The titles of the three chapters respectively indicate Hilton's intention: "How love, through gracious beholding of Jhesu, slayeth all stirrings of pride and maketh the soul meek perfectly; for it maketh the soul to lose savour in all earthly worship"; "How love slayeth all stirrings of wrath and envy softly, and reformeth in the soul the virtues of peace and patience and of perfect charity to his even-christian, as he did specially in the Apostle"; "How love slayeth covetise, lechery, and gluttony, and slayeth the fleshly savour and delight in all the five bodily wits softly and easily through a gracious beholding of Jhesu." It is charity, then, which effaces the deadly sins and leaves the virtues in their places, so that Hilton's remedy for the sins corresponds directly with the primary object of desire, God and his love. While charity is generally the basis of the virtues and ultimately underlies, for example, the specific *remedia* in the *Parson's Tale*, in *The Scale* it is emphatically the contemplative's remedy for the sins. Passages throughout *The Scale* enforce Hilton's teaching on this point. Contemplative means are valid whether one is combating the image of sin in general or a particular sin:

And therefore when thou shalt arise against the ground of sin in general or else against any sin in special, hang fast upon this desire and set the point of thy thought more upon Jhesu Christ whom thou desirest than upon the sin which thou reprovest; for if thou do so, then fighteth Jhesu Christ for thee and He shall destroy sin in thee. Thou shalt mickle sooner come to thy purpose if thou do so, than if thou leave meek desire to God principally, and wilt set thine heart only against stirring of sin, as thou wouldest destroy it by mastery of thy self. Thou shalt never bring it so about; but do as I have said, and better if thou mayest, and I expect by the grace of Jhesu thou shalt make the devil ashamed, and all such wicked stirrings thou shalt break away, that they shall not mickle harm thee. And upon this manner wise may this image of sin be broken down in thee and destroyed, by the which thou art forshapen from the kindly shape of the image of Christ. And thou shalt be shapen again to the image of Jhesu man by meekness and charity; and then shalt thou be fully shapen to the self image of Jhesu God, here living by a shadow in contemplation, and in the bliss of heaven by full soothfastness. (I, xci, pp. 218–19)

Of the means for the progress of the soul in contemplation—a desire for the love of God, meekness and charity, and grace—all are explicit in the above directions on how to destroy the sins. Grace and love, of course, were for any mediaeval Christian the fundamental weapons against sin, the means which were necessary to achieve a contrite heart and which, for example, kept penance from being a mechanical gesture. These means, however, are in the religious-handbook tradition often obscured by the practical or ascetic directions for combatting sin. In *The Scale* precisely the reverse is true. Hilton denigrates ascetic methods to emphasize the fundamentally spiritual weapons, even when dealing with individual sins:

But this travail against the ground [of lechery] namely shall be ghostly, as by prayers and ghostly virtues, and not bodily by no bodily penance. For wit thou well, though thou wake and fast and scourge thyself and do all that thou can, thou shalt never have that cleanness and that chastity without the gift of God and the grace of meekness. Thou shouldest be able rather to slay thyself than thou shouldest slay fleshly stirrings and feelings of lusts of lechery, either in heart or in thy flesh, by any bodily penance. But by the grace of Jhesu in a meek soul, the ground may be stopped and destroyed, and the spring may be dried; and that is very chastity in body and in soul. (I, lxxiii, pp. 181–82)

Indeed, chastity may be the virtue opposing lechery, but in *The Scale* chastity is the result of the destruction of lechery rather than a special means for combating it. In order to establish similarities between Hilton's remedy and that of the religious-handbook tradition, a critic might emphasize Hilton's comment that a contemplative must try to suppress all the deadly sins and "travail for to get all virtues" (II, xx, p. 298); even at this point, however, the critic would still have to recognize that Hilton specifically attributes the development of virtues to the means of progress in contemplation (I, lxxvi). Bloomfield has commented that "love (or grace or Jesus or God) is his [Hilton's] answer to the problem of the good life and the way to God. Through love we may conquer the real enemies of humanity—the cardinal sins."[52] Despite the popular tone of "enemies of humanity," which is not Hilton's phrase, and the equation of the "good life" with the contemplative one, Bloomfield's statement comes close to explaining Hilton's adaptation of the deadly sins to his higher goal in *The Scale*. The remedy for the sins suggests the real state of health Hilton is aiming at.

Understanding Hilton's treatment of the deadly sins in the light of his contemplative remedy for them leads to the clarification of two minor points concerning *The Scale*. The first of these underlies a disagreement between two critics, Dom Sitwell and Dom Noetinger. Dom Sitwell, explaining the effect of contemplation on covetousness, lechery, gluttony, and sloth, writes that "it is to be noted that he [Hilton] considers these sins in their gross and material sense. In this he is reminiscent of the surprising frankness with which the author of the *Ancren Riwle* discusses gross bodily sins for the benefit of the three sisters, and in contradistinction to St. John of the Cross, who in *The Dark*

Night confines himself to, for example, spiritual gluttony, a lack of restraint in seeking for spiritual pleasures which overflow into the senses." [53] Dom Noetinger, on the other hand, argues that Hilton is not particularly concerned with external or material sins at all: "True to his plan he does not dwell upon outwardly sinful acts, from which he supposes his readers already freed; he insists rather upon those interior motions and evil tendencies which remain in the soul, often without her own knowledge." [54] Many passages in *The Scale*, like the comment that there are two kinds of pride, the "bodily pride . . . of fleshly living men" and the "ghostly pride . . . of hypocrites and heretics" (I, lvii, p. 136) and the comment that love will eventually conquer "fleshly lusts of gluttony" which lead to indiscreet eating and drinking (II, xxxix, p. 411), rather obviously support Sitwell's view. Other passages in *The Scale*, however, lend at least partial support to Noetinger's contention that Hilton focuses attention on internal sins. Hilton devotes Book I, lxxiv, to emphasizing that a contemplative must be more concerned about suppressing temptations to ghostly sins than to bodily ones, and he further indicates his attitude about physical and spiritual sins when he says that "a man sinneth not commonly deadly in gluttony, but if he be encumbered with other deadly sins before done" (I, lxxii, pp. 178–79). While Sitwell's view is the more accurate, since he does not maintain that pride, wrath, and envy are treated basically as physical sins in *The Scale*, most interesting is the cause of Noetinger's view. Though not equating the remedies for the sins with the means of progress for the soul in contemplation, Noetinger recognizes that the means for destroying the deadly sins are spiritual, [55] so that he apparently believes that he should see the sins as spiritual also. What he fails to recognize is that while Hilton does differentiate between physical and spiritual sins and subordinate the former to the latter, he provides only one remedy for both kinds of sin, the contemplative remedy appropriate to his reader's goal. In other words, that Hilton treats some sins "in the gross and material sense" does not necessitate his balancing them with physical or merely ascetic remedies.

The second minor point clarified by a recognition of Hilton's contemplative remedy for the deadly sins concerns his attitude towards parts of his treatment of them. After explaining that moderation must prevail in eating if the contemplative is to avoid both gluttony and, conversely, distraction in his contemplation because of hunger, Hilton writes, "I speak further than I thought to have spoken in this matter, but nevertheless do if thou mayest as I thee say, and I hope God shall make all well" (I, lxxvii, p. 189). What is strange about his comment is that he has devoted only two very short chapters to eating and gluttony, and neither of the chapters is narrowly ascetic. A comment roughly similar in tone follows his explanation that a recluse may yet be covetous: "Peradventure thou hast not forsaken thy covetise, but thou hast changed it from great things into small, as from a pound into a penny and from a silvern piece into a disc of one half-penny. This is a simple change; thou art no good merchant. These ensamples are childish; nevertheless they betoken more" (I, lxxi, p. 172). The example is not especially childish, and the little space it takes hardly justifies Hilton's apology or his apparent desire to go on at once with his work. The explanation for Hilton's anxiety in this part of his treatment of the sins (and the explanation, I contend, for the relative paucity of popular examples and imagery in *The Scale*) is that Hilton does not care to spend time treating secondary methods for coping with the sins or even delineating the sins with practical examples, for he feels that the contemplative remedy will solve all problems anyway. Popular examples are "childish" exactly because they deal with the sins at the level of the sins, while the maturing contemplative ought to deal with the sins, no matter how grossly material the sins themselves are, on a higher, spiritual level.

While Hilton's contemplative remedy for the sins distinguishes his treatment of them from the treatments in the religious-handbook tradition, that he examines this major element with any completeness at all distinguishes *The Scale* from the works of the other fourteenth-century English contemplatives. Rolle, for instance, refers a number of times to the sins, but his references do not lead to careful analyses. In "Ego Dormio" the first degree of love is characterized by the keeping of the commandments, faith in the Church, and avoiding the deadly sins,[56] but the points are merely mentioned. In "The Commandment" Rolle distinguishes mortal from venial sins, adding, as Hilton does, that one who wishes to love God will try to flee all sins.[57] Rolle's remedies, however, are not like Hilton's contemplative one; in fact, they stand in direct contrast with Hilton's directions that, for example, the working against lechery shall not be by "bodily penance" (I, lxxiii, p. 181).[58] Rolle's treatments of individual sins, like his comment that pride and vanity keep one from God,[59] are neither systematically arranged nor generally more than a few lines long. Only his concern with lechery stands forth in any way. Arnould writes about the *Melos Amoris* that "the main source of temptation is, of course, the flesh, and its agent, woman," [60] and against lechery Rolle makes the Augustinian observation that bodies are beautiful not that we may take pleasure in them, but that we can recognize the excellence of the Maker through them.[61] If, however, Rolle's great concern about lechery is perhaps the result of peculiar personal problems, it should not be emphasized as a distinguishing factor in his treatment of the sins as an element from the religious-handbook tradition. In *The Cloud* the seven sins merit less attention than they do in the works of Rolle, and Bloomfield's comment that *The Cloud* "is not excessively concerned" with the sins is an understatement.[62] The author of *The Cloud* explains that consent is a main requirement for a mortal sin, and he lists and briefly explains the deadly sins; [63] also, he makes the point that being a wretched sinner should not discourage one from entering the contemplative life.[64] Nevertheless, his treatment of the deadly sins is very scant, most probably because of his view that a contemplative should regard sin as a "lump" [65] and act towards it accordingly:

Do thou, in the same manner, fill thy spirit with the ghostly meaning of this word SIN, and without any special regard unto any kind of sin, whether it be venial or mortal: pride, anger, or envy, covetousness, sloth, gluttony, or lust. What recks it in contemplatives what sin it be, or how great a sin it be? For all sins they think—I mean for the time of this work—alike great in themselves, when the least sin separateth them from God, and hindereth them from their ghostly peace. [66]

The teaching that the contemplative should flee all sin indiscriminately is, of course, parallel to points made by Rolle and Hilton. In Julian's *Revelations* the sins are very unimportant, though references to them occur. One should work spiritually without sloth, [67] and he should quietly accept scorn and mockery to make certain that he does not develop pride or vainglory. [68] While a critic might expect treatments of the sins in the *Revelations* because of Julian's opportunity to relate them with her visions of the Passion and because of her view that "we sin customably" though God loves us, [69] Julian's references to the sins are fleeting, and she develops no treatment of them in any way comparable to that in *The Scale*. In the *Book of Margery Kempe,* there are equally few references to the sins. In one passage God tells Margery that he will sometimes withdraw the grace of contemplation so that she will not become overly proud, [70] and in another he thanks her for having charity towards and weeping and praying for "all lecherous men and women." [71] Also, one of Margery's prayers is that ". . . if any man or woman be dead at this hour through deadly sin, if any prayer may help them, hear my prayers for them and make them live without end." [72] One might reasonably argue, of course, that the *Book of Margery Kempe* is autobiographical and consequently that one should not expect any formal treatment of the sins in it. But the fact remains that it, like the *Revelations, The Cloud,* and the works of Rolle, is very obviously distinct from *The Scale* because of its lack of an extensive treatment of the deadly sins.

Besides the sins, the other major elements of the religious-handbook tradition as enumerated in Peckham's *Constitutions* appear or are at least suggested in *The Scale*. None of the other elements, however, are treated nearly as fully as the sins are. Hilton refers to the works of mercy and the keeping of the commandments specifically as characteristic of the active life (I, ii), and he states that a reform in faith, the reform common to most good souls, requires of men a constant striving "for to keep the commandments of God upon their cunning" (II, x, p. 255). The articles of faith are not listed in *The Scale*, but Hilton's great concern for orthodoxy implies a belief in them, and they are in general at least suggested: "Also thee behoveth love and worship in thine heart all the laws and ordinances made by prelates and rulers of Holy Kirk, either in declaring of the faith, or of the sacraments or in general governance of all Christian men" (I, xxi, pp. 47–48). The virtues as they appear in the religious-handbook tradition are neither treated fully nor developed systematically in *The Scale:* lists of them are infrequent and short, and they are never examined in the categories of theological and natural. While the sacraments are referred to a number of times, only baptism and penance are individually recognized, and the emphasis on penance is, as I have argued, connected with Hilton's concern for orthodoxy rather than with his desire to treat the sacrament in especial detail. The appearance of these other major elements of the religious-handbook tradition in *The Scale* is completely altered by, consistent with, and subordinated to Hilton's contemplative goal and teachings. The works of mercy are not appropriate to a contemplative and a recluse, while a following of the commandments and a belief in the articles of faith would be expected of a soul sufficiently advanced to be interested in contemplation; since Hilton makes the development of the virtues of the religious-handbook tradition, like the destruction of the sins, the natural result of applying the means for progress in contemplation, his emphasizing the means of progress rather than the virtues is logical; finally, since he regards the sacraments as milk for children and not the food contemplatives seek (II, x), Hilton's cursory glance at them is explicable. That these other major elements of the religious-handbook tradition appear briefly in *The Scale* does not necessarily suggest a tie with the religious-handbook tradition, since their appearance could be coincidental and certainly represents no more than what one would expect from the natural overlap of all religious books. Also, the presence of these elements does not distinguish *The Scale* from the works of the other fourteenth-century contemplatives, for the elements appear at least in a slight degree in all of them. Perhaps the only critical value in recognizing their existence in *The Scale* is that it further illustrates Hilton's consistent and logical subordination of all his materials to the contemplative goal of his work.

Besides the elements enumerated in Peckham's *Constitutions,* many of the works in the religious-handbook tradition contain specific teachings on asceticism, especially in the form of detailed instructions on when to pray, how to fast and do penance, how to deal with individual temptations or difficulties, etc. Very often these ascetic teachings pertain to the external conduct of the person addressed. The *Benedictine Rule* and the *Ancrene Riwle,* for example, are filled with such instructions for leading the good life (in contrast to the contemplative life), and frequently one sees the kind of minute parallels which can argue for the strength of a continuing tradition. For instance, in the *Benedictine Rule* brothers who are away from the monastery for a day are forbidden to eat without the abbot's permission,[73] and in the *Ancrene Riwle,* maids who are sent on errands are enjoined in the same way: "Let her not go anywhere else than where she is sent, without permission, and let her not eat or drink while she is out." [74] In *The Scale,* however, there are few such teachings, for Hilton is not especially concerned with the details of his reader's external life, except that the contemplative be a recluse. When

Hilton does treat particular problems of the external life, like how much one should eat, his solution, again, is generally not embodied in a rule, but in the contemplative's application of the principle of moderation, since "the mean is best" (I, xxii, p. 51). Yet, a few examples of specific rules of conduct occur in *The Scale*, as in the passage in which Hilton explains how a recluse is to behave to a visitor:

If thou couldest well love thine even-christian, it should not hinder thee for to speak with them discreetly. Discretion shalt thou have upon this manner as me thinketh. Whoso come to thee, ask him meekly what he will; and if he come for to tell his trouble and be comforted of thy speech, hear him gladly, and suffer him say what he will for ease of his own heart. And when he hath done, comfort him if thou can goodly and charitably, and soon break off. And then after that, if he will fall in idle tales or vanities of other men's deeds answer him but little nor feed not his speech; and he shall soon be irked and soon take his leave. If it be another man, that cometh for to teach thee, as a man of Holy Kirk, hear him lowly with reverence for his order, and if his speech comfort thee ask of him, and make thee not for to teach him. It falleth not to thee to teach a priest, but in need. If his speech comfort thee not answer little, and he will soon take his leave. (I, lxxxiii, pp. 201–2)

While moderation still prevails in this direction, the specific trick of not answering or showing interest in what is being said in order to stop the conversation is very much like the advice one often finds in manuals for ascetics; however, though this passage is quoted fully by Chambers as an example of a continuing spirit appearing in fourteenth-century prose,[75] it is exceedingly atypical of *The Scale,* and it represents only a minor overlap between the religious-handbook and the contemplative traditions. Another example of specific directions for the external life appears in Hilton's warning to the contemplative not to "ask questions of ilk ghostly man what thou shalt do, how thou shalt love God, and how thou shalt serve God and speak of ghostly matters that pass thy knowing, as perchance some do" (II, xlii, p. 439). The remedy here, however, is contemplative, for the recluse is told merely to keep to her work towards contemplation, so that the problem is at once subordinated to the goal of *The Scale* rather than being treated specifically as an external difficulty. These very few specific ascetic teachings do not distinguish *The Scale* from the works of Hilton's contemporaries, since at least comparable touches occur in all of their works, nor do they suggest strongly a tendency on Hilton's part towards the religious-handbook tradition, since their slight appearance is easily explained as the result of overlap. And as with the elements other than the deadly sins enumerated in the *Constitutions,* perhaps the main value in noticing Hilton's treatment of these problems lies in the appreciation of the completeness of Hilton's subordination of his materials to his contemplative goal.

The major element of the religious-handbook tradition appearing in *The Scale* and not explicable by coincidence or overlap is, then, the deadly sins. Why Hilton chose and developed this element from a tradition distinct from the contemplative one, however, remains an important question, especially since Hilton recognizes that *The Scale* is unlike the books which teach "good living" (II, xx, p. 298). The answer is found, I think, on the contemplative level, generally because of Hilton's purpose in the whole of *The Scale* and specifically because of his contemplative remedy for the sins. In the first place, according to his teaching that "to receive ghostly fire of the love of God" one must cleanse himself from "all fleshly filth" (II, xxviii, p. 350), Hilton might stress the deadly sins to be certain that the aspiring contemplative ascends the ladder towards perfect contemplation rung by rung. Focusing attention on the sins would make the contemplative likely to recognize them in himself and consequently to strive for a pure foundation for contemplation rather than presumptuously attempting to achieve the highest levels of contemplation without purgation. Also, he may treat the sins to create a repulsion from them in the contemplative, a repulsion which conversely would intensify the desire for the love of God. Moreover, the desire for the love of God would be increased by a second result of the repulsion, the humility or meekness stemming from a recognition of the wretchedness of the soul. Thirdly, his emphasizing the sins would broaden the appeal of *The Scale* by making the contemplative goal appear to be within reach of those who truly desire it. While the author of *The Cloud* states the principle that an amended soul need not fear being presumptuous by seeking contemplation though he has been "the wretchedest sinner of this life," [76] Hilton makes the principle emphatic in practice when he discusses the sins and the means for completing their suppression as connected with the very means of progress for the soul in contemplation. A final explanation for Hilton's treatment of the deadly sins, an explanation which is very conjectural, is that he perhaps wanted to emphasize his anti-quietism. A passivity towards the sins and even a toleration of continued sinning easily develop as further abuses of quietism, and Hilton may have been somewhat driven by his general concern for orthodoxy to stress his teaching that the true passivity in contemplation, nought, is achieved only after the sins have been purged from the soul. Probably all of these causes are in some degree responsible for Hilton's inclusion of the deadly sins in *The Scale*. Whatever their relative importance may be, their effect distinguishes *The Scale* from the works of the other fourteenth-century contemplatives while at the same time it emphasizes, by the remedy for the sins, Hilton's subordination of all of his materials to his contemplative purpose.

The relation between *The Scale* and the religious-handbook tradition mirrors the eclecticism of the whole work. Though drawing on distinct traditions, Hilton avoids producing an *omnium gatherum* by integrating his materials carefully, and instead works towards real unity.

THE UNITY

OF *THE SCALE OF PERFECTION*

While explaining various elements of *The Scale*, I have indicated how they are different from or similar to the teachings of the other fourteenth-century contemplatives and how they represent traditional materials used by Hilton in either a traditional or a new way. I have also suggested possible causes for Hilton's emphasis on or treatment of particular points. But most pertinent to this chapter are the frequent references to the relations between various teachings in *The Scale* and especially to the real consistency of seemingly disparate elements as they are used by Hilton. These references and the words like "subordination" and "moderation" which often occur in them dictate in great part any final comment on the unity of *The Scale*, a unity evident in the teachings, the tone, and the structure of the work and a unity which itself emphasizes the purpose and helps to explain the success of the guide.

The teachings of *The Scale* illustrate the unity of the work by their focusing of attention on contemplation proper and especially the mystical experience rather than on any physical or spiritual matter which might merely be connected with contemplation. In his discussion of the three Christian lives, for example, Hilton views the active life briefly, differentiating it from the contemplative life and giving its main characteristics, and the mixed life only indirectly. He devotes almost all of his book to the contemplative life as led by a recluse and to the levels of contemplation, and he treats the levels themselves proportionately according to their proximity to and importance for the mystical experience. The first level of contemplation is disposed of in a few paragraphs, and the second and third levels and the teachings on the progress to them occupy more than ninety percent of Books I and II. The essential means of progress towards perfect contemplation are entirely spiritual and are effective and important as they contribute to the achieving of the primary object of desire, God and his love. And that grace is necessary for progress to contemplation further emphasizes contemplation proper by making a key to it something which is unattainable by man's efforts and which at the same time is directly identified with the object to be contemplated, God. The advancement of the soul in contemplation is explained according to spiritual stages, stages which, even though they might give pleasure in the alternation of pleasure and pain in the contemplative's progress, must always be regarded as stages and never confused with the contemplative's real goal: "Whoso hath this grace [the gift and the pleasure of the higher degree of the second part of contemplation], keep he himself in lowness, and look that he be aye desiring for to come to more knowing and feeling of God, in the third part of contemplation" (I, vii, p. 13). The nought which immediately precedes the mystical experience, moreover, is characterized negatively by an absence of regard for the finite and positively by a receptivity to the Infinite, so that even in this high spiritual state the potentiality for what is above rather than the graciousness of the state itself is most important. And increasing the impact of all the above teachings is Hilton's attitude towards pseudocontemplative phenomena, his distrust and denigration of what deviates from contemplation as a spiritual process directed towards a spiritual goal.

Contributing to the unity of his teachings is Hilton's eclecticism. Hilton maintains control over the materials at his disposal, ready to use whatever lends itself to his plan but not allowing any single influence to harm the proportion or effect of his work.

It has long been commonplace for critics to state that after Rolle, scholasticism and mysticism diverge and seem contradictory in England,[1] but apparently scholastic materials appear in *The Scale*. Many of Hilton's definitions are very close to St. Thomas', though here the similarities could result from the traditions of Patristic theology. Moreover, though Hilton stresses that the cognition of the third part of contemplation cannot be arrived at by "naked reason" (II, xxxii, p. 370), he states that the first part of contemplation, common to "lettered men, and great clerks," "lieth in knowing of God and of ghostly things, gotten by reason, by teaching of man, and by study in Holy Writ" (I, iv, p. 6). Yet, the scholasticism in *The Scale*, though Hilton may indeed be "well-versed in the arguments of the Schools,"[2] is never permitted to lead to theological disputes or to overshadow the spiritual means of progress of the soul. Rather, it remains a useful starting point in the spiritual process or merely a recognizable element in Hilton's method of explanation. Hilton's eclecticism and control are equally apparent in his use of the contemplative and the religious-handbook traditions. He is willing to accept Rolle's devotion to Jesus as proper for the second part of contemplation, which consists of a kind of knowing in the imagination, since scenes from the Passion or life of Christ make the best bases for meditation; however, he never allows Rolle's preoccupation with Jesus alone to alter his own view, similar to the view of the author of *The Cloud*, that the primary object of desire is God and that the mystical experience is a cognition of God, that is, of the total Being composed of three persons. In other words, he sees that for the beginning contemplative an effective means to a theocentric goal is Christo-centricism, but he never confuses the means with the end. Hilton's use of the matter of the deadly sins common to the religious-handbook tradition, a major use unique among the fourteenth-century English contemplatives, also suggests not only his eclecticism, but the control which keeps all the elements of *The Scale* focusing on contemplation proper. The sins are evil primarily in that they keep one from reforming his soul and consequently from contemplation, and the remedy for the sins is contemplative, so that Hilton's treatment of the sins becomes perfectly consistent with his contemplative goal.

The most important cause of the unity in Hilton's teachings, the cause responsible for his very controlled eclecticism as well as for his constant focusing of attention on contemplation proper, is his technique of subordination. No matter what they concern, his materials in *The Scale* are always developed according to his contemplative purpose, so that they are subordinated consistently by one standard and consequently assume a proportional importance in the scheme of the work. The elements other than the deadly sins from the religious-handbook tradition are barely touched on in *The Scale* since they are not appropriate specifically to contemplation, but the doctrine of grace, which one might expect to be developed in a theological rather than a contemplative work, is emphasized throughout *The Scale* because of its direct and continuing relation to the progress of the soul. All of the examples in the preceding paragraphs reflect the subordination of materials in *The Scale,* either by Hilton's proportional development or particular treatment of his materials.

Along with the unity of teachings in *The Scale* and very closely related to it is a unity of tone. The word "intellectual" now has a dubious connotation, but it is still probably the most accurate adjective one can use to describe the tone of *The Scale.* That the tone is intellectual does not mean that the work is coldly or uninvitingly analytical, seems discursive as a theological or philosophical work does, or is of little value practically. It means that the tone suggests careful, planned, intelligent direction, in contrast, for example, to mere devotional fervor. After stating that Rolle's contemplation is a "re-action of the heart" against scholasticism, Horstman makes the comment that Rolle "as exclusively represents the side of feeling as Scotus that of reason and logical consequence, either lacking the corrective of the other element,"[3] a comment which implies adequately the outstanding quality and deficiency many see in Rolle's works. But a few pages later Horstman adds that "Hilton's style and manner is almost identical with his [Rolle's]."[4] Indeed, Hilton does not believe that the cognition of the third part of contemplation can be achieved by dialectical means. Nevertheless, as I have argued, he does not run to the opposite extreme of the "fire-of-love" contemplation of Rolle, and the resulting tone in *The Scale,* due precisely to the fact that Hilton allows "the corrective of the other element" to influence him, is intellectual and very unlike the tone of Rolle's unqualified "side of feeling."

The intellectual tone of *The Scale* is partially the result of Hilton's tendency to rationalize, that is, to clarify his teachings on reasonable grounds. The passage on the Holy Name, which in fact explains away the popular devotion to the name of "Jesus," might be regarded as a deliberate effort to lift *The Scale* from the realm of the merely devotional. Certainly it contrasts strongly with the almost physical passion for Jesus which the works of Rolle sometimes suggest. Miss Gardner refers to this tendency to rationalize in her observation that when Hilton deals with terms like "rich nought," "characteristically he makes them unparadoxical, for Hilton's mind is not daring."[5] But rather than saying simply that "Hilton's mind is not daring," one might point out that his unwillingness to be mystifying or to attract by devices like oxymoron is a major cause for the intellectual tone of *The Scale.* The expediency apparent in *The Scale,* very closely related to Hilton's subordination of materials to his contemplative goal, also leads to the intellectual tone of the work. Hilton's means of avoiding problems for the contemplative, like his emphasis on orthodoxy to prevent the abuses of antinomianism, reflect his readiness to use what is practically effective to accomplish his goal. Expediency on this level is connected with careful planning and controlled rather than passionate execution, and resulting from these qualities is an increase in the intellectual tone. Finally, Hilton's teaching of moderation in all things except the desire for the love of God maintains the intellectual tone of his guide. It prevents the overdevelopment of the lower levels of contemplation, like passionate imaginings of scenes from the life of Christ, and it almost completely obviates the necessity of detailed instructions for the external life. Not only does this moderation keep the contemplative's progress from being erratic, but it is responsible in part for Hilton's alteration and curtailing of materials at his disposal, with the result, as Inge points out, that "his Mysticism is sounder and saner than even that of Eckhart or Tauler." [6]

Recognizing the intellectual tone of *The Scale* allows one to reconcile seemingly opposed interpretations of Hilton's contemplation. Miss Underhill writes that Hilton "is pre-eminently a lover, not a metaphysician," [7] with the obvious implication that his teachings on contemplation have little to do with dialectics or scholasticism and with at least a suggestion that his works are more passionate than precise. Father Pepler, however, distinguishes Hilton from Rolle, the author of *The Cloud*, and the author of the *Ancrene Riwle* by the statement that Hilton is the only one who sets down "with the precision of the theologian the whole way of progress to union," [8] with the obvious suggestion that Hilton is not merely a "lover," but one who betrays intellectual or scholastic tendencies. To justify both of these comments, one must differentiate the intellectual tone of *The Scale* from the essence of Hilton's teachings on the progress towards the mystical experience. The intellectual tone is the result of careful planning and controlled execution, the result of the conveyance of Hilton's teachings, but the teachings themselves, inasmuch as they stress purely contemplative means to knowledge and love, center about the love of God. Thus it is not a contradiction to assert that Hilton, "pre-eminently a lover," works "with the precision of a theologian." It is simply that the first criticism is of Hilton as a contemplative, while the second is of Hilton as a teacher.

The third unity in *The Scale* is one of structure. In the

preceding chapters Hilton's teachings have been grouped and discussed according to their relations to major contemplative ideas, like the levels of contemplation and the means of progress of the soul, and not according to their appearance chronologically in *The Scale*. Also, the possibility that Books I and II appeared separately has been ignored and *The Scale* has been treated as a whole, since there are no doctrinal differences between the two books. But the teachings as they appear in order in Books I and II and consequently in their chronological relation to the whole of *The Scale* reflect a structural unity based on a constant progress of the soul, the progress or specifically the reform from the image of sin to the image of God. Dom Sitwell has argued that the second book of *The Scale* "is in no sense a continuation of the first, but a rehandling of the matter with emphasis on the higher part of contemplation instead of on the attainment of the pre-requisite virtues." [9] But the total result of a rehandling with a different emphasis can be a constant progress. The parts of *The Scale* flow into one another rather than being artificially delineated, as they are in my analysis, and the flowing and overlapping are appropriate to a guide. After summarizing *The Scale* and commenting that Book I leads to the destruction of the image of sin, and Book II to the re-creation of the image of God, Noetinger most effectively points out the relation of these two goals, a relation which, in turn, explains the total structural unity of *The Scale* and, in fact, suggests the near impossibility of constructing such a guide without some rehandling or overlapping of materials:

In actual fact, the constructive work is inseparable from the destructive, and although he distinguishes them for the sake of clearness, Hilton does not make any practical severance between them. Indeed, it would be truer to say that he reinstates them in the position which they commonly held under the older mystical system. In order to cleanse and detach the soul, he begins by gathering her within herself; then, to foster her growth, he raises her above herself, up to Almighty God: *Ab exterioribus ad interiora; ab interioribus ad superiora.*[10]

An example of the kind of overlapping or repetition or rehandling of material apparent within the structure of the work is seen in the three important passages in which the deadly sins are treated. The long discussion of the sins in Book I (chapters lii–lx; lxiii–xci) consists of a focusing on the problem of the sins as they hinder contemplation and on Hilton's contemplative remedy for them. Hilton's treatment is very full and is probably designed, as I have suggested, to create in the contemplative a repulsion from the sins as well as to clarify the basis of the image of sin, antagonistic to the image of God. The length of the treatment is appropriate to the early stage of contemplation, purgation, and both the length and the treatment itself establish the sins at this point as significant primary blocks to the contemplative's progress. The second important appearance of the sins is in Book II, chapter xiv, where men led by individual sins are compared to particular beasts. Immediately preceding this passage is an explanation of the states of the three kinds of men, those not reformed, those reformed in faith, and those reformed in faith and feeling (II, xiii); immediately following it is an explanation of how "lovers of this world unable [sic] them in divers manners to the reforming of their own souls" (II, xv, p. 280). The treatment here is relatively brief, since the reader learned precisely the problem of the sins in the long passage in Book I, and it is consistent with Hilton's view that the sins are evil because they hinder contemplation. Not only do the surrounding chapters put the sins in the context of the reform necessary for contemplation, but chapter xiv itself ends with the advice that contemplatives "should lift up their heart for to love God, and they would busily seek and travail how they might be reformed to His likeness or [before] they passed hence" (p. 279), that is, it ends with Hilton's contemplative remedy for the sins. Finally, the brevity of the treatment is consistent with the more advanced stage of the contemplative at this time, a stage in which the sins are sufficiently suppressed so that he need only be guarded from a relapse. The third important treatment of the deadly sins occurs near the end of Book II, in chapters xxxvii–xxxix, in which the destruction of the sins by the love in contemplation is explained. The sins here are seen not as primary blocks *to* contemplation, but as evils destroyed *by* it, so that the treatment corresponds to the most advanced stage of the contemplative. Moreover, the length of the treatment and the fact that it touches on each of the sins individually provide a balance to the long treatment in Book I. The total effect of these three major appearances of the deadly sins or of this rehandling of material is to emphasize the structural unity of *The Scale* by emphasizing the constant progress. Just as *The Scale* as a whole teaches the movement from the image of sin to the image of God, the treatments of the sins present them first as evils to be conquered, then as evils being conquered, and finally as evils conquered. The interweaving of this material, while serving to keep the lower rungs of contemplation always in view, according to Hilton's scale idea, thus helps develop *The Scale* itself. Dom Sitwell, though he denies the unity of structure of the whole of *The Scale* based on constant progress, recognizes Hilton's use of progressive overlapping in the last twenty-six chapters of Book II, with which Sitwell's theological analysis is concerned: "He himself [Hilton] moves quietly backwards and forwards, elaborating his thought, sometimes repeating himself, but always building up his picture of the soul turning from creatures and seeking only God." [11] Sitwell's comment on Hilton's technique is valid for the entirety of *The Scale,* and it explains both the major structural unity based on the progress to the image of God and the overlapping of specific materials in Books I and II. The understanding of this structural unity must lead to the rejection of criticisms like Miss Underhill's, that Hilton's "whole method is discursive rather than orderly." [12]

Besides the progressive overlapping of materials, there are within the grand plan of *The Scale* many specific passages of varying lengths which contribute in minor ways to the structure of the work or which can be explained as consistent with its principle of progress. The first nine chapters of Book I, for instance, present a brief survey of the Christian lives and levels of contemplation, a survey which provides the contemplative with an outline into which he can fit the details from the teachings of the rest of *The Scale*. This over-all view not only clarifies the contemplative's goal, but gives him a basis on which to judge his development and to apply thoughtfully the directions in the work. The first sentence of Book II, besides serving as a prayer of sorts, represents the kind of brief introduction Hilton favors: "For as mickle as thou covetest greatly and askest it by charity, for to hear more of an image the which I have before times in party discried to thee, therefore I will gladly with dread fall to thy desire; and helping the grace of our Lord Jhesu Christ, in Whom I fully trust, I shall open to thee a little more of this image" (p. 225). In this passage the words "more" and "in party," while suggesting what is to follow, also provide a transition which indicates Hilton's own view of the relation between Books I and II and of the unity of his work. Also prevalent throughout *The Scale* are very brief transitional passages, like the one ending the chapter distinguishing the reforms in faith, in faith and feeling, and in feeling: "The first is good, the second is better, but the third, that is in the bliss of heaven, is altogether best. First begin we to speak of the one and then of the tother; and so shall we come to the third" (II, v, p. 242). Besides introductory and transitional passages, *The Scale* contains concluding or summarizing passages: chapter xxiii of Book I, offering "a rehearsing of things spoken before . . . ," reflects an obvious intention to clarify the movement from element to element within the whole of *The Scale*, and both Books I and II are given brief conclusions.

While the mere existence of these concluding and summarizing passages signifies little, since one expects conclusions and summaries in a long work, a characteristic of all of them emphasizes the constant progress Hilton is aiming at in *The Scale*. The passages, far from suggesting a note of finality, point to that which is to come. Chapter xxiii of Book I ends by drawing all together so that the contemplative may proceed to meditation, the second part of contemplation, and the last chapter of Book I with its advice to "take it [the book] as it will come, and not all at once" (p. 222) suggests the future state which the reader is to keep striving for rather than a goal reached. Even the last sentences of Book II suggest futurity and the continuation of progress: "These are the ghostly things that I spake of before, and they may be called new gracious feelings. And I do but touch them a little, for wissing of thy soul. For a soul that is clean, stirred by grace to use of this working, may see more in an hour of such ghostly matter, than might be written in a great book" (p. 464). These passages, because they unite or relate to specific teachings in *The Scale,* cannot be validly cited to indicate the unity of structure of the whole of the work. But regarded in the light of Hilton's plan based on the constant progress of the soul and with his progressive overlapping of materials, they can serve as details pointing to the practical effectiveness of Hilton's principle of unity.

Besides the specific passages contributing in minor ways to its structure, *The Scale* contains two chapters which are at first sight apparently incorrectly positioned but which might be explained as consistent with Hilton's unifying principle of progress towards contemplation. Chapters lxi and lxii of Book I, which explain the various kinds of rewards in heaven and which emphasize the teaching that one's highest reward is determined by his charity, break into the otherwise smoothly flowing treatment of the deadly sins, disuniting specifically the discussion of pride. Not only does the content, which might properly be placed after the discussion of the Christian lives and the levels of contemplation in chapters i–ix of Book I, seem out of place, but Hilton's opening words in chapter lxiii, which resumes the discussion of the sins, indicate his own awareness of the digression: "I have near forgot this image [of sin]; but now I turn again thereto. If thou wilt wit how mickle pride is therein, thou mayest . . ." (p. 152). These chapters represent what Dom Knowles is evidently referring to when he qualifies his comment that *The Scale* is "a methodical work, the outcome of deliberate planning" by saying that it is "not without its share of medieval digression and disorder." [13] Yet, the position of the chapters might be explicable according to Hilton's technique of teaching progress.

The chapters are (and the simile is not particularly inappropriate to the contemplative in the elementary stage of his work) like the carrots dangled in front of a donkey: the donkey may not receive his reward until the end of the day, but because the reward is in immediate view, he keeps plodding on. The beginning contemplative purging himself of the deadly sins is working towards an eventual reward also, and because his reward is sometimes put in his immediate view, he can plod on in his drudgery. This explanation is in accord with the principle of the alternation of pleasure and pain characteristic of Hilton's teachings. The pain of elementary purgation is followed by the pleasures of the second part of contemplation, but the pain of purgation is so extended that Hilton adds in its midst a view of the pleasure to come, a pleasure in expectation. Specific comments from the two chapters corroborate this view. Hilton prefaces his explanation of the common and special rewards of heaven by stating that it is "in comfort of thee and all others having the state of anker enclosed, and also by the grace of God in comfort of them all that enter any religion approved by Holy Kirk, that all those that by the mercy of our Lord shall be saved, they shall have a special meed and a singular worship in the bliss of heaven for their state of living, before other souls that had not that state in Holy Kirk, though they be never so holy" (lxi, p. 146). In the next chapter the comforting of the contemplatives in their work is turned into an impetus for continued work. Since the contemplative receives a special reward and at the same time has the opportunity to devote all his efforts to perfecting his charity, which determines the greatness of his general reward, he indeed has much to gain, especially in proportion to the mere earthly duty of suppressing the sins. And a new energy can easily result from such occasional reminders of future pleasure.

The unity of the teachings, the tone, and the structure of *The Scale* reveals and emphasizes both the purpose and the effectiveness of the work. The focusing of the teachings on contemplation and the subordination of elements according to their relative value for the contemplative's goal indicate Hilton's concern with contemplation proper rather than with spirituality in general or with the externals of the religious life, and they keep the aspiring contemplative from drifting from his goal or confusing means with end. The intellectual tone of *The Scale* corresponds with Hilton's desire to prevent excesses and with his explanation on a rational level of what are often considered the "mysterious" elements of contemplation, helping the contemplative to a practical view of contemplation and keeping him from mere passionate devotion and its abuses. The unity of structure, based on Hilton's principle of constant progress, always indicates the goal of *The Scale* while it keeps the contemplative securely advancing. And comments in *The Scale* like "this travail [the reforming from the image of sin to the image of God and contemplation] is cause of all this writing" (I, liv, p. 130; see also II, i) specifically point to Hilton's intention as it is revealed by the effect of *The Scale* itself. *The Scale* is a practical work and, as Noetinger says, not a theological treatise.[14] But contrary to Miss Gardner's assertion, it is not simply "an attempt to put into simple language and adapt for the needs of individual souls the general teachings of the Church."[15] It is a guide specifically to the contemplation of God, one which is to be read "not all at once" (I, xciii, p. 222), but which is to be a *vade mecum* for those aspiring to the mystical experience.

Consistent with the specific purpose of *The Scale* to direct the reader to contemplation is Hilton's insistence on a select audience for his work. *The Scale* begins with an address to a "ghostly sister in Jhesu Christ," and the first sentence of Book II with its reference to a request by the reader and its personal "thou's" implies a continuation of the select audience. It is true that critics have disputed the import of these references. Miss Gardner has argued about the introductory passage in Book II "that the friend who had asked for more information was a conventional excuse for writing," [16] and Dom Noetinger, commenting on the whole of *The Scale*, states the opposite: "His work is addressed to a recluse, and although nothing is known regarding her, it is unlikely that in this he was merely employing a literary device." [17] It is also true, however, that whether or not *The Scale* was written originally for a single person, Hilton obviously intended to limit his audience at least to contemplatives only. His admonition at the end of Book I, chapter xciii, that *The Scale* belongs "not all to a man which hath active life, but to thee or to any other which hath the state of life contemplative" (p. 223) clearly states his view. Moreover comments woven into *The Scale* indicate that his admonition is not merely conventional. Chapter lxi of Book I is written, as we have seen, to comfort those "having the state of anker enclosed . . ." (p. 146), enclosed for the purpose of contemplation. And chapter xxi of Book II, which contains the famous passage on the pilgrimage to Jerusalem, i.e., the way to contemplation, begins with a similarly limiting comment: "Nevertheless for thou covetest for to have some manner working by the which thou mightest be rather nigher to that reforming, I shall say thee as me thinketh by the grace of our Lord Jhesu, the shortest and the readiest help that I know in this working" (p. 303). The recluse striving for contemplation by reforming his soul to the image of God is, then, the reader to whom Hilton addresses the whole of *The Scale*.[18] Besides being consistent with his purpose, Hilton's limitation of his audience helps him to achieve the unity of *The Scale*. It makes unnecessary constant qualifications for those who have different goals or who are not devoting themselves totally to the contemplation of God while it gives Hilton a stable point to which he can relate what he says.

An analysis of *The Scale* reveals the unity of the work, and it is largely the unity of its parts, as chosen, refined, and altered by Hilton, that makes *The Scale* an effective guide to contemplation. Far more orderly than the works of Rolle because of Hilton's subordination of materials according to their importance to the contemplative goal and far more restrained than *The Cloud* because of his moderation and care that the contemplative not be distracted from his primary work, *The Scale* teaches a constant progress, one which slowly but surely leads the contemplative rung by rung to the top of the ladder of perfection. Understanding the teachings and unity of *The Scale* must lead immediately to the rejection of criticisms like Baugh's, "that one is frequently led to doubt his [Hilton's] place among true mystics." [19] Perhaps eventually it will lead to a general recognition of Hilton as the most impressive of the mediaeval English contemplatives.

REFERENCE MATTER

NOTES

CHAPTER I: A Background

1 Dom M. Noetinger and Dom E. Bouvet, trans., Walter Hilton, *Scala Perfectionis* (Tours, 1923), I, 54. The introduction to this edition is translated by an Oblate of Solesmes in *The Scale of Perfection* (London, 1927). For further information on the history of the text, see Helen L. Gardner's "The Text of *The Scale of Perfection*," *Medium Aevum*, V (1936), 11 ff., and S. S. Hussey, "The Text of *The Scale of Perfection*, Book II," *Neuphilologisches Mitteilungen*, LXV (1964), 75–92. A printing history is available in Gerard Sitwell, trans., *The Scale of Perfection* (London, 1953), p. v.

2 This tradition, discussed in its relation to *The Scale* in Chapter V, encompasses the "vernacular literature of religious manuals" associated with the *Parson's Tale* (W. F. Bryan and G. Dempster, eds., *Sources and Analogues of the Canterbury Tales* [New York, 1958], p. 724). The "religious-handbook tradition" will refer to all works that are religious or devotional but specifically neither contemplative nor speculatively theological.

3 *The Cloud of Unknowing and Other Treatises*, ed. Abbot Justin McCann (London, 1952), Prologue. Modernized quotations from *The Cloud* in my text are from this edition, though the reference by chapter as well as page permits the use of any edition, including the original (*The Cloud of Unknowing and The Book of Privy Counselling*, ed. Phyllis Hodgson, EETS, No. 218 [London, 1944]).

4 Walter Hilton, *The Scale of Perfection*, ed. Evelyn Underhill (London, 1923; second impression, 1948). All citations from *The Scale* in my text are from this edition. It should be noted

187

that the inclusion of references to books and chapters of *The Scale* (within parentheses in the text) allows the reader to trace materials in any standard edition (like the Penguin translation by Leo Sherley-Price).

5 Hope Emily Allen, "The Authorship of the *Prick of Conscience,*" *Studies in English and Comparative Literature* (Boston, 1910), p. 163.

6 Dom David Knowles, *The English Mystical Tradition* (London, 1961).

7 Conrad Pepler, O.P., *The English Religious Heritage* (St. Louis, 1958).

8 Eric Colledge, *The Mediaeval Mystics of England* (New York, 1961).

9 Helen L. Gardner, "Walter Hilton and the Mystical Tradition in England," *Essays and Studies,* XXII (1937), 103–27.

10 Joy M. Russell-Smith, "Walter Hilton and a Tract in Defence of the Veneration of Images," *Dominican Studies,* VII (1954), 199 and n. 75.

11 Underhill, ed., *The Scale,* p. vi.

12 Noetinger, trans., *Scala,* I, 7.

13 H. Gardner, "Walter Hilton," p. 108.

14 Russell-Smith, "Defence," pp. 209–10; 184–87.

15 Noetinger, trans., *Scala,* I, 53, note; I, 58, note.

16 William Ralph Inge, *Studies of English Mystics* (London, 1907), p. 81.

17 Underhill, ed., *The Scale,* p. xxi.

18 Pepler, *English Religious Heritage,* p. 375.

19 Underhill, ed., *The Scale,* p. xlv.

20 *Ibid.,* pp. xliv–xlv.

21 H. Gardner, "The Text," p. 23.

22 *Ibid.,* pp. 20–23.

23 Work has been begun, however, by a group of English scholars (see Knowles, *English Mystical Tradition,* p. 101, note).

24 Hussey, "The Text," pp. 91–92.

25 John Edwin Wells, *A Manual of the Writings in Middle English* (New Haven, 1926), p. 461.

26 Underhill, ed., *The Scale,* p. 365, note.

27 *Ibid.,* p. xlv.

28 H. Gardner, "Walter Hilton," p. 114.

29 Noetinger, trans., *Scala,* II, 192–93, note. For a clear and sensitive recent survey of these differences, see Joy M. Russell-

Smith, "Walter Hilton," *The Month*, XXII (Sept., 1959), 139–44. To her explanation of why Hilton wrote Book II (pp. 143–44), one might add that the more advanced state of the contemplative addressed in II would dictate a more advanced presentation than is available in I. Such an explanation is consistent with the tie between the books which Mrs. Russell-Smith has observed (p. 139, n. 3).

30 See Knowles, *English Mystical Tradition*, p. 103.

31 William Fairweather, *Among the Mystics* (Edinburgh, 1936), p. v.

32 Inge, *Studies of English Mystics*, pp. 80–81.

33 William Ralph Inge, *Mysticism in Religion* (Chicago, 1948), pp. 17–18.

34 Colledge, *Mediaeval Mystics*, pp. 3–4.

35 These comments, of course, are not intended to represent a survey of the problem of bias in mystical criticism, nor will they strike the experienced reader of contemplative literature as new. But for the general reader they provide a necessary caveat.

36 Evelyn Underhill, *Mysticism* (London, 1919), p. vii.

37 Dom Cuthbert Butler, *Western Mysticism* (London, 1951), pp. vii–viii.

38 William James, *The Varieties of Religious Experience* (London, 1916), p. 380.

39 Fairweather, *Among the Mystics*, pp. 12, 18.

40 St. Augustine, *Liber de videndo Deo,* quoted in Butler, *Western Mysticism*, p. 58.

41 *The Cloud*, ed. McCann, Chap. 26, p. 43.

42 *The Book of Privy Counselling* in *The Cloud of Unknowing and Other Treatises*, ed. Abbot Justin McCann (London, 1952), p. 119. Modernized quotations in my text are from this edition. References will also be given, in parentheses, to the original text, available in *The Cloud of Unknowing and The Book of Privy Counselling*, ed. Phyllis Hodgson, EETS, No. 218 (London, 1944); for this quotation, see Hodgson, p. 153, ll. 11–20.

43 *The Book of Margery Kempe*, trans. W. Butler-Bowdon (London, 1954), Chap. 83, p. 265. Modernized quotations in my text are from this edition, though the reference by chapter as well as page permits the use of any edition, including the original (*The Book of Margery Kempe*, ed. Sanford Brown Meech and Hope Emily Allen, EETS, No. 212 [London, 1940]).

44 Underhill, *Mysticism*, p. 9.
45 *The Cloud*, ed. McCann, Prologue, p. 4.
46 Walter Hilton, "Song of Angels," *The Cell of Self Knowledge*, ed. Edmund Gardner (London, 1910), p. 66.
47 Richard Rolle, *Incendium Amoris*, ed. Margaret Deanesly (Manchester, 1915), p. 145: "Admirabar magis quam enuncio quando siquidem sentiui cor meum primitus incalescere, et uere non imaginarie, quasi sensibile igne estuare."
48 Butler, *Western Mysticism*, p. 60.
49 Robert Alfred Vaughn, *Hours with the Mystics*, 3d ed. (London, n.d.), I, 267.
50 Arthur Edward Waite, *Studies in Mysticism* (London, 1906).
51 James, *Varieties of Religious Experience*, p. 387.
52 Fairweather, *Among the Mystics*, p. 41.
53 Meech and Allen, eds., *Book of Margery Kempe*, p. lxi.
54 In fairness, one must note that Miss Allen, on page lxvii in the 1940 "Addenda" to her "Prefatory Note" in *The Book of Margery Kempe*, wrote that her second volume would include a "more inclusive review of late-medieval English contemplative piety." Perhaps she intended to make distinctions there.
55 Fairweather, *Among the Mystics*, p. vi.
56 Robert Penn Warren, *All the King's Men* (New York, 1959), p. 306.
57 Rachel Carson, *The Sea Around Us* (New York, 1951), p. 14.
58 See "The Form of Living," *English Writings of Richard Rolle*, ed. Hope Emily Allen (Oxford, 1931), p. 118.
59 Geraldine E. Hodgson, *English Mystics* (London, 1922), p. 143.
60 Butler, *Western Mysticism*, p. 213.
61 Henri Delacroix, *Études d'histoire et de psychologie du mysticisme* (Paris, 1908), pp. 359–60. The translation is mine.

CHAPTER II: The Three Christian Lives and the Levels of Contemplation

1 *The Cloud*, ed. McCann, Chap. 74, p. 98.
2 P. Hodgson, ed., *The Cloud*, p. lxxi.
3 See *Privy Counselling*, ed. McCann, p. 128 (ed. P. Hodgson, p. 163, l. 28—p. 164, l. 6).
4 *Ibid.*, pp. 127–28 (ed. P. Hodgson, p. 163, ll. 5–28).

5 "Form of Living," *English Writings of Rolle*, p. 117, l. 19—p. 118, l. 34.
6 Butler, *Western Mysticism*, p. xl.
7 *Ibid.*, pp. 173–74.
8 Underhill, *Mysticism*, pp. 295–96.
9 "The Bee and the Stork," *English Writings of Rolle*, p. 56, ll. 50–59.
10 Richard Rolle, *The Fire of Love and The Mending of Life*, trans. Frances M. M. Comper (London, 1914), p. 94.
11 *The Cloud*, ed. McCann, Chap. 8, p. 18.
12 *Ibid.*, Chap. 19, p. 33.
13 *Ibid.*, Chap. 21, p. 37.
14 *Privy Counselling*, ed. McCann, p. 116 (ed. P. Hodgson, p. 149, ll. 20–26).
15 *The Mending of Life*, p. 241.
16 Deanesly, ed., *Incendium*, p. 47.
17 *The Fire of Love*, p. 59 (*Incendium*, pp. 179–80).
18 *The Cloud*, ed. McCann, Chap. 23, pp. 38–39.
19 *Book of Margery Kempe*, trans. Butler-Bowdon, Chap. 13, p. 36. For the possibility of a different and equally tenable interpretation of this passage, see the note on it, Meech and Allen, eds., p. 270.
20 For a general view that being a recluse is not a requisite for perfect contemplation, see Underhill, *Mysticism*, pp. 295–96, as quoted above, and pp. 210–11; Butler, *Western Mysticism*, p. lv. For the view applied specifically to *The Scale*, see Pepler, *English Religious Heritage*, p. 426.
21 Russell-Smith, "Walter Hilton," especially pp. 146–47.
22 Comper, trans., *The Fire of Love*, p. 267, note.
23 "The Book That Is Called Mixed Life . . . ," *Minor Works of Walter Hilton*, ed. Dorothy Jones (New York, 1929), pp. 1–77.
24 Pepler, *English Religious Heritage*, p. 427.
25 *Ibid.*
26 St. John of the Cross, *Subida del Monte Carmelo*, quoted in Underhill, *Mysticism*, p. 256.
27 *The Fire of Love*, pp. 95–96 (*Incendium*, pp. 206–7).
28 Butler, *Western Mysticism*, pp. 176–78.
29 St. Teresa, *Moradas Sétimas*, quoted in Underhill, *Mysticism*, p. 514.
30 Underhill, *Mysticism*, p. 535.
31 James, *Varieties of Religious Experience*, p. 413.

32 Noetinger, trans., *Scala*, I, 56, note.
33 *Ibid.*, p. 21, note.
34 "Mixed Life," *Minor Works of Hilton*, p. 23.
35 Butler, *Western Mysticism*, p. 180.
36 "Mixed Life," *Minor Works of Hilton*, pp. 27–28.
37 Butler, *Western Mysticism*, p. 184.
38 St. Teresa, *Moradas Sétimas*, quoted in Underhill, *Mysticism*, p. 514. Hilton uses the Martha-Mary contrast in "Mixed Life," pp. 10–11, but not to argue the superiority of the mixed life.
39 *The Mending of Life*, p. 241.
40 *Incendium*, pp. 206–7.
41 Allen, ed., *English Writings of Rolle*, p. xlv.
42 "Mixed Life," *Minor Works of Hilton*, p. 23.
43 Woodbridge Riley, *The Meaning of Mysticism* (New York, 1930), p. 34.
44 Inge, *Mysticism in Religion*, p. 84.
45 Pepler, *English Religious Heritage*, pp. 8–9; p. 36.
46 Comper, trans., *The Fire of Love*, pp. xvi ff.
47 Fairweather, *Among the Mystics*, p. 63.
48 E. Gardner, ed., *Cell of Self Knowledge*, p. xiii.
49 Riley, *Meaning of Mysticism*, p. 44.
50 Pepler, *English Religious Heritage*, pp. 38, 233.
51 Knowles, *English Mystical Tradition*, p. 91.
52 James, *Varieties of Religious Experience*, p. 408.
53 Gerald Bullett, *The English Mystics* (London, 1950), p. 44.
54 Underhill, *Mysticism*, p. 369.
55 See Delacroix, *Études*, pp. 347–48, for a careful statement on the regular system of contemplation.
56 Thomas W. Coleman, "Walter Hilton's 'Scale of Perfection,' " *The London Quarterly and Holborn Review*, CLX (April, 1935), 243.
57 G. Hodgson, *English Mystics*, p. 144.
58 Butler, *Western Mysticism*, p. xxviii.
59 *Incendium*, p. 157; *Privy Counselling*, ed. P. Hodgson, p. 172, l. 2.
60 *Privy Counselling*, ed. McCann, p. 105 (ed. P. Hodgson, p. 137, ll. 4–25).
61 Deanesly, ed., *Incendium*, p. 38.
62 P. Hodgson, ed., *Privy Counselling*, p. 213, note to p. 162, l. 19.
63 Noetinger, trans., *Scala*, I, 187, note; I, 228, note.
64 Knowles, *English Mystical Tradition*, p. 79.

65 *The Cloud,* ed. McCann, Chap. 73, p. 96.
66 *Privy Counselling,* ed. McCann, p. 124 (ed. P. Hodgson, p. 159, ll. 19–23).
67 *The Cloud,* ed. McCann, Chap. 40, p. 57.
68 Mother Julian, *Revelations of Divine Love,* ed. George Tyrrell, S.J. (London, 1902), p. 101.
69 "Ego Dormio," *Some Minor Works of Richard Rolle,* trans. Geraldine E. Hodgson (London, 1923), pp. 69–70.
70 Butler, *Western Mysticism,* p. 129.
71 "Form of Living," *English Writings of Rolle,* p. 96, ll. 1–4.
72 *Ibid.,* ll. 12–15; *The Cloud,* ed. McCann, Chap. 8, p. 19.
73 Margery Kempe's reaction to *"Noli me tangere"* is interesting. When "in her contemplation" she perceives Mary Magdalen told "touch me not" and yet go from Christ with happiness, she is perplexed and feels that if it were she who had been so spoken to, she could never have been happy. In fact, "the creature had such great grief and misery in that word that, whenever she heard it in any sermon, as she did many times, she wept, sorrowed and cried, as if she would have died, for the love and desire that she had to be with Our Lord" (*Book of Margery Kempe,* trans. Butler-Bowdon, Chap. 81, p. 260). Although she says she knows Hilton's work, Margery completely misunderstands the meaning of the quotation, indicating that she has not passed the second stage of contemplation, according to Hilton's definition.
74 Clare Kirchberger, editor of Hilton's *The Goad of Love* (London, 1952), pp. 31–33 and Chap. 27) points out that in translating the *Stimulus Amoris,* Hilton, by interpolations, emphasizes that while affection is to be enjoyed, it is not to be confused with the end of contemplation: "though this sweetness be of Christ, it is not Christ. . . ." Also, affection, even as it appears in the third part of contemplation, must be tested before being accepted, because of the possibility of false inspiration by the fiend in a proud soul.
75 *Privy Counselling,* ed. McCann, pp. 106–7 (ed. P. Hodgson, p. 139, ll. 12–14).
76 Butler, *Western Mysticism,* p. 20.
77 *Ibid.,* p. 34.
78 Jan van Ruysbroek, quoted in Waite, *Studies in Mysticism,* p. 17: "in vastissimum divinitatis pelagus navigare." The "enormous sea," for example, could be the experimental knowledge

of God one gains in the mystical experience or it could be the very union with the Infinite.

79 Butler, *Western Mysticism*, pp. 41–42.

80 *Privy Counselling*, ed. McCann, p. 115 (ed. P. Hodgson, p. 149, ll. 6–10); *The Cloud*, ed. McCann, Chap. 9, p. 21.

81 Gerard Sitwell, "Contemplation in 'The Scale of Perfection,'" *Downside Review*, LXVIII (Summer, 1950), 277–81.

82 *Ibid.*, pp. 283–89.

83 *The Cloud*, ed. McCann, Chap. 9, pp. 20–21.

84 *Book of Margery Kempe*, ed. Meech and Allen, Chap. 31, p. 78.

85 H. Gardner, "Walter Hilton," p. 123.

86 *Book of Margery Kempe*, trans. Butler-Bowdon, Chap. 36, p. 116. Julian (*Revelations of Divine Love*, p. 138) also speaks of God as father, mother, and "very spouse," but her imagery is not as striking.

87 *The Cloud*, ed. McCann, Chap. 1, p. 5; Chap. 9, p. 21.

88 St. Gregory, *Homilies on Ezechiel*, quoted in Butler, *Western Mysticism*, p. 66.

89 James, *Varieties of Religious Experience*, p. 381.

90 P. Hodgson, ed., *The Cloud*, p. lxx; ed. McCann, Chap. 71, p. 94.

91 *Privy Counselling*, ed. McCann, p. 112 (ed. P. Hodgson, p. 145, ll. 19–25).

CHAPTER III: The Progress of the Soul

1 Evelyn Underhill, "Walter Hilton," *Mixed Pasture* (New York, 1933), p. 199.

2 Tyrrell, ed., *Revelations of Divine Love*, p. vii.

3 *The Cloud*, ed. McCann, Prayer on the Prologue, pp. 3, 40.

4 *Ibid.*, Chap. 24, p. 40, and Chap. 60, p. 83.

5 *Book of Margery Kempe*, trans. Butler-Bowdon, Chap. 86, p. 279; and see note, Meech and Allen, eds., p. 339.

6 The terms "primary" and "secondary objects of desire" are mine and will be used consistently. In particular chapters Hilton makes the distinction by various means.

7 "Desyre and Delit," *English Writings of Rolle*, p. 57, ll. 6–9: "circumsysede gastely." Rolle's circumcision metaphor is a traditional one, though it is very appropriately used here to

characterize the lack of contamination in the singular desire for Jesus. The allegorical meaning of circumcision is clear in Rabanus Maurus: "tunc purissimi, hoc est omnibus carnalis concupiscentiae vitiis et corruptionibus, in quibus maxime luxuria regnat, exspoliati" (*Comment. in Genesim, Patrologia Latina*, ed. J. P. Migne [Paris, 1844–64], Vol. CVII, cols. 561–62). Alanus de Insulis explains the meaning further, specifically drawing the relation between a Christian's circumcision and his ideal spiritual state, one close to Christ: "Non vacat a mysterio quod puer Christus circumcisus est. Per hoc enim significatur quod nos pueri, non aetate, sed puritate, debemus nos circumcidere a puerilitate; vel, quod a prima aetate, nos a vitiis debemus circumcidere" (*Sententiae, P.L.*, Vol. CCX, col. 236, sec. 12).

8 Allen, ed., *English Writings of Rolle*, pp. 159–60, note to p. 106, ll. 66–68. Evidence of the early devotion to the Holy Name is found outside of the contemplatives as well, as Miss Underhill points out (*The Scale*, p. xxvii).

9 Hope Emily Allen, *Writings Ascribed to Richard Rolle* (New York, 1927), p. 245.

10 *The Mending of Life*, pp. 231–32, *et passim*.

11 *Encomium, Canticles*, quoted by Allen, ed., *English Writings of Rolle*, p. 159, note to p. 106, ll. 66–68. The translation is mine.

12 Allen, ed., *English Writings of Rolle*, p. lvii.

13 *The Cloud*, ed. McCann, Chap. 45, p. 62, and P. Hodgson, ed., p. 197, note to p. 86, ll. 5–12.

14 *The Cloud*, ed. McCann, Chap. 51, p. 69.

15 P. Hodgson, ed., *The Cloud*, p. 198, note to p. 90, ll. 14–15.

16 Meech and Allen, eds., *Book of Margery Kempe*, pp. 255–56, note to p. 1, n. 2.

17 *Book of Margery Kempe*, trans. Butler-Bowdon, Chap. 1, p. 11.

18 That Hilton uses "Jesus" to refer to God and to the second person of the Trinity made man has been pointed out by Dom Sitwell in his edition of *The Scale*, pp. 71, 73, notes, but he has not attempted to explain any distinction in Hilton's use.

19 As Sitwell points out, "It is inevitable that at least in the early stages of the spiritual life the imagination will occupy itself with the humanity of Christ" ("Contemplation in the 'Scale,'" *Downside Review*, LXVII [1949], 284). The same point is made by St. Bernard in his explanation that while the final

love of Christ is a spiritual one, in which, in Butler's words, "the images of the Sacred Humanity no longer form part," the love starts as being "in a certain sense carnal, in that it chiefly moves the heart of man towards the flesh of Christ and what Christ in the flesh did and said" (*Western Mysticism*, p. 118).

20 Noetinger, trans., *Scala*, I, 195, note; Sitwell, trans., *The Scale*, p. 67, note.

21 Underhill, ed., *The Scale*, pp. xliv–xlv.

22 *Ibid.*

23 *Ibid.*, pp. xxvi–xxvii.

24 Inge, *Studies of English Mystics*, p. 111.

25 Although Hilton uses "Jesus" to mean God, he does not use "God" to refer to Jesus specifically as the second person of the Trinity.

26 Knowles, *English Mystical Tradition*, p. 104.

27 H. Gardner, "The Text," p. 29.

28 H. Gardner, "Walter Hilton," pp. 119–20.

29 Knowles, *English Mystical Tradition*, p. 116; Underhill, ed., *The Scale*, p. xliv.

30 Bullett, *English Mystics*, p. 49.

31 *The Cloud*, ed. McCann, Chaps. 13, 14, pp. 25–27.

32 Both Hilton and the author of *The Cloud* (ed. McCann, Chaps. 29, 30, pp. 45–46; *Privy Counselling*, ed. P. Hodgson, p. 161, ll. 23–24) are especially insistent that a contemplative not judge another man. The frequent admonitions would seem to indicate that much judging of one's fellow man was going on, and Hilton specifically says that any deeds with "the likeness of goodness" must not be judged by men and that only "the open heretic" and "the open cursed man," "rebels to God and Holy Kirk," must be avoided (I, lxvii, p. 160).

33 Meech and Allen, eds., *Book of Margery Kempe*, p. 325, note to p. 156, l. 26.

34 *Incendium*, p. 170.

35 James, *Varieties of Religious Experience*, p. 381.

36 Underhill, *Mysticism*, p. 102.

37 Noetinger, trans., *Scala*, II, 269, note. The translation is mine.

38 Butler, *Western Mysticism*, p. 68.

39 *Ibid.*, pp. 107–8.

40 *Privy Counselling*, ed. McCann, p. 113 (ed. P. Hodgson, p. 146, ll. 11–15).

41 *Ibid.*, p. 110 (ed. P. Hodgson, p. 142, ll. 25–26).

42 *Revelations of Divine Love,* p. 216.
43 "Ego Dormio," *Minor Works of Rolle,* p. 63.
44 "Form of Living," *English Writings of Rolle,* p. 114, l. 212—p. 115, l. 246.
45 *The Mending of Life,* p. 235.
46 Pepler, *English Religious Heritage,* pp. 384, 390.
47 Noetinger, trans., *Scala,* I, 46.
48 Kirchberger, ed., *Goad of Love,* pp. 33, 37.
49 *Book of Margery Kempe,* trans. Butler-Bowdon, Chap. 82, p. 262.
50 *Ibid.,* Chap. 14, p. 40.
51 *Ibid.,* Chap. 11, p. 32.
52 *Revelations of Divine Love,* p. 22.
53 "Ego Dormio," *English Writings of Rolle,* p. 69, ll. 263–69.
54 Allen, ed., *English Writings of Rolle,* p. 123, note to p. 4, l. 8.
55 P. Hodgson, ed., *The Cloud,* p. lvi.
56 *The Cloud,* ed. McCann, Chap. 32, p. 47; *Privy Counselling,* ed. McCann, p. 127 (ed. P. Hodgson, p. 162, ll. 14–18).
57 Sitwell, trans., *The Scale,* pp. 249–50, note.
58 Knowles, *English Mystical Tradition,* p. 17.
59 *The Cloud,* ed. McCann, Chap. 45, p. 63.
60 Underhill, *Mysticism,* pp. 384–85.
61 *Catholic Encyclopedia* (New York, 1913), under "quietism," pp. 608–10.
62 Inge, *Studies of English Mystics,* p. 30.
63 Butler, *Western Mysticism,* p. lvii.
64 Knowles, *English Mystical Tradition,* p. 12.
65 Noetinger, trans., *Scala,* I, 27.
66 James, *Varieties of Religious Experience,* p. 381.
67 *Book of Margery Kempe,* trans. Butler-Bowdon, Chap. 86, p. 276.
68 *The Fire of Love,* p. 72 (*Incendium,* p. 190).
69 *The Cloud,* ed. McCann, Chap. 34, p. 49.
70 Sitwell, "Contemplation in the 'Scale,'" *Downside Review,* LXVIII, 274.
71 *Ibid.,* LXVII, 288.
72 It is possible that Hilton knew of the condemnation in 1329 of the quietistic principles in Eckhart's teachings. Eckhart had earlier studied in Paris and had received his degree there, and though the posthumous condemnation was at Cologne, it certainly would have been known in Paris, a great theological

center. If Hilton studied and received his degree at Paris, as the manuscript which refers to him as *"Parisius"* suggests, he probably would have heard or read of the heresy, especially in view of his interest in contemplation.

73 *Revelations of Divine Love*, p. 149.

74 Fairweather, *Among the Mystics*, p. 12. For a brief but excellent account of the influence of Plotinus on St. Augustine and consequently on the Middle Ages, see Dom David Knowles, *The Evolution of Medieval Thought* (New York, 1964), Chapters II and III. As Dom Knowles points out, "there is a practical rule which rarely fails the commentator on Augustine's philosophy; it is that when a source for his thought is wanting the *Enneads* of Plotinus should be searched" (p. 43).

75 Sitwell, trans., *The Scale*, p. 63, note; Noetinger, trans., *Scala*, I, 187, note.

76 *The Cloud*, ed. McCann, Chaps. 62–66, pp. 85–89.

77 Noetinger, trans., *Scala*, I, 36.

78 Knowles, *English Mystical Tradition*, pp. 102–3; Underhill, *Mixed Pasture*, p. 194.

79 Underhill, *Mysticism*, p. 247.

80 Waite, *Studies in Mysticism*, p. 10.

81 William R. Inge, *Christian Mysticism* (London, 1948), p. 115.

82 Riley, *Meaning of Mysticism*, p. 28.

83 Butler, *Western Mysticism*, pp. 69–70.

84 *The Cloud*, ed. McCann, Chap. 70, p. 92.

85 *Ibid.*, Chap. 5, p. 13.

86 The states of the soul in its progress become increasingly difficult to separate and delineate: a contemplative's rejection of the world may not yet be complete when he begins to find God in his soul, and indeed his perceiving faintly the image of God while he is yet struggling with worldly vanities may aid him to continue to struggle. My explanations of the various states of the soul in its progress are ideal in that they are of states which may never exist in a pure form.

Also, much of the terminology I use, like "recollection" and "introversion," is not found in Hilton, but is the standard terminology of critics, such as Dom Butler and Miss Underhill. I explain the terminology in this book specifically according to Hilton's teachings in *The Scale*.

87 See *Enarratio in Psalmum xli*. Augustine includes there a concise statement of the search: "Quaerens ergo Deum meum

in rebus visibilibus et corporalibus, et non inveniens; quaerens ejus substantiam in meipso, quasi sit aliquid qualis ego sum, neque hoc inveniens; aliquid super animam esse sentio Deum meum. Ergo, ut eum tangerem, *Haec meditatus sum, et effudi super me animam meam*" (*P.L.*, Vol. XXXVI, col. 469, sec. 8).

88 St. Gregory, *Homilies on Ezechiel*, quoted in Butler, *Western Mysticism*, p. 70.

89 Fairweather, *Among the Mystics*, p. 8.

90 *Deonise Hid Divinite and Other Treatises on Contemplative Prayer*, ed. Phyllis Hodgson, EETS, No. 231 (London, 1955), p. 43, ll. 5–6. The translation is mine.

91 Inge, *Christian Mysticism*, p. 141.

92 Fairweather, *Among the Mystics*, p. 14.

93 Inge, *Christian Mysticism*, p. 200.

94 P. Hodgson, ed., *The Cloud*, p. lv.

95 Knowles, *English Mystical Tradition*, pp. 69–70.

96 *The Cloud*, ed. McCann, Chap. 26, p. 42.

97 *Privy Counselling*, ed. McCann, p. 114 (ed. P. Hodgson, p. 147, ll. 11–15). It has been customary to read *The Cloud* and *Privy Counselling* according to the ideas of pseudo-Dionysius, especially his ideas on the negative way, since the author of *The Cloud* says his teachings can be found in Denis (ed. McCann, Chap. 70, p. 93) and since he translated the *Mystica Theologica* of Denis. But modern critics point out the differences in emphasis between the author of *The Cloud* and pseudo-Dionysius. Miss Hodgson writes, "The exercise of contemplative prayer taught by the English author involves more than the negative process of freeing oneself from all images and all discursive thought stressed by Dionysius. It is a positive reaching up of love towards God. The English writer lays alternate stress now on the one aspect, now on the other" (*The Cloud*, p. lxiii). And Dom Sitwell, following Dom McCann, admits that the author of *The Cloud* may attach "more importance to the positive action of the will than did Denis himself" ("Contemplation in the 'Scale,'" *Downside Review*, LXVII, 287). In contrast, Dom Knowles' view that Hilton's nought is active while the dark night of the author of *The Cloud* is passive (*English Mystical Tradition*, pp. 69–70) is difficult to accept.

98 Rufus M. Jones, *The Flowering of Mysticism* (New York, 1940), p. 223.

99 Underhill, *Mysticism*, pp. 462–63.

100 Pepler, *English Religious Heritage*, p. 416.
101 The first part of contemplation, reasoned knowledge, does not fit into this scheme, for it is not a necessary step and in itself not necessarily a good step: only the learned can achieve it, and heretics and hypocrites can abuse it. Yet, it could fit into the scheme without disturbing the principle of alternation. If one uses it correctly, with meekness, he gains the pleasures of knowing about God as the finite mind without grace can know Him, but after these pleasures he must yet go through rejection, recollection, and introversion to progress to the second part of contemplation. If one abuses it, he is a heretic and enjoys the false pleasures of pride, which must be purged in the normal way, involving pain.
102 Sister M. Madeleva, *Pearl: A Study in Spiritual Dryness* (New York, 1925).
103 *Ibid.*, p. 27.
104 Underhill, *Mysticism*, p. 472.
105 Sister Madeleva, *Pearl*, p. 35.
106 *Privy Counselling*, ed. McCann, p. 131 (ed. P. Hodgson, p. 167, ll. 17–22).
107 *Ibid.*, p. 132 (ed. P. Hodgson, p. 168, ll. 3–5).

CHAPTER IV: Orthodoxy, Moderation, and Pseudocontemplative Phenomena

1 Underhill, *Mysticism*, p. 178.
2 Waite, *Studies in Mysticism*, pp. 15–16.
3 Bullett, *English Mystics*, p. 47.
4 Allen, ed., *English Writings of Rolle*, p. 135, note to p. 30, ll. 106 ff.
5 "Meditations on the Passion," *English Writings of Rolle*, p. 30, l. 107—p. 31, l. 114. The translation is mine.
6 Allen, ed., *English Writings of Rolle*, p. 162, note to p. 114, ll. 189–211.
7 P. Hodgson, ed., *The Cloud*, p. lxxxii.
8 *The Cloud*, ed. McCann, Chap. 31, p. 46.
9 *Ibid.*, Chap. 75, p. 98.
10 *Revelations of Divine Love*, p. 121.
11 Meech and Allen, eds., *Book of Margery Kempe*, p. 273, note to p. 32, l. 6.

12 *Book of Margery Kempe,* trans. Butler-Bowdon, Chap. 86, p. 278.

13 Knowles, *English Mystical Tradition,* p. 116.

14 Noetinger, trans., *Scala,* II, 36, note. Other critics disagree, however. In a note on the passage in his translation, Leo Sherley-Price argues that "Hilton would not intend to imply that an unbaptized child is doomed to eternal punishment" (p. 255). Dom Gerard Sitwell seems to maintain the same view, principally in his citing "the general opinion of theologians" that an unbaptized infant suffers only a "pain of loss" and not a "pain of sense" (*The Scale,* p. 155, note). But this distinction does not appear in *The Scale,* and the severity of Hilton's language might argue against introducing it.

15 Waite, *Studies in Mysticism,* p. 18.

16 Pepler, *English Religious Heritage,* p. 33.

17 *Catholic Encyclopedia,* under "Lateran," p. 18.

18 Noetinger, trans., *Scala,* II, 39, note.

19 Gerard Sitwell, "Walter Hilton," *The Clergy Review,* XLIV (June, 1959), 331–32.

20 Achille Luchaire, *Innocent III: Le Concile de Latran* (Paris, 1908), p. 85.

21 Inge, *Studies of English Mystics,* p. 31.

22 Fairweather, *Among the Mystics,* p. 8.

23 Blessed Jan van Ruysbroek, *The Spiritual Espousals,* trans. Eric Colledge (London, 1952), pp. 16–17.

24 St. Ambrose's explanation of the verse, an explanation appearing later in the commentaries of Rabanus Maurus and Peter the Lombard, provides a basic view of the text in the Middle Ages: "Quoniam Deus Spiritus est, per Christum legem dedit Spiritus: non litteris utique scriptam, sed per fidem animis intimatam; non quae visibilia doceat, sed invisibilia credi suadeat; quae animus spiritaliter colligat, non quae oculus cernat. Haec lex dat libertatem, solam fidem poscens; ut quia quae non videt, credit, de conditione erui mereatur" (Ambrosius, *Comm. in. Epist. ad Cor. Sec., P.L.,* Vol. XVII, col. 288; Rabanus Maurus, *P.L.,* Vol. CXII, col. 177; Peter the Lombard, *P.L.,* Vol. CXCII, col. 28).

25 "An Epistle of Discretion in Stirrings of the Soul," *Cell of Self Knowledge,* p. 106.

26 The relation between pride and error is made by Augustine in the prologue to *De Doctrina Christiana* (*P.L.,* Vol. XXXIV,

cols. 17–18). Here, as elsewhere, Hilton uses traditional Patristic materials to enforce a point appropriately and effectively.

27 Allen, ed., *English Writings of Rolle*, p. xlvii.

28 Waite, *Studies in Mysticism*, p. 15.

29 Delacroix, *Études*, p. 356.

30 Underhill, *Mysticism*, pp. 268–71.

31 Owen Chadwick, *Western Asceticism* (London, 1958), p. 105.

32 *Ibid.*, p. 106.

33 *The Cloud*, ed. McCann, Chap. 41, pp. 57–58.

34 P. Hodgson, ed., *The Cloud*, p. 190, note to p. 38, l. 16.

35 *The Fire of Love*, p. 78 (*Incendium*, p. 194).

36 *The Mending of Life*, p. 210.

37 *Book of Margery Kempe*, trans. Butler-Bowdon, Chap. 3, pp. 16–17.

38 Meech and Allen, eds., *Book of Margery Kempe*, p. 261, note to p. 12, l. 29.

39 *Book of Margery Kempe*, trans. Butler-Bowdon, Chap. 36, p. 115.

40 Phyllis Hodgson (*The Cloud*, p. lxxx) says that the discretion in ascetic and devotional practices which the author of *The Cloud* teaches also has its basis in the idea of subordination of means to end. That Hilton's basis for moderation is like that of the author of *The Cloud* and not like that of Rolle, who maintains that discretion is primarily of value because it keeps virtues from becoming vices (*The Mending of Life*, p. 210), supports my earlier contention that regarding the third part of contemplation and what is immediately relevant to it, Hilton's teachings are like those of the author of *The Cloud* rather than like Rolle's.

41 Butler, *Western Mysticism*, p. xxxvii.

42 Clarence Herbert Hamilton, *A Psychological Interpretation of Mysticism* (Chicago, 1916), p. 73.

43 Underhill, *Mysticism*, p. 334.

44 Butler, *Western Mysticism*, p. 126.

45 Inge, *Christian Mysticism*, pp. 16–17.

46 *Revelations of Divine Love*, p. 179.

47 *Ibid.*, p. 25.

48 Knowles, *English Mystical Tradition*, p. 124.

49 "Form of Living," *English Writings of Rolle*, p. 91, ll. 58–74.

50 *Ibid.*, p. 93, ll. 125–40. Rolle's is the traditional classification from St. Gregory, as Miss Allen notes (p. 154).
51 *Book of Margery Kempe*, trans. Butler-Bowdon, Chap. 41, pp. 128–29.
52 *Ibid.*, Chap. 85, p. 272.
53 "Song of Angels," p. 69.
54 Riley, *Meaning of Mysticism*, p. 53.
55 Underhill, *Mysticism*, p. 72.
56 Herbert Thurston, S.J., *The Physical Phenomena of Mysticism* (London, 1952); for the official position of the Church, see p. 104.
57 Inge, *Studies of English Mystics*, pp. 85–86.
58 Inge, *Mysticism in Religion*, p. 13.
59 Butler, *Western Mysticism*, p. 127.
60 *Incendium*, p. 145; "Form of Living," *English Writings of Rolle*, p. 105, ll. 35–42.
61 Allen, ed., *English Writings of Rolle*, p. 158, note to p. 105, ll. 38 ff.
62 *Revelations of Divine Love*, p. 185; see also p. 181.
63 *The Cloud*, ed. McCann, Chap. 52, p. 71.
64 *Ibid.*, Chap. 48, pp. 66–67; see, however, Chap. 53, p. 73, in which the principle of differentiation implied seems to be that physical phenomena are bad if they control the man. Whether they are automatically good if they do not control him is not clear.
65 *Ibid.*, Chap. 53, p. 72.
66 *Ibid.*, Chap. 57, p. 78.
67 *Ibid.*, Chap. 53, p. 73.
68 *Book of Margery Kempe*, trans. Butler-Bowdon, Chap. 17, pp. 51–52.
69 *Ibid.*, Chap. 28, p. 88.
70 *Ibid.*, Chap. 60, p. 192.
71 *Ibid.*, Chap. 62, p. 201.
72 *Ibid.*, Chap. 89, p. 289.
73 Meech and Allen, eds., *Book of Margery Kempe*, p. xlii.
74 *Ibid.*, p. 214, ll. 5–7, and note.
75 Hilton's apparent acceptance of heat as physical here is inconsistent with his teaching that heat, specifically the fire of love, is not physically felt (I, xxvi). However, the qualification "as it were fire" may be intended to put the possibility of

physical heat in doubt. See also his warning about accepting as good "any sensible heat as it were fire glowing and warming the breast . . ." (I, x, p. 19).

CHAPTER V: *The Scale of Perfection* and the
Religious-Handbook Tradition

1 H. G. Pfander, "Some Medieval Manuals of Religious Instruction in England and Observations on Chaucer's *Parson's Tale*," *JEGP*, XXXV (1936), 244.

2 R. W. Chambers, *On the Continuity of English Prose from Alfred to More and His School*, EETS, No. 191A (London, 1957), pp. xcci–cxxii; reprinted from *Harpsfield's Life of More*, EETS, No. 186.

3 H. Gardner, "Walter Hilton," p. 120.

4 *Ibid.*

5 *Ibid.*, p. 103.

6 Underhill, ed., *The Scale*, p. vi.

7 Hope Emily Allen, "Wynkyn de Worde and a Second French Compilation from the 'Ancren[e] Riwle' with a Description of the First," *Essays and Studies in Honor of Carleton Brown* (New York, 1940), p. 185.

8 Cassian, *Conferences*, quoted in Chadwick, *Western Asceticism*, pp. 193–94.

9 Knowles, *English Mystical Tradition*, p. vii. Dom Gerard Sitwell, though he argues that the author of the *Riwle* expected to achieve contemplation, agrees that the work is primarily ascetic and distinct from the works of the mystics ("Introduction," *The Ancrene Riwle*, trans. M. B. Salu [London, 1955]).

10 Knowles, *English Mystical Tradition*, p. 110.

11 *Ibid.*, pp. 117–18.

12 Rev. R. Garrigou-Lagrange, O.P., *Christian Perfection and Contemplation*, trans. Sister M. Timothea Doyle, O.P. (St. Louis, 1939), p. 39.

13 Pfander, "Some Medieval Manuals," p. 256.

14 For the original text, see *The Book of Vices and Virtues*, ed. W. Nelson Francis, EETS, No. 217 (London, 1942), p. ix.

15 *Ibid.*, p. 6, l. 20—p. 9, l. 31.

16 *Ibid.*, p. 6, ll. 12–18.

17 Robert Mannyng, *Handlyng Synne,* ed. Frederick J. Furnivall, EETS, Nos. 119, 123 (London, 1903), p. 6, note following line 124 of the *Manuel.*

18 *Ibid.,* p. 25, l. 687—p. 28, l. 774.

19 *Ibid.,* p. 2, l. 43: "For lewde men y vndyr-toke."

20 *Book of Vices and Virtues,* p. 206, l. 33—p. 207, l. 9.

21 *Ancrene Riwle,* trans. Salu, p. 183. Quotations from the *Riwle* in my text are from this edition.

22 Pfander, "Some Medieval Manuals," p. 244.

23 *Handlyng Synne,* p. 349, l. 11303—p. 396, l. 12630.

24 D. W. Robertson, Jr., "The Cultural Tradition of *Handlyng Synne," Speculum,* XXII (1947), 185.

25 Pfander, "Some Medieval Manuals," p. 255.

26 *Book of Vices and Virtues,* p. 183, ll. 2–9. The translation is mine.

27 *Ancrene Riwle,* pp. 133–53.

28 *Book of Vices and Virtues,* pp. 121–71.

29 *Handlyng Synne,* p. 69, l. 1917—p. 72, l. 2008.

30 *Ancrene Riwle,* pp. 125–26.

31 Geoffrey Chaucer, *Works,* ed. F. N. Robinson (Boston, 1957), p. 243, l. 515.

32 Morton W. Bloomfield, *The Seven Deadly Sins* (Michigan State College Press, 1952).

33 *Ibid.,* p. 72.

34 *Medieval Handbooks of Penance,* ed. John T. McNeill and Helena M. Gamer, Columbia University Records of Civilization, No. XXIX (New York, 1938), pp. 98–117, 226.

35 Bloomfield, *Seven Deadly Sins,* pp. 124–25.

36 *Book of Vices and Virtues,* p. 26, l. 24—p. 30, l. 4.

37 *Ancrene Riwle,* p. 96.

38 *The English Text of the Ancrene Riwle,* ed. R. M. Wilson, EETS, No. 229 (London, 1954).

39 *Handlyng Synne,* p. 179, ll. 5481–5484.

40 *Book of Vices and Virtues,* p. 12, ll. 25–27. The translation is mine.

41 *Works of Chaucer,* p. 239, ll. 387–89.

42 Bloomfield, *Seven Deadly Sins,* pp. 245–49.

43 *Book of Vices and Virtues,* p. 10, ll. 21–24.

44 *Ancrene Riwle,* pp. 86–92.

45 Contrast in the *Works of Chaucer,* pp. 239–42 (devoted to pride) with pp. 251–54 (devoted to avarice).

46 Bloomfield, *Seven Deadly Sins*, p. 176.

47 *Book of Vices and Virtues*, p. 22, l. 22—p. 23, l. 26.

48 *Ancrene Riwle*, pp. 88–89.

49 For a fuller account of such imagery, see Bloomfield, *Seven Deadly Sins*, pp. 181 ff.

50 See also *The Scale*, I, xv, in which a list of the deadly sins seen in reflection is followed by a list of opposing virtues.

51 Noetinger, trans., *Scala*, II, 251, note.

52 Bloomfield, *Seven Deadly Sins*, p. 182.

53 Sitwell, "Contemplation in the 'Scale,'" *Downside Review*, LXVIII, 276.

54 Noetinger, "Introduction," *The Scale*, trans. an Oblate of Solesmes, pp. xxix–xxx.

55 *Ibid.*, p. xxx.

56 "Ego Dormio," *English Writings of Rolle*, p. 63, ll. 85–88. My references to the sins in the works of Hilton's contemporaries are, of course, intended not to be complete, but only to suggest peculiarities of treatment.

57 "The Commandment," *English Writings of Rolle*, p. 74, ll. 13–18.

58 See "Form of Living," *English Writings of Rolle*, p. 90, ll. 43–46, and *The Mending of Life*, p. 204.

59 "The Commandment," *English Writings of Rolle*, p. 77, ll. 129–31.

60 E. J. F. Arnould, ed., Richard Rolle, *Melos Amoris* (Oxford, 1957), p. xli.

61 *Incendium*, p. 275. Cf. Augustine, *Confessions*, trans. Rex Warner (New York, 1963), IV, xii.

62 Bloomfield, *Seven Deadly Sins*, p. 179.

63 *The Cloud*, ed. McCann, Chap. 10, pp. 22–23.

64 *Ibid.*, Chap. 16, p. 29.

65 *Ibid.*, Chap. 36, p. 52, and Chap. 43, p. 60.

66 *Ibid.*, Chap. 40, pp. 56–57.

67 *Revelations of Divine Love*, p. 31.

68 *Ibid.*, p. 71.

69 *Ibid.*, p. 213.

70 *Book of Margery Kempe*, trans. Butler-Bowdon, Chap. 14, p. 40.

71 *Ibid.*, Chap. 84, p. 269.

72 *Ibid.*, p. 333 (ed. Meech and Allen, p. 253, ll. 26–29).

73 *Benedictine Rule,* quoted in Chadwick, *Western Asceticism,* p. 323, sec. 51.

74 *Ancrene Riwle,* p. 189.

75 Chambers, *Continuity of English Prose,* pp. civ–cv.

76 *The Cloud,* ed. McCann, Chap. 16, p. 29.

CHAPTER VI: The Unity of *The Scale of Perfection*

1 C. Horstman, ed., *Yorkshire Writers: Richard Rolle . . . and His Followers* (London, 1895–96), I, xiii. See also R. M. Wilson, "Three Middle English Mystics," *Essays and Studies,* N.S. IX (1956), 88.

2 Noetinger, "Introduction," *The Scale,* trans. an Oblate of Solesmes, p. vi.

3 Horstman, ed., *Richard Rolle,* II, xxxv.

4 *Ibid.,* p. xxxix.

5 H. Gardner, "Walter Hilton," p. 116.

6 Inge, *Christian Mysticism,* p. 200.

7 Underhill, *Mysticism,* p. 555. In a later edition the phrase was altered to "pre-eminently a spiritual director, . . . not a metaphysician" (New York, 1961, p. 466), but the contrast remains.

8 Pepler, *English Religious Heritage,* p. 375.

9 Sitwell, "Contemplation in the 'Scale,'" *Downside Review,* LXVII, 277.

10 Noetinger, "Introduction," *The Scale,* trans. an Oblate of Solesmes, pp. xxvii–xxviii.

11 Sitwell, "Contemplation in the 'Scale,'" *Downside Review,* LXVII, 290.

12 Underhill, ed., *The Scale,* p. xli.

13 Knowles, *English Mystical Tradition,* pp. 100–101.

14 Noetinger, trans., *Scala,* I, 234, note.

15 H. Gardner, "Walter Hilton," p. 120.

16 *Ibid.,* p. 114. Dom Knowles (*English Mystical Tradition,* p. 102) agrees with Miss Gardner.

17 Noetinger, "Introduction," *The Scale,* trans. an Oblate of Solesmes, p. x. Father Pepler (*English Religious Heritage,* p. 420) agrees with Dom Noetinger.

18 That Hilton addresses *The Scale* to contemplatives does not

mean, of course, that much in it cannot be valuable to anyone else, or as Wells very carefully says, "though perhaps it was composed for a recluse, its doctrine is capable of broader application" (*Manual of Writings in Middle English*, p. 461).

19 A. C. Baugh, ed., Kemp Malone, Tucker Brooke, George Sherburn, and Samuel Chew, *A Literary History of England* (New York, 1948), p. 230.

WORKS CITED

Allen, Hope Emily. "The Authorship of the *Prick of Conscience*," *Studies in English and Comparative Literature*, pp. 115–70. (Radcliffe Monographs, No. XV.) Boston, 1910.

——. *Writings Ascribed to Richard Rolle*. (Modern Language Association Monograph, No. III.) New York, 1927.

——. "Wynkyn de Worde and a Second French Compilation from the 'Ancren[e] Riwle' with a Description of the First," *Essays and Studies in Honor of Carleton Brown*, pp. 182–219. New York, 1940.

The Ancrene Riwle, trans. M. B. Salu, "Introduction" by Gerard Sitwell, O.S.B. London, 1955.

The Ancrene Riwle, The English Text of, ed. R. M. Wilson. (Early English Text Society, No. 229.) London, 1954.

Augustine, St. *Confessions*, trans. Rex Warner. New York, 1963.

Baugh, Albert C., ed., Kemp Malone, Tucker Brooke, George Sherburn, and Samuel Chew. *A Literary History of England*. New York, 1948.

Bloomfield, Morton W. *The Seven Deadly Sins*. Michigan State College Press, 1952.

The Book of Vices and Virtues, ed. W. Nelson Francis. (Early English Text Society, No. 217.) London, 1942.

Bryan, W. F., and G. Dempster, eds. *Sources and Analogues of Chaucer's Canterbury Tales*. New York, 1958.

Bullett, Gerald. *The English Mystics*. London, 1950.

Butler, Dom Cuthbert. *Western Mysticism*. London, 1951.

The Catholic Encyclopedia, ed. Charles Herbermann et al. 17 vols. New York, 1907–22.

Chadwick, Owen. *Western Asceticism*. (The Library of Christian Classics, Vol. XII.) London, 1958.

Chambers, R. W. *On the Continuity of English Prose from Alfred to More and His School.* (Early English Text Society, No. 191A; reprinted from *Harpsfield's Life of More*, Early English Text Society, No. 186.) London, 1957.

Chaucer, Geoffrey. *The Works of Geoffrey Chaucer*, ed. F. N. Robinson. Boston, 1957.

The Cloud of Unknowing and Other Treatises, ed. Abbot Justin McCann. London, 1952.

The Cloud of Unknowing and The Book of Privy Counselling, ed. Phyllis Hodgson. (Early English Text Society, No. 218.) London, 1944.

Coleman, Thomas W. "Walter Hilton's 'Scale of Perfection,'" *The London Quarterly and Holborn Review*, CLX (April, 1935), 241–45.

Colledge, Eric. *The Mediaeval Mystics of England.* New York, 1961.

Delacroix, Henri. *Études d'histoire et de psychologie du mysticisme.* Paris, 1908.

Deonise Hid Divinite and Other Treatises on Contemplative Prayer . . . , ed. Phyllis Hodgson. (Early English Text Society, No. 231.) London, 1955.

Fairweather, William. *Among the Mystics.* Edinburgh, 1936.

Gardner, Helen L. "The Text of *The Scale of Perfection*," *Medium Aevum*, V (1936), 11–30.

————. "Walter Hilton and the Mystical Tradition in England," *Essays and Studies*, XXII (1937), 103–27.

Garrigou-Lagrange, Rev. R., O.P. *Christian Perfection and Contemplation*, trans. Sister M. Timothea Doyle, O.P. St. Louis, 1939.

Hamilton, Clarence Herbert. *A Psychological Interpretation of Mysticism.* Chicago, 1916.

Hilton, Walter. *The Goad of Love*, ed. Clare Kirchberger. London, 1952.

————. *The Ladder of Perfection*, trans. Leo Sherley-Price. (Penguin Classics L74.) London, 1957.

————. *Minor Works of Walter Hilton*, ed. Dorothy Jones. New York, 1929.

————. *Scala Perfectionis*, trans. Dom M. Noetinger and Dom E. Bouvet. 2 vols. in one. Tours, 1923.

————. *The Scale of Perfection*, trans. Gerard Sitwell. London, 1953.

————. *The Scale of Perfection*, trans. an Oblate of Solesmes. London, 1927.

————. *The Scale of Perfection,* ed. Evelyn Underhill. London, 1923; second impression, 1948.

————. "The Song of Angels," *The Cell of Self Knowledge,* ed. Edmund Gardner, pp. 61–73. London, 1910.

Hodgson, Geraldine E. *English Mystics.* London, 1922.

Hussey, S. S. "The Text of *The Scale of Perfection,* Book II," *Neuphilologisches Mitteilungen,* LXV (1964), 75–92.

Inge, William Ralph. *Christian Mysticism.* London, 1948.

————. *Mysticism in Religion.* Chicago, 1948.

————. *Studies of English Mystics.* London, 1907.

James, William. *The Varieties of Religious Experience.* London, 1916.

Jones, Rufus M. *The Flowering of Mysticism.* New York, 1940.

Julian, Mother. *Revelations of Divine Love,* ed. George Tyrrell, S.J. London, 1902.

Kempe, Margery. *The Book of Margery Kempe,* ed. Sanford Brown Meech and Hope Emily Allen. (Early English Text Society, No. 212.) London, 1940.

————. *The Book of Margery Kempe,* trans. W. Butler-Bowdon. London, 1954.

Knowles, Dom David. *The English Mystical Tradition.* London, 1961.

————. *The Evolution of Medieval Thought.* New York, 1964.

Luchaire, Achille. *Innocent III: Le Concile de Latran.* Paris, 1908.

Madeleva, Sister M. *Pearl: A Study in Spiritual Dryness.* New York, 1925.

Mannyng, Robert. *Handlyng Synne,* ed. Frederick J. Furnivall. (Early English Text Society, Nos. 119, 123.) London, 1901, 1903.

Medieval Handbooks of Penance, ed. John T. McNeill and Helena M. Gamer. (Columbia University Records of Civilization, No. XXIX.) New York, 1938.

Patrologiae Cursus Completus: Series Latina, ed. J. P. Migne. 221 vols. Paris, 1844–64.

Pepler, Conrad, O.P. *The English Religious Heritage.* St. Louis, 1958.

Pfander, H. G. "Some Medieval Manuals of Religious Instruction in England and Observations on Chaucer's *Parson's Tale,*" *JEGP,* XXXV (1936), 243–58.

Riley, Woodbridge. *The Meaning of Mysticism.* New York, 1930.

Robertson, D. W., Jr. "The Cultural Tradition of *Handlyng Synne,*" *Speculum,* XXII (1947), 162–85.

Rolle, Richard. *English Writings of Richard Rolle,* ed. Hope Emily Allen. Oxford, 1931.

———. *The Fire of Love . . . and the Mending of Life . . . ,* trans. Frances M. M. Comper. London, 1914.

———. *Incendium Amoris,* ed. Margaret Deanesly. (University of Manchester Publications, No. XCVII.) Manchester, 1915.

———. *Melos Amoris,* ed. E. J. F. Arnould. Oxford, 1957.

———. *Some Minor Works of Richard Rolle,* trans. Geraldine E. Hodgson. London, 1923.

———. *Yorkshire Writers: Richard Rolle of Hampole and His Followers,* ed. C. Horstman. 2 vols. London, 1895–96.

Russell-Smith, Joy M. "Walter Hilton," *The Month,* XXII (Sept., 1959), 133–48.

———. "Walter Hilton and a Tract in Defence of the Veneration of Images," *Dominican Studies,* VII (1954), 180–214.

Ruysbroek, Jan van. *The Spiritual Espousals,* trans. Eric Colledge. London, 1952.

Sitwell, Gerard, O.S.B. "Contemplation in 'The Scale of Perfection,'" *Downside Review,* LXVII (Summer, 1949), 276–90; cont. LXVIII (Winter, 1949/50), 21–34; LXVIII (Summer, 1950), 271–89.

———. "Walter Hilton," *The Clergy Review,* XLIV (June, 1959), 321–32.

Thurston, Herbert, S.J. *The Physical Phenomena of Mysticism,* ed. J. H. Crehan, S.J. London, 1952.

Underhill, Evelyn. *Mysticism.* London, 1919.

———. "Walter Hilton," *Mixed Pasture,* pp. 188–208. New York, 1933.

Vaughan, Robert Alfred. *Hours with the Mystics.* 2 vols., 3d ed. London, n.d.

Waite, Arthur Edward. *Studies in Mysticism.* London, 1906.

Wells, John Edwin. *A Manual of the Writings in Middle English 1050–1400.* With 9 supplements. New Haven, 1926–51.

Wilson, R. M. "Three Middle English Mystics," *Essays and Studies,* N.S. IX (1956), 87–112.

INDEX